Education . . . beyond tomorrow

Education . . . beyond tomorrow

Edited by

Richard W. Hostrop

An ETC Publication
1975

CIP

Library of Congress Cataloging in Publication Data

Hostrop, Richard W.   comp.
    Education . . . beyond tomorrow.

    ([Education futures, no. 3])
    CONTENTS: Eye, G.G. and others. Instructional technology reshapes the school: its impact on faculty and administrators. — Eurich, A., Gores, H.B. and Sand. O. High school, 1980. — Southworth, W.D. The elementary school principalship, 1980. [etc.]
    1. Educational planning — Addresses, essays, lectures. I. Title.
    LB41.H75   371.2'07   74-5233
    ISBN 0-88280-016-7

No part of this publication may be reproduced or transmitted in any form or by any means, electronic or mechanical, including photocopy, recording, or any information storage and retrieval system now known or to be invented, without permission in writing from the publisher, except by a reviewer who wishes to quote brief passages in connection with a review written for inclusion in a magazine, periodical, newspaper, or broadcast.

Copyright © 1975 by ETC PUBLICATIONS
18512 Pierce Terrace
Homewood, Illinois 60430

All rights reserved.

Printed in the United States of America

CONTENTS

FOREWORD, vii

PART I   THE FUTURE OF ELEMENTARY AND SECONDARY SCHOOL EDUCATION

Instructional Technology Reshapes the School: Its Impact on Faculty and Administrators,
Glen G. Eye, Stephen J. Knezevich, Martin B. Garrison, Angelo Giaudrone, Wilma L. Victor, D. Richard Wynn, **3**

High School, 1980,
Alvin Eurich, Harold B. Gores, Ole Sand, **29**

The Elementary School Principalship — 1980,
William D. Southworth, **45**

PART II   THE FUTURE OF HIGHER EDUCATION

Fuller: Who will Man Spaceship Earth?
Michael Sheldrick, **57**

The University in the Learning Society,
Robert M. Hutchins, **65**

Higher Education in the United States in 1980 and 2000 — From the Perspective of the Carnegie Commission,
Clark Kerr, **69**

Space-Free/Time-Free Higher Learning: New Programs, New Institutions, and New Questions,
Michael Marien, **97**

Toward an Unknown Station: Planning for the Seventies,
Lewis B. Mayhew, **112**

Utopian Perspectives on the University,
John S. Brubacher, **132**

The Alberta Academy,
Commission on Educational Planning for the Cabinet Committee on Education
(Edmonton, Alberta, Canada) **150**

PART III SCENARIOS: FACTS OR FANCIES ABOUT THE FUTURE?

Uncritical Lovers, Unloving Critics
John W. Gardner, **169**

Letter from Tomorrow
John Caffrey, **180**

The School System: A Look into the Future,
Robert T. Grant, **186**

Leave the Teaching to Us!
Stephen Dobbs, **191**

1996: Where You May Go When You Can Go Anywhere,
Frank K. Kelly, **196**

Looking Back from 1999 — The Noise and the Quiet of the Sixties,
Louis Shores, **208**

View from the Year 2001,
Nell Eurich, **221**

2002: An Education Odyssey,
M. Chester Nolte, **232**

Educational Plan for Atomia,
John E. Tirrell, Albert A. Canfield, **245**

PART IV ADVOCATES AND DISCLAIMERS OF FUTUROLOGY

Is the Past Relevant?
William S. Banowsky, **267**

The Attractive and Utterly Falacious Time Machine: Futurology,
Robert Nisbet, **276**

The Future as Myth,
Daniel Roselle, **288**

Futurism in Higher Education: Fad or Fulfillment?
John A. Creager, **294**

Trying to Know Tomorrow Today,
Donald W. Robinson, **311**

INDEX, 317

FOREWORD

In 1963 the *Education Index* listed but one entry under "Future." Ten years later there were more than thirty such entries. This more than thirty-fold increase in the number of articles appearing in educational periodicals concerned with the future of education is symptomatic of the intense interest in the millenial benchmark soon to be reached. This interest also comes about in recognition that in our global metropolis today's novelty soon becomes tomorrow's antique. Tomorrow's innovation is soon replaced with day-after-tomorrow's still newer invention. To just stay even in today's googol paced world demands a mind-attitude which is gyroscoped into a looking ahead direction, an attitude which, at the very least, considers alternative rather than linear tomorrows.

Not only has there been a proliferation of futuristic articles on education (and in other fields), but futurists have their own journals (e.g., *Futures* and *The Futurist*), their own organizations (e.g., The Futuribles, Mankind 2000, the Institute of the Future, the International Society of Educational Planners, and The World Future Society), and even their own "think tanks" (e.g., the Educational Policy Research Center at Stanford University and Syracuse University respectively). Moreover, probably the fastest growing new subject to find its way into the curriculum of secondary and postsecondary institutions is the "study of the future."

That there should be such interest in the serious study of the future should not be surprising. What is more surprising is that it has taken this subject this long to break open the curriculum door. Just as we study the past to better understand today's events, the study of the future can aid us to better understand tomorrow's events. There are some futurists (and historians) who go beyond this difficult enough objective by asserting that it is imperative not to just plan *for* the future, but to actually plan *the* future. That is, futurology should be devoted to shaping in advance what tomorrow's world *should* be. It thus appears that there are two groups emerging and diverging among futurists/historians (the two sides of the same coin), the speculators and the interpreters on the one hand vis-a-vis the planners and the utopianists on the other. And as Victor Hugo aptly said, "Greater than the tread of mighty armies is an idea whose time has come." The time to begin the serious and earnest study (and planning) of the future of education in a systematic and holistic way has surely come.

The authors of the twenty-four selections included in this anthology represent a virtual 'Who's Who' among educational practitioners and futurists. The reader will find the speculators and the interpreters alongside the planners and the utopianists, the disdainers and the disclaimers alongside the ecstatics and the evangelists, and the futurist alongside his complementarian, the historian.

The contents of *Education . . . beyond tomorrow* have been taken from a rich variety of little known as well as well known sources. But each source represents a unique facet or presents a unique aspect of futurism as it particularly relates to the field of education. Taken together, the Gestalt of futurology reveals and illuminates itself.

A brief pause to define several frequently used futurological terms, some already used and others to be used, may prove helpful to some readers new to the new discipline.

Futurists (or "Futurologists") as defined by Alvin Toffler are individuals "who concern themselves with the alternatives facing man as the human race collides with an onrushing future."

Futures may be defined as conditions, events, and happenings which may occur in the future. Because the future is unknown, usually futurists pose and consider *alternative* futures that may occur or would be desirable to *make* occur.

Futurology (or "Futuristics" or "Futurism") is defined by I. Bestuzhev-Lada as "both a complex combination of specific social prognoses and prognostication proper, a new, gradually developing science of the laws, methods, and ways of prognostication."

The Delphi Technique is described by Theodore J. Gordon as "a method of seeking a group consensus which avoids some of the problems of face-to-face confrontation. Generally a Delphi exercise engages experts in an anonymous debate, their opinions being exchanged [via questionnaires] through an intermediary."

The *Cross-Impact Matrix Analysis* is a forecasting method by which the probability of each item in a forecasted set can be adjusted in view of judgments relating to potential interactions of the forecasted items. It has special importance in the attempt to prevent future shock by regulating the pace of change. It does this by tracing the effects of one innovation on another, making possible for the first time, anticipatory analysis of complex chains of social, technological and other occurrences — and the rates at which they are likely to occur.

Simulation is the approximation of complex systems by dynamic models. They may be mechanical analogs, mathematical analogs, metaphorical analogs, or game analogs.

Finally, a term frequently encountered in futurology is *scenario*. Scenario has been defined by Theodore J. Gordon as " . . . 'future history' . . . a narrative description of a potential course of developments which might lead to some future state of affairs." Herman Kahn and Anthony J. Wiener describe its use thusly: "Imagination has always been one of the principal means for dealing in various ways with the future, and the scenario is simply one of many devices useful in stimulating and disciplining the imagination."

Familiarity with the frequently encountered preceding terms will considerably aid the reader in his understanding and enjoyment of the selections which follow.

The purposes of *Education . . . beyond tomorrow* are multi-varied. This work serves to bring together in one convenient place most every aspect of futurology as it is being discussed and practiced in education today. It introduces to the reader the futurist thinkers and their thoughts. Many of these thoughts, when seized by enough educational practitioners, will result in profound educational changes locally, nationally, and globally. This work can aid the reader to become more future conscious and future oriented, to plan more and to react less. Finally, *Education . . . beyond tomorrow* can be used as a basic or supplementary textbook in courses on the future and courses concerned with planning. Adjunct to these serious purposes is the not inconsequential aspect that the selections are simply interesting and fun to read.

Homewood, Illinois   Richard W. Hostrop

Publisher's Note:

Education . . . beyond tomorrow is the third work published by ETC concerned with education futures. *Foundations of Futurology in Education* (Education futures no. 1 — $7.95) has three major parts to it: Introducing the Future; Forecasting and Specifying Educational Futures; Conceptual Views of the Future. *The Future: Human Ecology and Education* (Education futures no. 2 — $8.50) chapter titles are: The Brain; The Nervous System; Electrical Stimulation of the Brain; Biofeedback; Biology of Human Violence; Chemicals Which Shape the Mind; The Hyperkinetic Child; Birth Research; A Look Back and Ahead. Orders for any of these companion books on education futures may be ordered directly from the publisher:

ETC PUBLICATIONS
Department EBT
18512 Pierce Terrace
Homewood, Illinois 60430

Education . . . beyond tomorrow

Part I
THE FUTURE OF ELEMENTARY AND SECONDARY SCHOOL EDUCATION

*The electronic age is literally one of illumination.
Just as light is at once energy and information,
so electric automation unites production, consumption,
and learning in an inextricable process.
For this reason,
teachers are already the largest employee group
in the U.S. economy,
and well may become the only group.*

MARCHAL McLUHAN

"Automation: Learning a Living"

Instructional Technology Reshapes the School: Its Impact on Faculty and Administrators

Glen G. Eye, Stephen J. Knezevich, Martin B Garrison, Angelo Giandrone, Wilma L. Victor, D. Richard Wynn

....THE HUMAN...HAS THREE INCOMPARABLE ADVANTAGES (OVER MACHINES): IT IS HIGHLY MOBILE, IT REQUIRES RELATIVELY LITTLE MAINTENANCE FOR AN AVERAGE OF 70 YEARS OF SERVICE, AND FINALLY, ITS GREATEST ADVANTAGE, IT CAN BE MASS PRODUCED BY RELATIVELY UNSKILLED LABOR.

It is an intriguing but difficult task to examine the impact of technology on the local educational system. What will be the role of the teacher in the forthcoming age when technology will play a dominant role in learning in a school setting? What happens to the role of the principal under such conditions? Of the superintendent? What new educational specializations will emerge? How will the professional staff and students be deployed? What will be the effect of technology on attendance areas and administrative units? And, finally, will the school itself survive or will it be replaced by a new social institution with educational purposes? The answers to these queries are not easy to come by. Speculation provides the only answers at a time when technology is still a primitive art in

Reprint of Chapter 7 of *Instructional Technology and the School Administrator*, American Association of School Administrators, 1970, with the permission of AASA and the Editor, Stephen J. Knezevich.

Part I

education. Nevertheless, it is well to remember Galsworthy's warning: "If you do not think of the future, you cannot have one."

RESHAPING THE ROLE OF THE TEACHER

Thomas Edison may have been the first to comment on the impact of technology on the role of the teacher. In 1891, he predicted that his motion picture projector would eliminate the need for teachers. Sixty-seven years later, Alexander Stoddard, then with the Ford Foundation, was quoted in the New York Times as saying that nationwide use of television could save 100,000 teaching positions and half a billion dollars in teachers' salaries annually. Since then, however, other articles by educational technology enthusiasts have assured readers that the machine will not replace the teacher. These assurances are so categorical and confident that one wonders whether the proponents of technology, like the Queen in Hamlet, "doth protest too much." As the federal Commission on Instructional Technology[1] puts it, the public and the education profession have been bombarded by optimistic predictions that technology will quickly transform schools and colleges. The legacy of the Luddites and the fear of the machines as a threat to human employment were manifest in many occupations before they were manifest in teaching. This has prompted some to speak to the myths of instructional technology.

Will the machine replace the human teacher in the classroom? One is reminded of the argument of the scientist and the humanist over the relative capabilities of the computer and the human mind. The scientist extolled the virtues of the former: it is

The future of Elementary and Secondary School Education

faster, more accurate, requires no vacations, demands no overtime pay, requires no psychological ingenuity in its management, and is unconscious of status. The humanist conceded these advantages to the machine, but insisted that the human mind had three incomparable advantages: it is highly mobile, it requires relatively little maintenance for an average of 70 years of service, and finally, its greatest advantage, it can be mass produced by relatively unskilled labor.

Will the machine replace the human teacher in the classroom? The experts give no clear answer. Suppes, of Stanford University, one of the pioneers in the development of CAI, states confidently that there seems to be little reason to think that computers will ever replace teachers or reduce the number of teachers needed. However, Broudy, of the University of Illinois, believes that the machine will displace the teacher because, to some extent, the machine will be doing what a live teacher might be doing. There would be no profit in machines if they did not somehow replace human labor. Most of the widely quoted authorities on this issue believe that technology, at least in its present prototype form, will not displace live teacher-student ratios as a consequence of the introduction of most new technology. The federal Commission on Instructional Technology reported that school teachers in 1969 were beginning to see the value of using technology, but few teacher-training institutions gave even passing attention to technology.[2]

Will the role of the teacher be affected by the use of educational technology? The literature provides no decisive answer. Some authorities argue that the

Part I

teacher's role will be more significant and professionally challenging primarily because it will be the teacher's responsibility to prepare materials for the machines--programs, televised lessons, filmed demonstrations, audio and visual illustrative materials, demonstrations, and evaluation instruments. Others contend that machine-mediated instruction will be "teacher-proof"; teaching and curricular and instructional decisions will not be made by teachers but by the producers of the materials and the controllers of media transmission.

Will educational technology relieve the teacher of his role of tutor, or will it make him a full-time tutor? Broudy contends that under ideal conditions teaching machines will function as a surrogate for the teacher in the "tutor-tutee" relationship and will instate this relationship for all pupils equally. Previously, because it was the most expensive of all forms of instruction, it was restricted to a very few. Coulson, of System Development Corporation, on the other hand, contends that the teacher will spend most of his time in diagnosing individual learning problems and remedying them in close tutorial interactions with pupils.

Suppes believes that computer-assisted tutorial systems, particularly in the well-structured subjects such as reading and mathematics, will carry the main load of teaching those subjects and that it will be the teacher's responsibility to help students who are not proceeding successfully with the tutorial program and who need special attention. The teacher's major task in this circumstance--that of salvaging the machine's failures--is perhaps less exhilarating

than the teacher's present role. Although there may
be challenges in becoming a remedial specialist
in the skill subjects, the teacher presumably will
no longer enjoy the satisfactions of guiding the learning of able students. The ultimate effect on morale
of teachers in this role remains to be measured.

One of the most enthusiastically proclaimed advantages of the new technology is that it will liberate
the teacher from many of the pedestrian tasks of the
classroom--preparing lessons, correcting papers,
and recording grades, among others. This blandishment is alluring indeed, but the amount of routine
work required, even in computer-managed instruction systems, is still an open question.

New patterns of deployment of live teachers, various
specialists, paraprofessionals, and machines will
undoubtedly emerge. Joyce has proposed an organizational model which illustrates one of the various
possible "man-media-machine" systems.[3] The
model consists of a "direct instructional team" and
"support centers." The instructional team includes
the team leader, an assistant team leader, other
teachers, and several paraprofessionals including
interns and teacher aides. This direct instructional
team is supported by specialized staff and technology
from (a) a computer support center, (b) a self-instruction center, (c) an inquiry center (a library
with abundant materials for listening and viewing),
(d) a materials creation center, (e) a human relations center, and (f) a guidance and evaluation
center. These centers, which support several direct
instructional teams, employ computer programmers,
media specialists, couselors, writers, and other
specialists, in addition to paraprofessionals. The

Part I

model includes a teacher leader who is not simply
a master teacher in charge of a conventional teaching
team but the leader of a large and complex staff. This
leader "orchestrates the environment" of rich resources of specialists, media, and machines so that
curricular patterns are tailored to the unique needs
of individual students.

Will teachers survive the teaching machine and the
computer, as secretaries have survived the type-
writer and the dictation machine? Or will they go the
way of the blacksmith and the coal miner? If teachers
do become organizers of systems of instruction, coordinators of media and methods of instruction, authors of instructional materials, diagnosticians of
learning difficulties, and prescribers of remediation,
there is a chance that teachers will eagerly seek the
allurements of educational technology. But if teachers
become simply button-pushing robots, clerks in instructional supply rooms, or scavengers of the machines' failures, then their resistance to the "technological revolution" in education will be understandable
and probably effective.

Clearly it is too early to answer these questions. Much
more experience and research are needed before final
decisions can be reached regarding the optimum deployment of human teachers, media, and machines.
Educational theorists have spoken freely of the idealized role of the human teacher as an exemplar of
scholarly behavior; a leader of cooperative inquiry;
a guide of students' intellectual, social, and emotional
development among others. Judging from available
studies of teacher behavior, very few teachers fulfill
these roles sufficiently well. The importance of human
teachers, particularly by those concerned about the

Future of Elementary and Secondary School Education

humanizing of education, can hardly be overemphasized.

Important as the future role of the teacher may be, this consideration is clearly subordinate to the more compelling question of whether the machine or human instruction or some combination of each contributes most to the total development of the learner.

RESHAPING THE ROLE OF SPECIALISTS

Educational technology will require the services of specialists not commonly employed in traditional programs of instruction and will modify or perhaps eliminate the roles of others.

This point is consistent with the observation of the federal Commission on Instructional Technology. To quote this Commission,

Technology can achieve its fullest potential in schools and colleges only with technical and paraprofessional support-- "media coordinators" serving as advisors on the use of instructional technology, experts on the production and procurement of instructional materials, plus specialists in many different disciplines working with teachers in research and development.[4]

In the next breath this same group observed that the lack of such specialists "could well be the Achilles heel of instructional technology." The scarcity of quality programmers handicapped the development of programed instruction presented with or without machines.

Some attribute the downfall of the so-called teaching

Part I

machines in the early 1960's to poor programing. Personnel with the competency necessary to produce quality instructional materials for modern technology are still in very short supply.

The installation of more sophisticated educational communications systems will require various kinds of media specialists with strong technical training in such fields as broadcasting, television, audiovisual projection, photography, sound recording, and related technical fields.

Many school systems will probably need an "educational engineer" to supervise and to coordinate the work of these communications specialists. Ideally, the educational engineer will have general knowledge of technical aspects of communication engineering and general professional knowledge of instruction. The closest existing counterparts to the "educational engineer" are probably the coordinators of instructional materials centers, many of whom began as audiovisual coordinators. Whether the coordinators of instructional materials centers (whose backgrounds are typically stronger in pedagogy than in engineering) can acquire a technical competency in communication engineering for this new position is an open question. If not, we may turn to the schools of engineering rather than to the schools of education for recruits for this new position.

The installation of computers will require the employment of programmers--people who can talk to the computer. These people will be subprofessional but with salaries and status well above the clerical level. The programmers' skills will be narrow but precise and important and will require a moderately high intellectual level. Within this classification, subspecializations will probably emerge in such areas as instructional programing, information storage and retrieval, research, and others. This group of paraprofessionals will require mastery of the science of programing but not of pedagogy or subject matter. Their work will be supervised by specialists in computer-assisted instruction who are capable of linking computer capabilities with the problems of curriculum and instruction. These specialists will articulate the work of technicians and teachers and will themselves be expert in both technology and pedagogy. They will supervise the preparation of instructional materials for transmission through the instructional media. One of the CAI specialist's most important roles will be to advise the school district on the purchase of instructional software. These specialists will serve as change agents of the enterprise, identifying worthwhile new technologies and relating them to the district's educational goals. This position may preempt many of the responsibilities now held by curriculum directors, assistant superintendents for curriculum and instruction, coordinators of curriculum and instruction, and similar functionaries. Whether the present incumbents of these positions can acquire the new competencies required or whether they will be replaced by a new breed of "coordinators of computer-assisted instruction" remains to be seen.

The most sophisticated specialization to emerge from educational technology may be that of the "systems analyst." He may serve in a staff position analogous to the research and development officer found on many university administrative staffs or in a line position analogous to the vice-president for research and development in many industrial corporations. The position of systems analyst has no precursor in public school organizations, which have been notoriously unmanned to undertake operations research, the forerunner of systems analysis and systems management. Whether this new functionary will serve in a staff position, advising and serving the administrative organization of the school system, or in a line position, perhaps as deputy superintendent of schools, cannot yet be predicted. In either case, this will be a position of potentially enormous power in the school system. Its incumbent will sit at the nexus of communication and the locus of decision making in the school system. He will bring an intellectual discipline to decision making that may be little understood by most of his administrative colleagues and therefore difficult to refute. The present short supply of systems analysts is jeopardizing the full and rapid application of systems theory to educational administration.

What the place of present specialists in conventional school organizations will be in new organizations is not certain. Supervisors of teachers, as we know them today, will probably become increasingly obsolete under systems of educational technology. As the computer assumes an increasing burden of managing instruction, so may it assume a greater share of the burden in improving instruction. The computer will force greater scientific analysis of the curriculum and will perhaps centralize decisions with respect to instructional methods and materials. Many decisions which classroom teachers formerly made regarding the scope and content of the curriculum and the choice of instruction methods and materials may be preempted by central office personnel. It has been in these realms of decision making at the local classroom level that the supervisor has typically applied his art, which will now become increasingly obsolete. His other major function has typically been the diagnosis, evaluation, and remediation of instructional methodology. The computer will be able to gather a plethora of data on both student performance and teacher performance and will analyze the correlation of the two in a far more sophisticated and thorough manner than the human supervisor was ever able to do. The task of feeding back and interpreting these data to the teacher and the task of imposing quality control over the teacher will remain in someone's job description. Whether this quite limited function of what was formerly known as supervision will be assumed by the principal or a smaller number of supervisors specializing in this function remains to be determined.

Counselors will undoubtedly remain and play an increasingly important part in the educational enterprise as the computer assembles, stores, analyzes, and disseminates a vastly increased volume of data on each student.

The future of teachers of special education is also uncertain. If, as several authorities on CAI suggest, all teachers will become increasingly occupied with remedial instruction for students who are rejected by the machines, then the present distinctions between special education teachers and regular classroom teachers may become increasingly obscured. It is probable, on the other hand, that educational technology will accommodate a vastly larger range of individual differences than the conventional classroom and that the number of student rejects from good CAI systems will be greatly reduced. There is evidence to suggest that many students who can-

Part I

not or will not learn in conventional systems do much better in some of the newer instructional systems. Should this prove to be the case generally, it is possible that the load of special education teachers will be materially reduced but perhaps never completely eliminated.

RESHAPING THE ROLE OF THE PRINCIPAL

Consider the role of the school principal in the new technological systems. The computer can already relieve the principal of much of the drudgery of his job: processing records, analyzing student achievement, formulating school schedules, assigning students to classes, forecasting school enrollments, monitoring the school budget, and accounting for finances, among others. The computer can perform these tasks far more swiftly and more reliably in most cases than the principal. By using computers more time is made available for the principal to fulfill his role as leader and educational planner.

Cybernation will undoubtedly have its greatest impact upon the principalship in the realm of educational decision making. In this discussion, distinction is made between the principal's participation in group decision making relative to the entire school system and his responsibility for making decisions for his school building. The current ethos with respect to the former is that, except for very large school systems, the principal should be a member of the administrative cabinet or council which, under the leadership of the superintendent, formulates many administrative decisions throughout the realm of the enterprise and shapes recommendations of educational policies for consideration by the board of education.

Future of Elementary and Secondary School Education

This strategy has been justified in part because the superintendent may have been too far removed from the action to gather and weigh all of the relevant facts, to conceive and evaluate all possible alternatives, and to formulate decisions confidentaly alone. In other words, the application of many minds was thought to be essential to collecting and processing the data and to weighing and selecting the alternatives. Cybernation now permits the storage and analysis of far greater amounts of data as well as more swift and accurate formulation and assessment of alternatives. To be sure, value questions remain beyond the capability of the computer. But whether the value questions will be seen as sufficiently compelling to justify the far greater time and expense involved in group decision making is questionable.

Some predict that the computer and the systems manager may largely displace the principal in the major decision-making councils of the school systems. Regardless of whether this development would have a salubrious effect upon the quality of decision making (some would disagree), it is obvious that the displacement would lessen the prestige of the principalship. However, predictions of this variety fail to take into account the many intangibles that are part of high-level decision and beyond the modeling and programing capabilities of systems analysts. Computers may help administrators sharpen judgments but will not reduce the importance of judgments. Data processing guided by a defensible model may generate alternatives, but it will not do away with the significance of the human decision maker in the principalship.

Consider the possible effects of the computer on the principal's role in making decisions about the opera-

Part I

tion of his building. Recently there has been a strong trend in educational thought, and to some degree in practice, toward the decentralization of decision making in the management of individual building units in school systems. This strategy has been defended on the grounds that this authority should (a) be as close to the information relative to the decision as possible, (b) be as close as possible to the people who must implement the decision, and (c) permit subordinates to exercise more creativity and adaptability. The computer now permits the collection, storage, and retrieval of information from local units in the central office and thereby abrogates the first requirement. Of course, printouts of the necessary information could also be transmitted to the principals' offices so that the first requirement is no longer a determinant. Whether instructional technology places more responsibility for implementing decisions at the central headquarters than it does at the building level and whether it will encourage creativity and flexibility remain to be seen. Argument can be made both ways. Therefore, the impact of cybernetics on decentralization or recentralization of decision making relative to individual schools is at present indeterminable. If industrial experience can provide an object lesson for education, the trend will probably be toward recentralization of administrative decision making. Most industries with computerized information systems have established huge centralized management centers which have preempted much of the decision making performed previously at the local plant level.

In any event, it is essential that fateful decisions about decentralization or centralization of administrative decisions in school systems be reached thoughtfully in terms of the welfare of the total enterprise. It may be tempting to permit consideration of administrative convenience or the logistics of the communication system to preempt concern of more compelling considerations. Should this happen, the role and responsibility of the principal might change in significant ways. In any event, in most school systems cybernation and systems theory will influence the principal's responsibilities as a manager of instructional resources. The computer, in conjunction with the application of systems theory, will probably relieve the principal of making decisions that control the actions of more and more individuals and will thereby reduce the number of principals required for a given enrollment. The primary consideration is, of course, not the unreasoned protection of any functionary's role and prestige but rather the application of that system of authority for decision making that contributes most to the accomplishment of the school system's goals.

It was suggested that the creative use of a wide variety of specialists will be demanded to make instructional technology work. This, in turn, will point to the increased importance of the coordination role of the principal. Making sure that the right specialist is available in the right place will be a major responsibility of the school executive at the attendance level. Synchronizing the efforts of men and machines to optimize learning opportunities for pupils will continue to be a challenge for most principals in the future, even though the relationship between men and machines may be changed dramatically.

RESHAPING THE ROLE OF THE CENTRAL STAFF

Mention was made earlier of the probable appearance

Part I

of new specializations in the administrative hierarchy: the systems analyst, the educational engineer, the coordinator of CAI, and others. The new specialists will probably preempt some of the authority presently exercised by supervisors, principals, and classroom teachers. They will be part of the new central staff team--a team the configuation of which will be quite different from its predecessor. We need not conclude before the fact that this necessarily will be bad.

Consider, for example, the differences in considerations between a school district's adoption of arithmetic textbooks and its adoption of a computer-managed instructional program in arithmetic. In the adoption of textbooks, it is perfectly feasible to delegate responsibility for a decision to committees composed of teachers, principals, and supervisors of arithmetic. It is conceivable that individual schools within the system might adopt different arithmetic series. In adopting a computer-managed instructional program in arithmetic, however, the locus of decision making changes. Important questions will arise concerning the logistics of the proposed innovations, compatibility of hardware and software, unit costs, comparative benefits, demands on computer time, scheduling, and so forth. Most of these considerations will be beyond the competence of the classroom teacher, the subject matter supervisor, and the principal. Although these persons may continue to be consulted with respect to pedagogical considerations of the software, they will not be able to challenge the educational engineer's judgments in the esoteric domain of his competency.

Other examples could be cited to suggest that the new educational technology specialists will preempt many of the former prerogatives of the principal, supervisor, and teacher. In so doing, the decision-making responsibility of the central office will be escalated while the decision-making responsibility of middle managers will be reduced. The degree to which this will prove true will depend to an extent on the narrowness of the specialization of these new central office personnel. If their specialization is narrow, they will manifest the phenomenon of "trained incapacity" to which Veblen called attention a generation ago. The amount of line responsiblity written into the job descriptions of these new specialists will also be a factor. However, it is probable that their job descriptions will emerge from their capabilities and their behavior rather than the other way around. The level of sophistication and the commitments of the line administrators, particularly the superintendent, will be another determinant. A superintendent or principal who is not knowledgeable and confident in the deployment of new educational systems will probably delegate more responsibity to the new specialists or will acquiesce in the specialists' reach for greater authority. As one writer observed, the systems approach at the top gives way to a vast morass of pushing and shoving--which is publicy cloaked as the refining of the programs and procedures. Sometimes it is, but often it most definitely is not. Highly cybernated school systems will probably be characterized by more centralization of control and a reduction in the number of echelons in the administrative hierarchy.

Part I

RESHAPING THE ROLE OF THE SUPERINTENDENT

The aspects of educational technology that have the greatest potential for redefining the role of the superintendent of schools are systems management theory, the revolution in information processing, and the emergence of new specializations. These related phenomena will have tremendous potential impact on the most fateful function of the administrator: decision making. By combining the discipline of systems management with the data processing capability of the computer, it is conceivable that the decision-making process in school administration may be revolutionized. Such a revolution would surely have considerable impact upon the role of the superintendent. The task of coordination of specialists will be greater at the superintendency level than at the principalship level.

Some forces vastly increase man's intellectual reach. Systems theory permits conceptualization of virtually the entire context of the world of school administration --the objectives, the resources, the required inputs, the constraints, the controllable var-
the various subsystems and their dynamic relationships, the complete range of alternative subsystems, their costs, their benefits, and the consequences for all of these factors of any change made in the total system. Systems theory yields the theoretical model that charts all of these relations and interactions. The computer provides the capacity for the collection, storage, retrieval, and analysis of much of the data which are relevant to any and all parts of the theoretical model. With its infallible memory, its unbelievable speed and accuracy, and its lack of bias, the computer is able to make de-

tailed analyses in a few seconds that would take a team of administrators years to perform.

The electronic computer is perhaps the first creation of man that has demonstrated anything even remotely resembling human intelligence. Miraculously, some of the newer computers have built into them the capability that is not always built into their human counterparts. Computers are limited only by the creativity and wisdom of the programmers who command them; that is, the computers can do well only those things they are told to do. The computers of the twenty-first century, we are told, may be capable of creative thought and of programing themselves eventually. Should this occur, will the administrator himself become Prometheus?

The prospect of this synthetic machine intelligence frightens some; they fear that the machine, which already surpasses man in memory, may eventually surpass him in creativity, reducing the administrator to an intolerably inferior role in an enterprise which he once controlled. Others believe that the machine can never be more creative than the man who creates it and that, therefore, it cannot supplant human intelligence or eliminate the crucial role of the administrator in the decision-making process. Nevertheless, the administrator and his social milieu, unlike the computer, are bound up in an inextricable network of feelings, emotions, values, tastes, needs, and motives that must impinge upon the decision-making process; these factors are inevitably beyond the domain of the computer.

For the foreseeable future at least, administration without the human administrator is practically incon-

Part I

ceivable. Nonetheless, the potential impact of the computer on the work of school administration is formidable. Most important, it promises to bring a far greater degree of rationality to the decision-making process, certainly none too soon in the beleaguered world of school administration. Our hero may soon be liberated from his dependence on intuition, hunches, guesses, and biases in the decisions he faces daily. The computer will force him to think more objectively, to define his purposes more explicitly, and to examine the full range of alternatives more carefully. The superintendent will probably be forced to concentrate more effectively on long-range planning, policy making, and evaluation. We are told that the computer revolution will relieve top managers of their minor burdens and will increase enormously the pressures on them to come to grips with the moral and ethical consequences of their decisions. In the past, the administrator could claim that he had too little information to anticipate all of the consequences of all possible alternative decisions. The new computer capability will deprive tomorrow's administrator of this excuse.

Finally, the superintendent may discover that decisions and policies will emerge from the wisdom put into the systems theory by the systems analyst, the rationality of the data processing program put into the computer by the programmer, and the value judgments derived from the outcome by the superintendent. As noted earlier, this procedure probably will supplant his administrative council's consensus. Perhaps that group will be rendered much less important, although it undoubtedly will still function in making value judgments. Administration may then have come full circle from classical scientific management to democratic administration to behavioral administration to computer-assisted classical management.

NEW PATTERNS OF DEVELOPMENT OF TEACHER AND STUDENTS

At this juncture in history, one can comment only generally on the deployment of professional employees and students in a cybernetic educational system. Contemporary student-teacher ratios will rapidly become obsolete, but new ratios cannot be predicted because they will vary so much. For example, one might predict that a "computer-assisted" secondary school guidance counselor could deal effectively with more than his present 350 students if the computer handled all of the data processing, analysis, record keeping, and even some of the conferencing with students. On the other hand, the instantaneous availability of a vastly increased volume of data about each student may decrease his case load. With installation of mass media and multimedia instruction, along with computer-managed individual study, it is conceivable that classrooms may be replaced entirely by auditoriums, conference rooms, and individual study carrels. The impact of this new deployment of space on the deployment of teachers and students is apparent at once. Perhaps all that can be said is that the new patterns will be quite different from those of the present, varied within the school system and varied in time, and therefore not subject to generalized description.

NEW ATTENDANCE UNIT AND ADMINISTRATIVE UNIT CONFIGURATIONS

Educational technology is likely to have a profound

Part I

effect on the organization of attendance units and administrative units. Current principles about optimum size of school buildings may become obsolete. With such innovations in communications as dial access to remote computers, the miniaturization of electronic equipment, the cybernation of instructional resources and perhaps even many pupil personnel services, neighborhood elementary schools of from 10 to 20 students housed in an apartment house or remodeled store may become very feasible. On the other hand, instructional systems requiring direct access to computers and mass media of communication might require attendance units of several thousand. Perhaps all that we can be sure of is that different instructional systems will require different sizes of attendance units or, as suggested later, perhaps no school buildings at all.

The enormous costs at least at present, of electronic installations will probably require much larger administrative units to make pupil unit costs tolerable. Well-stocked instructional materials centers with supporting hardware will represent enormous expenditures that can be justified only by high volume of utilization and therefore large administrative units. An alternative would be interdistrict compacts for time-sharing of computers and cooperative purchase and use of facilities and perhaps certain personnel on a regional basis.

WILL THE SCHOOL ITSELF SURVIVE?

We come now to the most profound question of the entire discussion: Will the school as a formal institution disappear in a new era of totally cybernetic education? This query may not be as fanciful as it seems. One of the more knowledgeable observers of the new educational technology believes that, by combining mass instructional technology with the individual instructional technology, it would be technically possible (but prohibitively expensive for some time) to eliminate not only the teacher but also the entire school system. According to some, totally automated education may be achievable almost immediately.

Our own powers of forecasting may not equal those of Wells, Orwell, or Huxley, but let us nevertheless examine the various components of educational technology that are either operational or nearly so at the moment to see how a totally automated educational system might appear.

Consider each student of school age having at his disposal a television receiver, either in his home or in a publicly supported neighborhood center. Assume also that each student has available a dial-access facility which permits him access, via laser, to a central learning center equipped with a large, high-speed computer plugged into a library of televised, programed, recorded, and printed materials serving whole cities or regions. By using microwave communication via orbiting satellites, the students could have access to any knowledge that is programed into any learning resource center anywhere in the world.

Assume also that each student has a light-pen and a teletypewriter which permit him to feed back to the computer his responses to questions posed by the program and to ask questions of the computer. (Eventually, the student and the computer will communicate through spoken language.) The computer records and analyzes the student's responses to determine

Part I

whether he is ready for the next learning step or whether he should be sent along a branched program uniquely designed to remedy his particular difficulty with the task at hand. When the student is ready to stop, he signs off and the computer dutifully remembers the point at which the student must begin when he signs in again.

Data on the quality of each student's performance could be researched for the continual refinement of the program. Data on student performance could be monitored to assure that each student was putting sufficient effort into his learning. Essential pupil personnel services that cannot be automated could be given by human agents in home visitation. If the child moved to another community, a complete printout of his entire academic record and biological data could be provided in seconds for the computer at the learning resource center in his new community.

Through the miracle of miniaturization, all of the equipment at the student's home terminal could be packed into a suitcase.

It is conceivable that the student's cognitive development might be handled as effectively, perhaps more effectively, through this fully automated educational environment at home as it could be in conventional schools. Whether the student's affective and psychomotor development could be equally well developed in this environment is, of course, another matter. Any reasonably complete view of education is concerned with social, emotional, physical, moral, and aesthetic as well as intellectual growth. Clearly, a completely automated educational environment cannot provide the social interaction essential for the refinement of one's interpersonal relations, self-understanding, values, tastes, feelings, and physical and mental health--a refinement which is essential to the well-educated student.

Some will regard this Orwellian possibility, the elimination of the formal public school, which Horace Mann regarded as "the greatest discovery made by man," as the final conquest of the machine in its historic struggle with man. Others may regard it as the ultimate triumph of man over the machine in the liberation of the educational process from the constraints of time and space.

IN SUM

In this chapter we have speculated about the impact of the new instructional technology in shaping education in the future. We have examined its possible impact on the role of the teacher, the instructional specialists, the principal, the superintendent, the deployment of staff and students, the attendance and administrative units. Finally we have speculated a bit on the destiny of the school itself as a formal institution.

These speculations, no doubt, will titillate the fancy of the scientists and trouble the souls of the humanists. We implore the thoughtful educator to neither accept nor reject a priori speculations about the future, but to ask rather that both the technological innovations and the conventional instructional systems which they may replace be appraised experimentally and that the benefits of each be measured against the objectives we hold for education. We implore that judgment not be contaminated either by passion for novelty or by an unreasoned commitment to the con-

Part I

ventional. We suggest that now is the time to begin the necessary planning for smooth transition into the age when technology is harnessed (rather than grafted) to the purposes of instruction.

Glen G. Eye is Professor of Education, University of Wisconsin; Stephen J. Knezevich is Professor of Educational Administration, University of Wisconsin; Martin B. Garrison is President, Henderson College, Arkadelphia, Arkansas; Angelo Giandrone is Superintendent, Tacoma, Washington; Wilma L. Victor, is Superintendent, Intermountain School, Brigham City, Utah; D. Richard Wynn is Chairman, Department of Educational Administration, University of Pittsburgh, Pennsylvania.

Notes and References

1. Commission on Instructional Technology. To Improve Learning. A Report to the President and the Congress of the United States. Washington, D.C.; Government Printing Office, 1970. p. 20
2. Ibid., p. 55
3. Joyce, Bruce R. The Teacher and His Staff; Man, Media and Machines. Washington, D.C.: National Education Association, 1967. 28 pp.
4. Commission on Instructional Technology, op. cit., p. 57.

High School, 1980

.... THERE'S A CONSIDERABLE DIFFERENCE
BETWEEN PREDICTION AND INVENTION. IN
INVENTION, WE LAY PLANS FOR THE FUTURE
AND ATTEMPT TO CARRY THEM OUT; IN
PREDICTION, WE MAKE GUESSES OF WHAT IS
LIKELY TO HAPPEN WITHOUT BEING CONCERNED
ABOUT CARRYING OUT PARTICULAR PLANS.

Alvin Eurich

I'm particularly pleased to take part in a conference concerned with common-sense priorities for the seventies. This means that you are looking ahead toward new developments for the American high schools. Some of us have tried to do this in the book to which Mr. Malone referred, High School, 1980. In fact, there are five of us on the platform this morning who have written chapters for that book.

In the book we were concerned mainly not with predicting the future of the American high school but with helping to invent the future. There's a considerable difference between prediction and invention. In invention, we lay plans for the future and attempt to carry them out; in prediction, we make guesses of what is likely to happen without being concerned about carrying out particular plans. So this morning, as has been true in your other sessions here, we

Reprinted with the copyright permission of The Bulletin of the National Association of Secondary School Principals May, 1971.

Part I

are looking to the future. But we can't look to the future very well unless we take a quick look back at the past. I'm going to highlight very briefly some of the things that have happened to American education in the 1960's.

It was a period during which there were tremendous developments. In fact, I think we can say that we probably saw more developments in American education in the 1960's than in any other decade in our entire history. There was tremendous support for the schools--local, state, and federal support. In fact, from 1963 to 1968, more legislation was passed by the federal government concerning education than was passed in our entire previous history. Also, larger sums of money were appropriated for education during that period of years from 1963 to 1968 than the federal government appropriated in our entire previous history. In other words, it was a recognition of the federal government that education is a very important and vital part in the planning of our futures. Enrollment skyrocketed, not only in this country but around the world. We began to make a variety of curriculum adaptations; we developed "upward bound" programs, acceleration, early admission, admission with advanced standing; we produced ethnic material for the curriculum. We introduced, too, a wide variety of new instructional practices: language laboratories, team teaching, the use of paraprofessionals, teaching aides, television, programmed learning, continuous progress techniques, directional learning, independent study. We also made great progress with school integration, with special attention to the disadvantaged. We made new efforts to reach students normally considered failures by schools, and we

The Future of Elementary and Secondary School Education

successfully reached them.

It was a period of great progress. But as great as progress was in the sixties, I think we can say that we will see even greater changes between now and 1980. Why do I say that? Because of certain things we see in the current picture.

THE FINANCIAL PROBLEMS

First of all, we are all aware of the financial problems with which our schools and colleges are confronted. Those financial problems grow out of a lessening of support for education. In the state of Ohio, for example, on the ballot last November, there were 243 new operating levies and of those only 14 or 23 percent were passed. This is typical of a change that has been occurring throughout the country in contrast with the sixties, where in many communities every levy that was placed on the ballot was approved by the voters. I don't think we can say that the voters are now turning down school bond issues primarily because they are concerned with the taxes that are going higher and higher. We can't say that, because the voters were much more generous with bonds for recreation, highways, or combatting pollution. In almost all of our 50 states where bond issues were on the ballot regarding those particular areas a much larger percentage passed.

So for the 1970's we're not talking about curtailing school expansion or cutting back on ancillary programs. We're really talking about closing some of the schools, closing them early, because they can't meet the payroll. We are talking about bankrupt school systems. Therefore, the first reason

Part I

I predict that changes will come much faster in the seventies is the financial reason.

The second reason for early change is student unrest. We're all aware that during the period from 1967 to 1969, 53 percent of the high schools in the United States reported conflicts with students. These conflicts have already brought about drastic changes in the curricula, in teaching methods, in relationships with the community, and in the goverance of our schools. And these changes will continue at a rapid pace during the 1970's.

A SYSTEM THAT DOESN'T FIT THE TIMES

The third reason why changes will come much more rapidly is that we're beginning to recognize that we're trying to perpetuate an anachronistic educational system, an educational system that does not fit the times. Our teacher-pupil ratio, 1:25 or 1:20, goes back to the Talmud, recorded in the middle of the third century. The exact quotation reads, "There should be one teacher for 25 pupils; if more than 25, there should be an assistant; if more than 40, there should be two teachers." So this general ratio of 1:20 or 1:25 was recorded in the middle of the third century, before we had any other means of communication except word of mouth. And yet today we use that formula as the basis for constructing our schools. It determines the size of the classroom, which in turn determines the number of teachers who need to be employed, which in turn determines the operating and construction budgets of our schools.

I've looked for some years now to see whether there

The Future of Elementary and Secondary School Education

is any other generally practiced rule upon which so much depends, a rule based upon a man-made formula that goes back as far as the middle of the third century. To date, I have not been able to find such a formula. That type of school system is beginning to break down because of the recognition that we have other means of communicating, other means of setting up learning situations than we have had in the past. And, because of the general situation in which we find ourselves at present, we are adopting new means of communication at a much more rapid pace than we have in the past decade.

SCHOOLS, COLLEGES NOT CENTRAL

The fourth reason I say changes will come faster in the period ahead is that we are just beginning to recognize that schools and colleges are no longer central to our educational system. They are no longer the top means of carrying on education. Why do I say that? Because the average high school senior finishing school this year has spent 15,000 hours, in his lifetime, looking at the television screen. He spent 11,000 hours in school. In other words, he has spent 4,000 hours more looking at television than he has spent in the classroom. In addition, television has had a powerful influence because it has dealt with the basic human emotions that motivate the actions of men; fear, love, hope, terror, and so on. The schools have not dealt with these emotions. Consequently, television has had a greater impact on the development of our youth than the schools have had. Quantitatively and qualitatively, the schools have become the Avis in education, no longer the Hertz. I hope that we can say in the period of the seventies that, like Avis, we'll try harder.

Part I

Now what do we get by relying so much upon televison? Newton Minnow, when he was chairman of the Federal Communications Commission, called television a great American wasteland. Nicholas Johnson, in a speech at the University of California a short time ago (he is at present serving on the FCC), said television is perhaps our nation's greatest single tragedy. Not only has it failed to make us a better race of men, it has actually made us worse. This national crisis has come about in large measure because of our willingness to turn over our minds and the development of our emotions to the instruments that program them and to the exclusive control of commercial television.

These, then are the basic reasons why it seems to me that education changes need to and will come more rapidly in the seventies. Because we need these changes, such meetings as you have had here in Houston are exceedingly important for planning. What can be done about this? You with the Association have sponsored a report on the urban schools. That report was discussed in a meeting in Milwaukee a short time ago. Out of that meeting a series of recommendations were developed and reported by Ralph Tyler. I hope that many of those recommendations can be carried out one way or the other under the sponsorship of this Association. They involve more experimental work, such as rotating faculty members. They involve a more active, aggressive program on the part of this Association, on the part of the school principals, upon parents, in order to bring about adjustments in the school and to gain further desperately needed financial support.

RECOMMENDED: COMMISSION ON EDUCATION IN THE COMMUNITY

The Future of Elementary and Secondary School Education

So we do need greater flexibility, we need new programs, we need new arrangements for learning. But even more, it seems to me, we need to recognize that not all learning goes on in the schools. The entire community provides a learning situation. We have not made full use of the learning resources that we have in every community of the United States. And in recognition of that, I should like to suggest that every urban area in the country set up a new commission on education in the community. And it would be the purpose of this commission to make full use of the educational resources that are in the community. More specifically, the function of the commission would include the following:

1. To make an inventory of all the educational resources in the community--programs of various kinds, theaters, museums, galleries. There are many facilities and human resources in the community that could be used for educational purposes that are not now being used.
2. To develop a master plan for using the educational resources of the community for every individual, from birth until death.
3. To stimulate the development of new types of educational programs to fill in gaps and improve the total patterns.
4. To stimulate and coordinate research on the value of different types of educational programs, including the television programs seen there.
5. To develop the case, show the need for, and urge further support on a community-wide basis, financial and otherwise, of the total educational program.

In other words, such a commission could highlight the learning that goes on in the community, within

Part I

the schools and outside the schools, and thereby
gain greater confidence and support from the public.
It seems to me that, with such coordination and
with the imagination principals and staffs of the high
schools throughout the country possess, we can move
forward during the period of the 1970's and by the
1980's We can have a more extensive and more effective educational program to help every person
in the community become all he is capable of being.

Alvin Eurich is president of the Academy for Educational Development in New York City. This article
is drawn from the author's oral presentation at the
NASSP 1971 convention in Houston, edited by the
Bulletin staff.

Harold B. Gores

I have great respect and admiration for principals.
Many are caught in the riptide where the culture of
the elders of the tribe conflicts with the culture of
the young. There the principal sits in his dory in
the riptide, in his dory called the principal's office,
tossed and buffeted by the collisions of these tides,
the waves cresting around his neck. The youth expect, of course, that he will be their leader and will
make new victories for humanity, whereas the elders
expect him, as keeper of the conventional wisdom,
to make sure that youth does not do anything that
will rock the boat.

Some time ago, the president of a school board asked
me to write the specifications for a high school principalship, there being one coming into vacancy in that
community. The longer I thought of it, the clearer

The Future of Elementary and Secondary School Education

it became to me that I could sum up the whole requirement by writing that it would be useful in the candidate's past if he had been a kamikaze pilot.

However, my remarks necessarily take off from my more recent professional life, which has to do with the solids of education as distinguished from the liquids (the people who flow in and out of education), and the gases (the curriculum). I deal with those parts which you can, with impunity, kick with your foot. I believe education is a fluid process and, like fluids, tends to take the shape of its container. To be sure, what's most important is the people, the ideas, and the places. I will talk about the places of education. I remind you that buildings, the places of education, cost ultimately about six percent of the total cost to fulfill the purposes for which the buildings were built in the first place. Or, to put it another way, two teachers in suburbia, at least in the Northeast, over a total career through to retirement, will cost the equivalent of one million dollars in buildings. Yet the man in the street sees these buildings as very expensive and beyond our grasp in this affluent society. Actually, of course, it is people that cost money. The most I might claim for the productivity of the environment might be 15 percent, arguing by analogy from a study made of the productivity of office workers. This indicated that the quality of the environment made about a 15 percent difference in what people do, their productivity, how they feel.

THESE ARE THE WORST OF TIMES

Let me comment quickly on the financial situation in which we find ourselves, the situation to which Mr.

Part I

Eurich has made reference. These are not the best of times and the worst of times, as Dickens said of another age. These are the worst of times. The National economy appears to have bottomed out-- the stock market thinks so anyway--but the economic curve of education, if the 1930's are to be repeated in pattern, probably won't bottom out for another 18 months. For example, economic historians agree that 1932 was the bottom of the Depression then, but it was not until the academic year 1933-1934 that most school systems were hurt. If the present follows that pattern, it will be late '71 or early '72 before the curve in education turns up. Five years ago, 80 percent of school bond issues passed; two years ago, 63 percent; last year, 43 percent. What's it going to be this year? It's clear that it's down, but that too will pass, and I would guess about 1972.

NEW CONSTRUCTION METHODS

In my remaining time, let me list some things relating to the environment about which principals will have to be making decisions in the 1970's because these things will be within our grasp. First of all, if you are still building your schools, stick on stick, largely handcrafted, go to Florida and look at the systems buildings going up there. (It's a good idea at this time of year to inspect Florida schools.) Look especially at the experiment in Fort Lauderdale, Broward County, where last August commissions were given to two architectural firms for occupancy of 16 million dollars' worth of schools next September. Fifteen months from the time of commissioning, there were two high schools of 2,000 pupils each, two middle schools, and two elementary schools. Or look at Toronto, where they built 23 schools at once, all of

The Future of Elementary and Secondary School Education

modular, pre-engineered components, and not by stick-on-stick cutting and fitting that has been our inheritance from an agrarian, nonindustrial past. Or look at Montreal, Canada, if you're up that way; look at the new additions in Detroit that are building systems, all seeking to get quick response. Quick response is extremely important in an escalating market where it takes four years from the time you decide to build a school till a child walks in the door. Slow construction is a luxury that escalating costs put beyond reach. We must get quick response--and the savings are substantial.

Another development that will challenge planners, particularly until the money flows again toward education, is called "found space." To see new found space, when you are in New York City, look at Harlem Prep, which was formerly an air-conditioned supermarket; now it is an air-cooled environment for learning. It just happens to have been a supermarket. Or look at the General Electric factory in Cleveland, a vocational school now, where the youngster when he is enrolled goes on the payroll. One way to fight dropouts, especially among adolescent boys, is to make sure that they have "walking around" money. So they go on a payroll when they enroll in the school. Or look at an excellent place for teachers and students to learn together--despite the fact that it was a mattress factory originally--in the Bronx: P.S. 211. Or look at El Central in Dallas, an excellent setting for a community college. It was once a department store.

You'll be under pressure to create new schedules and to de-schedule--a good reason to go to Las Vegas. When you're there, look at Four O'clock High, a high school that will start at four o'clock in the

Part I

afternoon. Many youngsters are nocturnal in their life-styles, and if you spread open the option over the whole day all the way until ten o'clock, you will get the most amazing response, frequently from the most creative people who are blinded by the sun. The moon is their satellite. You'll be surprised how much trade you can pick up at night, how many there are of these creative, sleepless characters.

In instructional technology you'll have to choose frequently which route you'll go. Will you institutionalize a single piece of information and then give intricate access to whoever wants it, after he has synchronized his watch against the master clock? For the major institutions that will have to be the route, because of the eventual economics of the matter. The other route is individual access devices, which will increasingly come into your schools as we miniaturize materials.

My concluding word comes from G. Stanley Hall, a great psychologist at the turn of the century. He observed that intellect is just a speck on the sea of emotion. As we establish learning environments, the greatest dividends will come from paying more attention to the emotions, although not necessarily less to the intellect. The symbol of our business is the lamp of knowledge. We've always been very good with light. We've been less good with warmth. Wouldn't it be nice if our symbol, the lamp of knowledge, were located on the mantle of a fireplace?

Goethe's dying words were, "Light, light, more light," but a philosopher said he was wrong. He should have said, "Warmth, warmth, more warmth."

The Future of Elementary and Secondary School Education

It is not the darkness of the night that kills; it is the frost.

Stand back and look at your school; it's a pretty chilly place. It's ceramic, indestructible, antiseptic, reverberating, hard, glistening, slippery. That's the municipal response to the feeling that people are more evil than good, and that children naturally (although birds won't) destroy their own nests. If you can warm up some of these places, take the chill of the frost out of some of the places we gather together, then maybe more people will like to be there, in a more friendly setting, and more often.

Harold B. Gores is president, Educational Facilities Laboratories, New York City. This article is drawn from the author's oral presentation at the NASSP 1971 convention in Houston, edited by the Bulletin staff.

Ole Sand

My purpose for being here, because all the ideas I had have already been stated, is to tell you five stories and hope that their points will help you back home.

My first point is that in your common-sense priorities the first one ought to be to take a firm stand and make things happen. For example, make sure that your library is larger than your gymnasium and that you will not focus on interscholastic sports. I predict that by 1980 the day of intercollegiate and interscholastic sports will be over and we'll have physical education for every youngster. (I know that

Part I

very few principals come from the field of coaching or physical education, so I feel comfortable saying this.)

I'd like to tell the story now that Robert Maynard Hutchins told when he was testifying before a Congressional committee, when he convinced them that the Fund for the Republic was not subversive. A congressman from Alabama asked him if he wasn't the man who made them quit football at the University of Chicago. Hutchins answered that that was one of his minor accomplishments, adding that they did discover atomic energy under the bleachers at Chicago. The congressman kept after him and Hutchins finally told him that he was convinced that if he ever went back into university administration he would support intercollegiate athletics but that there would be no football. Instead, they would have racing stables and the jockeys would wear school colors and the horses would not have to pass entrance examinations.

LEADERSHIP IS FUNCTION, NOT POSITION

My second point, which is a serious one for the eighties, is that leadership is a function, not a position. I am delighted that all the principals I know are aware that they are not the bosses simply because they hold the position of principal. They know for sure that command is power over people and leadership is power over problems. They know that genuine power is power with, and pseudo power is power over. In some instances they may have perceived teacher militancy as a restraining force in the sixties, but I believe that it will be one of the great supporting forces in the seventies. I

The Future of Elementary and Secondary School Education

predict that the power that the organized teaching profession has shown for economic benefits and working conditions will be a tremendously important channel to make things happen. My hypothesis for the seventies is that change can and will happen if the power of the organized teaching profession is really used to make things change.

My third point is that the power groups in society today--black power, brown power, student power, etc.--can make things change. I'd like to see a community group run a school for six months or a year. I believe we need options.

Another very practical idea is not to have any faculty meetings from four to six in the afternoon. We should cut down on the teacher load and have a maximum of 15 teaching hours, with 30 hours for research, planning, and development. We've got to change the notion of what the role of the teacher is.

SOME GOOD NEWS

Now I have good news for you. There is one problem that has been solved, the birth control problem in India. All you do is send 12 high school English teachers to India. If they teach sex the way they teach English, I guarantee you the Indians will lose interest in the subject and the problem will be solved.

There's another problem that's solved, too, the counseling and guidance problem. We have very firm evidence on this one. We have done extensive study and Ralph Tyler has helped us validate it. All you have to do is draw a picture of a cow and you ask the youngster a question. "If you call the cow's tail a leg, how

Part I

many legs will he have?" If he answers five, you obviously counsel him into mathematics. If he says calling the tail a leg doesn't make it one, there are still four legs, then you counsel him into science. If he gets a dreamy look on his face and says that it might be 18 or 27, you counsel him into the arts and the humanities. If he says, "That was a good question; I will have to think about it," counsel him into administration.

What are we going to do in the seventies to make these things happen in the eighties is to teach the kids to write love letters and lab notes. Doesn't that take care of the sciences and the humanities?

Now I quote from Harold Gores: "Make sure that we move from memory to inquiry." If we can please help change school-teachers from walking, talking oracles who hand out information to conductors of a dialogue who discuss the meaning of it all, I will be happy for the seventies. I want to make sure that our schools move from a spiritless climate to one with a zest for learning. Learning is fun."

Ole Sand is director, Center for the Study of Instruction, National Education Association. This article is drawn from the author's oral presentation at the NASSP 1971 convention in Houston, edited by the Bulletin staff.

The Elementary School Principalship — 1980

William D. Southworth

BY 1980, EDUCATIONAL PRACTICE WILL HAVE CAUGHT UP WITH EDUCATIONAL THEORY TO THE POINT THAT ACTIVE STAFF PARTICIPATION IN ALL ASPECTS OF ELEMENTARY EDUCATION WILL BE THE NORM IN EVERY GOOD SCHOOL.

The principalship of 1980, is not going to change radically from what it is today. It is certainly not going to disappear into some vague "relevancy" relationship that would eliminate the principalship.

The reason that it will not change is that it has developed from decades of experience, and it continues in being because it is needed. There must still be someone in the building, who has the responsibility for the building; and that responsibility will not be turned over to a committee of teachers. Specifically, principals of 1980 will still work directly with parents, and for two good reasons. Parents will continue to want to see the principal because he is in charge. They will not be satisfied meeting with a committee of teachers, however designated. Next, teachers will want the principal to continue in this principal's role because that is the set-up that they know, the set-up that works.

Somehow there seems to have developed the odd idea

Reprinted with the copyright permission of
The Clearing House, November, 1971.

Part I

that there is a basic conflict between the elementary school principal and his staff, that the two have more in conflict than they have in common. This odd idea is based on the attempt of some people to reduce subtle and sophisticated relationships to a simplistic, clear-cut, black-and-white relationship, primarily that of management and labor. The analogy of principal and teachers to management and labor is completely untenable; and it is the attempt to make it tenable that adds to the already complicated relationship existing between principals and teachers.

What will be the staff relations of the principal of 1980? His staff relations will not be changed materially from what they are today in the better-run schools. There will be some change of emphasis as roles become more clearly defined, but the change will be more minor than major.

The principal will recognize, and work on the basis of, the two discrete professional relationships of the teachers in his building. First, all teachers of the building are primarily teachers of the district. They are selected by central office personnel and assigned as their need in the individual building dictates. As district personnel they join with their counterparts in other buildings to form a district-wide teachers' organization. Thus, they have two pulls on their loyalty, toward other teachers and toward their common organization. Second, teachers of the building form a group, with their principal to nurture the development of the children of the building; and as this group, develop loyalties to the group, and to the principal.

In matters of salary, job security, working conditions,

and personal security, teachers want to have a strong teachers' association, and most teachers realize that they must participate in such an organization. While teachers recognize the need for collective strength, they are not avid for such strength, for most teachers would prefer not to have to be concerned about such things as salary, job security, working conditions, etc., for they would really like to concentrate on what they were educated for--to teach. But modern American life being what it is, teachers must participate and must work for their own benefits, for they cannot expect a benevolent, all-knowing school board to proffer what the teachers consider to be fair.

The teachers of a building are, in effect, riding two horses, both of which are going in the same direction, generally but not always. As district teachers, their relationship with their principal is attenuated, for decisions are made about their work in their own building by the district-wide group without consultation with the principal.

Obviously, a point is reached where the interests of the teachers and the interests of the principal come into conflict. For example, the limitation of class size, as defined in the negotiations agreement, limits the options for scheduling of personnel that a principal has. When, therefore, teachers are able to get a class size limitation as part of the negotiations agreement that they have developed with their school board, they are acting as district personnel, and not as building personnel; and as district personnel, they come in conflict with their building principal who is functioning solely as the building principal.

Part I

While the point made here may appear obvious, it is not obvious to many elementary principals. How pathetic is the principal who said, "I know that all my teachers are loyal to me." meaning that "his" teachers will function only as teachers of the school and not as district teachers. He must learn to differentiate between strictly local building matters, concerning which his teachers will act "loyally" to him, and district matters in which the teachers will act "loyally" to their own organization.

By 1980, principals will have learned to live easily with contracts drawn between boards and teachers. While some traditional options will be denied them, such as sole determination of the placement of children, there will be the compensation of not carrying the heavy load of responsibility of educational leadership of the building alone, but sharing it with other competent, dedicated professional teachers.

By 1980, educational practice will have caught up with educational theory to the point that active staff participation in all aspects of elementary education will be the norm in every good school. Participation of staff in policy-making for the school, for example, has been a tenet of good school administration for 25 years; but the theory too often has been more honored in the breach than in the observance. By 1980 satisfactory relationships among school people will have developed to the point where an easy relationship will exist, based on each group's knowing its role and participating in that role.

The reason that group participation will become a way of professional life for the principal of 1980 is

The Future of Elementary and Secondary School Education

that the principal of that time will have grown up in the profession when participation was practiced and not just talked about. To the principal of that time, group participation will be the basis on which he makes most of his decisions.

The role of the principal with the community will be largely unchanged. The proposal, advanced in some areas, that the principal not even have the responsibility of meeting with parents who want to talk about their children's progress, that the parents meet with the teachers involved and their union representative, will long since have disappeared. No other system than the one now in use will work nearly as well as the present system. However, it must be pointed out that the teachers are becoming more skillful in parent-teacher conferences, and that the actual participation of the principal in many conferences can be lessened because of the increased skill of the teachers.

In other areas of the principal's responsibilities, he will find that teachers do not really want to assume his role. Certainly they will not want to assume the day-by-day responsibilities and irritations of the principalship. They will continue to scrutinize his role and function as building leader critically; but not with the idea of taking it over. The teachers will demand to know what the principal does, and why he does what he does; but they will not try to eliminate his position as principal. Nor will they want the primary functions of the principalship parceled out to committees. They will want their own responsibilities and privileges respected by the principal. What they will demand, via the negotiations route, is clear role definitions and role functioning.

Part I

The principal will continue to have rating of teachers as major responsibility. He will work with two colleagues of the teachers being rated, so that the final decisions concerning the rating of teachers will come from this committee. The principal will thus function in a committee where he can always be outvoted, if the teachers vote as a bloc. But functionally, the committee will most often agree unanimously in its decisions; a split decision will be unusual; and two teachers voting against the principal will be rare.

The matter of inventory control will figure importantly in a well-run school. It is obviously poor management for paper, for instance, to become dried out and useless on storeroom shelves while teachers run short of paper in the classrooms. Since the supplies exist for the use of the teachers in the classrooms, it seems reasonable that a representative committee of teachers work with the principal in ordering, inventorying, and issuing supplies. Specifically, grade level representatives, elected by their peers, can serve with the principal in the above functions. Perhaps representatives of the primary and intermediate groups can serve on such a committee, so that it not become too large, with careful attention given to the special needs of the kindergarten teachers.

An alternative to a supplies committee is a responsible and fair secretary who would carefully carry out instructions of the committee, following carefully designed guidelines for her direction, and the teachers' protection. If such guidelines are not carefully spelled out, the secretary can accumulate partial control over the instructional program by by determining herself what teachers will receive what supplies and in what amounts. The committee must always remember and act upon the knowledge that authority not clearly assigned will be seized.

The principal will still have multi-faceted responsibilities, not startlingly different from those of the past, but more clearly spelled out. For example, he will consider himself, and his staff will consider him, to be the leader of the school in many areas, but not always in curricular areas. He will be wise enough to know that he does not know as much about kindergarten teaching as do the kindergarten teachers, for instance. He will continue, however, to know more about the overall curriculum of the school than anyone else, and his expertise will continue to be recognized by the staff. He will serve frequently as the "first among equals." His real leadership will weigh more heavily than his status leadership, with its title of principal.

One tenet of the democratic process is that the good leader deliberately assumes less authority than he can seize. In fact, the good leader graciously offers to share as much of his authority as he can. For example, when a matter of building procedure comes up, such as lunchroom serving lines, the administrator can rather easily devise a good system, particularly if he works with the lunchroom people. If he consults with the staff, or a committee of the staff, he may come out with the same results; but, the fact that the results are the same is not justification for not consulting with the staff. Granted that not consulting with the staff will "save time," there is the larger issue

Part I

that the staff will feel that it has been by-passed in an area where it should have been consulted. Therefore, no matter the results, no matter how efficient the principal's plan, there can remain a residue of resentment if the staff feels that they are not important enough to have their opinions considered.

One more tenet of the democratic process that the wise leader learns is that of giving as many opportunities as possible to get many people involved in decision making. What is not readily apparent is the lack of desire on the part of the staff members to participate. What staff members frequently want is the opportunity to participate. If the opportunity is really available to them, staff members enjoy an option that they do not have to exercise, for decision making is hard work and consumes large amounts of time that can be more pleasantly occupied otherwise. Suppose, for example, that the administrator asks if the staff would like to have a committee set up agendas for staff meetings. They would probably prefer that the principal do so, knowing that they, as staff members, would have ample opportunity to participate in each meeting themselves, and can at that time bring up pertinent items. The point is that an opportunity to participate was presented to the members of the staff, and they did not want the opportunity.

On the other hand, suppose that the staff wanted an agenda committee. Practically, the principal would be the chief architect of the agenda because he would have a wider view. However, it is the gracious offer to share authority that, strangely, strengthens the authority of the principal, for the

The Future of Elementary and Secondary School Education

staff will feel that he is not trying to accumulate power for the sake of power, but that he is trying to help the school to run more effectively. If the principal is the real leader, and not just the status leader, the staff will gladly assign to him areas of decision that might otherwise be denied him.

The principal of 1980 will be convinced that every pertinent decision that he makes and every pertinent action that he takes must relate to the welfare of the children and of the members of the staff. If the staff members know that he operates on this basis of concern for others, their professional sights will be raised; and matters that might otherwise deal in personalities, can deal in policies and practices for the promotion of the best interests of the people of the school.

Professional preparation for the principalship will become more sophisticated and demanding. One particular area of preparation will be budget management. By 1980 the budgets of most school systems will be programmed; that is, the cost of each program in the school will be priced, and each program will be considered as a unit. For example, the instructional costs of teaching reading in first grade are found in several places in the usual, current-day budget. The cost of teaching comes under instructional costs; the costs of supplies under supplies; the costs of textbooks under textbooks, Under program budgeting the total cost of the reading program will be developed so that any intelligent adult can determine immediately just how much it costs to teach first graders to read. And if there should be a marked disparity between the cost of teaching first graders in Washington School to read, as compared with the cost of

Part I

teaching first graders in Jackson School to read, the question will arise, "Why the difference?" The answer to that question will reveal a great deal more about the two schools than simply that one spends more money for teaching first graders than the other does.

Altogether, the elementary principalship of 1980 will be a more professionally demanding position than it is today, because of the increased subteties that will characterize the society of that time; and the schools will always reflect the society which they serve. While more will be demanded of the principal in the area of professional leadership, he will have the compensation of additional salary, more clearly defined role responsibilities, and a relationship with his staff that is grounded in agreements carefully hammered out, and clearly understood by teachers and principals. In short, the principal of 1980 will find his work satisfying because he will know what he is to do and under what circumstances he is to function. Therefore, while not greatly different from his counterpart of today, he will be a more "professional" man, and will function more effectively as an educational leader than his counterpart today.

Dr. Southworth is Chairman of the Department of Administration and Supervision, School of Education, at St. John's University in Jamaica, New York.

Part II
THE FUTURE OF HIGHER EDUCATION

We must create new models for adults who can teach their children not what to learn, but how to learn and not what they should be committed to, but to the value of commitment.

MARGARET MEAD

"The Future: Prefigurative Cultures and Unknown Children"

Fuller: Who Will Man Spaceship Earth?

Michael Sheldrick

....WHAT USUALLY HAPPENS IN THE EDUCATIONAL PROCESS IS THAT THE FACULTIES ARE DULLED, OVERLOADED, STUFFED AND PARALYZED, SO THAT BY THE TIME THE STUDENTS ARE MATURE, THEY HAVE LOST MANY OF THEIR INNATE CAPABILITIES.

Buckminster Fuller is a man of many parts--he is a philosopher, an engineer, a poet, a mathematician, an architect, a machinist, a cartographer, and even an ·educator. He is all these and none of them, for Richard Buckminster Fuller inhabits a synergistic world unknown to most of us. In an age of specialization, he is the consummate generalist--in his own words, a "self-disciplined comprehensivist." Still, his awesome grasp of general principles has permitted him to become no mean practitioner of many esoteric specialties.

Mr. Fuller's view of things starts invariably with the universe. Those who look to him for immediate answers to specific problems will be disappointed, for he will offer none. He is always a viewer and explainer of patterns. "I have to start with what I think the human's function in the universe may probably be," he says. "Next I explore the way humans

Reprinted with permission from the September, 1971 issue of College & University Business. Copyright 1971, McGraw-Hill Pubs., Inc., Chicago. All rights reserved.

Part II

and other biological species subconsciously cooperate in the successful regenerative balance of nature. Next, I think about what is happening to only subconsciously functioning man on earth, and next about what is happening to the chemically, biologically invisibly, and unselconsciously coordinated evolution of the little spaceship earth, and lastly, about whether that dynamically evolute earth and its passengers are trending and wending."

Each of Mr. Fuller's thoughts constitute a system: that is, his lines of "thought interrelationships..... return cyclically upon themselves in a plurality of directions, as do various circles around the great sphere." Nonetheless, his views on education can be conveniently divided into four main pillars which support the structure of the idea.

Mr. Fuller's analysis begins with a unique view of the collective history of universities: "All universities are organized today on the working assumption that specialization is essential. Now, how did that come about? Universities are quite new in the history of man. The technical ones go back to military undertakings and the like. I find that there were some very strong men and some very strong illiterate men... The strong man was able to organize himself into a powerful position by making it perfectly clear that he was stronger than the other fellow. Then came the followers who said, "Well, I'd better go along with him because he seems to organize things here. Everybody gets out of his way and lets him have those things that are necessary to survive."

In this Fullerian world, the top man recognized

The Future of Higher Education

among those gathered around him some exceptionally bright men who conceivably could plot against him. He intellectually disarmed them by assigning each of them specialized tasks. One man, good at languages, was told to find out the enemy's plans, and thus was born military intelligence. Another, interested in fashioning swords, was assigned the task of producing better weapons.

"The patterns," Mr. Fuller continues, "is one of the head man saying, "All right, you mind your own business, you mind your business, and you mind your own business. I'm the only one who minds everybody's business. Is that quite clear? Now this is where specialization begins. I've just given you the scheme and strategy of Oxford University."

Once the university was founded along these lines, he says, it was a short step for the head man to discover that "anticipatory divide and conquer" was better than plain, unadorned divide and conquer. "And that's exactly what the top man was doing when he took in all the bright ones and made them specialists," he continues. "He didn't bother with the dull ones at all. The bright ones weren't allowed to talk to one another very much and in time, they became so specialized and their languages so different they couldn't talk to one another anyway."

On the college level, as an alternative to the specialization Mr. Fuller calls "brain slavery," he is likely to recommend a course much like the one he followed at the Naval Academy early in World War I. "The naval officer who would command the fleets of our nation's ships had to operate autonomously," he says. "They were selectively promoted for com-

Part II

prehensive capability. They had to be entrusted with supreme authority at sea for the simple reason that there was no other authority present. Naval officers had to be prepared to make comprehensive, epochal and solo decisions on behalf of their nation. They had to be extraordinarily familiar with world commerce and the broad range of technology. They had to know chemistry, physics, mathematics, logistics, ballistics, economics, biology, law, psychology and engineering. They had to be able to set up industrially-tooled bases in foreign parts."

Belief in the boundless capacity of the individual to learn is the second component of Mr. Fuller's thoughts on education. Although man is by nature a generalist, the almost infinite capability of the individual to learn, he thinks, is destroyed by the institutions of society.

"I am convinced," Mr. Fuller says, "that neither I nor any other human being, past or present, was or is a genius. I am convinced that what I have, every physically normal child also had at birth. We could, of course, hypothesize that all babies are born geniuses and quickly get degeniused. Unfavorable circumstances, shortsightedness, frayed nervous systems, ignorantly articulated love, and fear of elders tend to shut off many of the child's brain capability valves. I was lucky in avoiding too many disconnections."

Mr. Fuller's view is that the function of schools on all levels should be to preserve what is natural and instinctive in human beings--an insatiable desire to learn. This constrasts sharply with most of American education, which postulates that the function of the school is to teach students what is useful to them. But, according to Mr. Fuller, "what usually happens in the educational process is that the faculties are dulled, overloaded, stuffed and paralyzed so that by the time the students are mature, they have lost many of their innate capabilities. My long-time hope is that we may soon begin to realize what we are doing and may alter the educational process in such a way only to help the new life to demonstrate some of its very powerful, innate capabilities."

A third important part of Mr. Fuller's outlook is what he sees as a coming reunification of science and the arts. The break, according to Mr. Fuller, came when the scientist discovered a number of phenomena beyond those that could be perceived simply by the senses, such as x-rays, for example. Literary men turned to familiar analogies to explain the new phenomena, such as water running in pipes to explain the flow of electricity through wires. These analogies were unsatisfactory to scientists, so they began to deal increasingly with abstract mathematical models. Finally, the scientists communicated without use of the common language and without reference to the sensate world. Thus, the public, including those in the arts, was unable to comprehend.

Now, says Mr. Fuller, "artists are extraordinarily important to human society. Many who have been called artists are healthy human beings who have kept their innate endowment of capabilities intact. The greatest of all faculties is the ability of the imagination to formulate conceptually. I feel that it is the artists who have kept the integrity of child-

Part II

hood alive until we reach the bridge between the arts and the sciences."

Mr. Fuller's fourth pillar is the utilization of technology to free man from routine, thought-stifling tasks so that he can fulfill what Mr. Fuller calls his integrative function. At the same time, says Mr. Fuller, such a step would give man greater physical and energy wealth than he could achieve through "brain-reflexed, manually controlled production." The result, according to Mr. Fuller, is that even as we are gaining more wealth, "it is very clear that the computer is already making man obsolete as a differentiator, that is, as a specialist."

One of the things holding back what otherwise would be a considerable use of the computer for tasks of differentiation is fear: "Our labor world and all salaried workers, including school teachers and college professors, are now at least subconsciously if not consciously afraid that automation will take away their jobs," he says. "On the other hand, humans alone can foresee, integrate and anticipate the new tasks to be done by progressively automated, wealth-producing machinery. To take advantage of the fabulous magnitudes of real wealth waiting to be employed intelligently by humans and to unblock automation's postponement by organized labor, we must give each human who is or becomes unemployed a life fellowship in research and development or just plain thinking."

In viewing this new era, Mr. Fuller perceives an important role for the universities, even if he is vague about the future of the institution itself: "U.S. labor will have to persuade Congress to under-

The Future of Higher Education

write 50 million lucrative university scholarships with life benefits of every type in order to persuade labor's rank and file to unblock and mandate full-cry automation."

Education, says Mr. Fuller, "is going to be number one among the great world industries, within which will flourish an educational technology that will provide tools such as the individually selected and articulated two-way TV and an intercontinentally networked documentaries call-up system, operative over any home two-way TV set."

From these ideas, a broad picture of Mr. Fuller's ideal university in 1996 can be drawn. It will have a comprehensive curriculum without disciplines as we now know them. Because automation will deliver great wealth there will be no need for the strong men of the past and no one to force students into specialties to intellectually castrate them.

The university will not be filled mainly with young people in the age bracket of 18 to 25 as is the case now, but will cater to all ages. Because of the diverse needs of its new student body and its huge size, the university will be forced to utilize every form of new technology to serve its students. All will be thirsting for knowledge. University officials will regard themselves as middlemen in the educational process, disseminating knowledge and ideas to students. They will no longer think of themselves as dispensers of bitter, though eminently necessary, educational pills to resisting patients.

The university will not regard itself as an institution, a physical entity, a builder and maintainer

Part II

of dormitories, an upholder of morals, an indefatigable in loco parentis, but as an information utility. Many of its students may never appear on campus; instead, they will be studying at home, working with their computer terminals and light pens in a modern correspondence school setting. "We will probably keep the schools open in the evenings because of the growing need for babysitters," Mr. Fuller says. "Real education, however, will be something to which individuals will discipline themselves spontaneously."

In 1927, R. Buckminster Fuller began determining how best to utilize the earth's mental and physical resources in 1980, when he hypothesizes, the world will be joined into a cooperative community.

Michael Sheldrick is a reporter for the McGraw-Hill World News.

The University in the Learning Society

Robert M. Hutchins

IN THE COMING AGE THE UNIVERSITY COULD BE TRANSFORMED INTO A CONTEMPORARY VERSION OF THE PLATONIC ACADEMY. IT COULD BE A CENTER OF INDEPENDENT THOUGHT AND CRITICISM, BRINGING THE GREAT INTELLECTUAL DISCIPLINES TOGETHER SO THAT THEY MIGHT SHED LIGHT ON ONE ANOTHER AND ON THE MAJOR ISSUES FACING MODERN MAN.

A cybernated world is likely to be one in which a few highly trained experts and a small labor force, whose qualifications are that they can see a red light or hear a whistle, can operate an industrial plant. We need education in science and technology in a scientific age not to train us for the work we have to do but to understand the world we are living in.

The report of a special Task Force on education of HEW ends with an absurd question: "How can students be freed from the infatuation of American society with the form rather than the substance of learning?" The students cannot be freed of this infatuation until the form rather than the substance of learning ceases to satisfy those upon whom their educational, economic and social future depends.

Reprinted with permission from the September, 1971 issue of College & University Business. Copyright 1971 McGraw-Hill Pubs., Inc., Chicago. All rights reserved

Part II

The real question is, why is American society infatuated with the form rather than the substance of learning? The answer must be that if you don't know what the substance is you have to be content with the form. Or if you are confused about the substance you can at least identify and seek the form. You may not be able to tell whether a person is educated, but you can always count his credits, grades and diplomas and the number of years he has been in school.

We must look forward to an immense decentralization, debureaucratization and deinstitutionalization if we are to have a learning society. Here technology can help us. The electronic devices now available can make every home a learning unit for all the family. All the members of the family might be continuously engaged in learning. Teachers might function as visiting nurses do today--and as physicians used to do. The new electronic devices do not eliminate the need for face-to-face instruction or for schools, but they enable us to shift attention from the wrong question, which is how can we get everybody in school and keep him there as long as possible, to the right one, which is how can we give everybody a chance to learn all his life?

The new technology gives a flexibility that will encourage us to abandon the old self-imposed limitations. They are that education is a matter for part of life, part of the year, or part of the day, that it is open in all its richness only to those who need it least, and that it must be conducted formally, in buildings designed for the purpose, by people who have spent their lives in schools.

The Open University in England, if it can hold off

the Tories and avoid suffocation from its credits
and degrees, gives us some intimation of what the
educational future could look like. The Open University is nothing less than a national commitment
to use all the intellectual and technological resources
of the country in a coherent way to give every citizen,
no matter what his background or academic qualifications, a chance to learn all his life. In this country,
the University Without Walls, which is just getting
started, appears to be contemplating the same thing.

Then there are cables, cassettes, computers and
videotape. It is reported that a cable system is
now being built in San Jose that will have 48 channels. It is hard to accept the proposition that all of
these must be dedicated to the kind of triviality
that is now the common fare on commercial television. The San Jose people would have to make a
tremendous effort to avoid using some of these channels for cultural, artistic and educational purposes,
and in particular for the discussion of political, economic and social issues.

I do not say we will use the new instruments technology has given us in order to create a new learning
society. I say only that we can. We can have a
learning society. Its object would be to raise every
man and woman and every community to the highest
cultural level attainable. In such a society the role
of educational institutions would be to provide for
what is notably missing from them today, and that
is the interaction of minds.

In the coming age the university could be transformed into a contemporary version of the
Platonic academy. It could be a center of independent thought and criticism, bringing the great

Part II

intellectual disciplines together so that they might shed light on one another and on the major issues facing modern man. The university is that institution which should lead in the achievement of critical consciousness. It must use and contain within it all the major modes of understanding and transforming reality. Thus the university would represent and constitute the circle of knowledge, in which everything is understood in the light of everything else.

Such a university could preside over the progress of the learning society.

In 22 years as president and chancellor of the University of Chicago, Robert Maynard Hutchins gained world fame for his humane and democratic approach to education. Today he is president of the Center for Study of Democratic Institutions. His most recent book is "The Learning Society."

Higher Education in the United States in 1980 and 2000 — From the Perspective of the Carnegie Commission

Clark Kerr

TODAY, IF I WERE TO PICK ONE REAL DISASTER AREA IN HIGHER EDUCATION, IT WOULD BE GENERAL EDUCATION.

During the 1960's, American higher education was faced with growing pressures from within and without. As a result, the late 1960's ushered in a period of intensive reassessment, a period in which faults in the existing system as well as certain new directions became more visible, a period of transition to respond to new clienteles and to the needs of a rapidly changing society.

In this period of transition, inevitably, task forces and commissions arose under various auspices to examine the goals and structure of higher education in its rapidly changing context. In 1968 the President requested Wilbur Cohen, Secretary of Health, Education and Welfare, to prepare a long-range plan for federal financial support for higher education. Again, in 1970, a special presidentially appointed task force under the chairmanship of James Hester was asked to report on federal priorities in higher

---

Reprinted by permission of the American Association for Higher Education and Jossey-Bass. From the Expanded Campus: Current Issues in Higher Education 1972, Dyckman W. Vermilye, Editor(San Francisco:Jossey-Bass, 1972)Chapter one,"Policy Concern for the Future," by Clark Kerr, pp. 3-21.

Part II

education. In 1969, the American Academy of Arts and Sciences appointed a group under the chairmanship of Martin Meyerson to suggest and develop new possibilities for defining the missions of universities and the means of carrying them out. And, about the same time, then Secretary of HEW, Robert Finch, appointed a task force chaired by Frank Newman to appraise and propose needed changes in higher education. As you know, this last task force has been reorganized somewhat to develop more specific recommendations growing out of its proposals. In specific response to turbulence on campus, President Nixon appointed a special committee under the chairmanship of William Scranton to look into the causes of unrest on America's campuses. At the national level several other commissions, including many working under the auspices of particular higher education associations, examined specific aspects of higher education. The 1960's also gave rise to numerous state commissions created to study particularly questions concerning the status of private higher education, the need for coordination and control at the state level, and development of future plans to meet the state's demands for postsecondary education.

The proliferation of commissions and task forces in a period of transition is to be expected; what is somewhat less expected is that commissions operating under quite different auspices and with substantially different membership characteristics, funding patterns, and methods of operation, should have so many significant areas of agreement on both the weaknesses in the present system and the measures to remedy those weaknesses.

The Future of Higher Education

The work of the Carnegie Commission has been aided by the work of these many other groups studying higher education. Whether in the future the Carnegie Commission will be looked upon as one of the more influential commissions studying higher education in the 1960's and 1970's is difficult to predict, but it will probably be viewed as having undertaken the most comprehensive survey of higher education, not only in American history but in the history of any nation.

The very breadth of scope predisposes the Carnegie Commission to a measure of impact on at least some areas of higher education. But as our publications are completed with little logical sequence, readers may find it difficult to perceive the central thrusts of the Commission. Hopefully, our final report in 1973 will supply the unifying themes, but in the meantime I have been asked to give you some notion of the Carnegie Commission's view of higher education as we now see it, what the relative certainties and uncertainties are for the period ahead to 2000, and what aspects of higher education might be subject to policy control to develop a higher education system more suited to our present and changing needs. This view from the perspective of the Carnegie Commission is being given at a time when the work of the Commission is about two-thirds completed, when nearly half of our research reports have been published, and when 11 out of our estimated 18 Commission reports have been issued. Through our profile series, of which 8 profiles have already been issed and 10 more are in process, we have tried to provide new descriptive and analytical material on the several types of institutions and significant functions that com-

Part II

prise American higher education. Through a series of essays by foreign observers, we are gaining international perspective on American higher education. And through over 65 individual research projects on particular aspects of higher education, of which 30 have been completed, we are seeking the necessary information to guide policy recommendations.

Our studies to date have led us to identify several relative certainties about higher education that confront us over the next few decades.

First of all we know the general magnitude of the numbers of students that must be served. In the 1970's places must be found for an additional 3 million students. This is the same additional number we accommodated in the 1960's, but it represents a smaller proportional gain. The addition of 3 million students in the 1960's constituted a 100 percent growth. In the 1980's we face some years in which the absolute numbers will go down in peace time and in prosperity (if in fact we have peace and prosperity) for the first time in more than 335 years since the founding of Harvard. There will be a reduction in some years and no net increase over the decade. In 1990, in fact, there may be slightly fewer students in our traditional colleges and universities than it now appears there will be in 1980. This will be a traumatic experience for colleges and universities that have been geared for decades to growth and for the last two decades to particularly rapid growth.

It is likely that there will be one further spurt in the enrollment of colleges and universities in the

The Future of Higher Education

1990's, when the grandchildren of the GI's enroll. But after that period, higher education will be growing at a slower rate than it has historically. Since 1870, we have doubled the number of students in college every 12 to 15 years. If we were to continue that doubling, beginning with 1970, we would have 16 million students in 1985; we would have 32 million students in the year 2000; we would have 64 million students in the year 2015. But this continued rate of growth is absolutely impossible and will never again occur in higher education. In the past we have grown at a rate much faster than American society. In the future, the higher education growth rate is much more likely to parallel that of society.

The second relative certainty with which we enter the next few decades concerns the general magnitude of the costs of higher education. The cost of higher education has grown enormously over the last few decades. Part of this growth can be attributed to the increase in numbers of students, but a part must also be attributed to rising costs per students. A study made for us by the Brookings Institution shows that since 1930 cost per student per year has gone up at a rate which is a combination of the general rate of inflation plus 3 percent. At the present time, our institutions of higher education have expenditures of about 20 billion dollars. Even if there were no general inflation, given the anticipated increase in the number of students and the 3 percent per year increase in costs, we can anticipate an expenditure of $40 billion in 1980, of $60 billion in 1990, and $100 billion in the year 2000. Not only are absolute costs rising, but they are becoming a larger proportion of our gross national product. And as the cost threatens to push upward

Part II

toward 3 percent of our gross national product, further increases are meeting increased resistance, particularly at a time when the nation's many other priorities--the renovation of our cities, the adequate financing of early, elementary, and secondary education, growing welfare costs, and the preservation of our physical environment, must also be met.

Third, we now have what is probably the best and most complete information ever available on the attitudes of students and faculty members. These findings emerge from a study sponsored by the Carnegie Commission in which 70,000 undergraduates, 30,000 graduates, and 60,000 faculty members were surveyed. While we can't be certain that these attitudes will continue throughout the twentieth century, certainly they must be a factor in policy determinations in the immediate future, and next few decades. Although the overall level of general satisfaction seems to be relatively high, with only 12 percent of undergraduates in all types of institutions indicating they were dissatisfied or very dissatisfied with the education they were getting at their colleges, and an additional 22 percent indicating they were on the fence, there were relatively higher levels of criticism on specific aspects of the educational process.

Ninety-six percent of the students favor an open access system. While such a system exists in some states and areas, we have far to go to achieve it across the nation. Students also are overwhelmingly in favor of putting the emphasis on teaching effectiveness rather than on publications as the major criterion for hiring and promoting faculty members. Ninety-five percent of the students surveyed indicated this preference, and 86 percent of the faculty agreed with this preference. Ninety percent of the students believed that course work should be more relevant to contemporary life and problems.

Other findings suggest further need for reassessment of present structures and programs. Sixty-seven percent of the students feel that colleges should have a responsibility for helping solve the social problems of society and not just through research; 62 percent believe that colleges should be governed primarily by faculty and students; 59 percent believe that all grades should be abolished; 53 percent feel that all courses should be elective; 48 percent believe that every student should be required to undertake a year of national service.

There is more dissatisfaction among graduate students (23 percent) but the general trend of opinions suggests similar changes. And finally, we know that our college graduates if educated in the traditional college and university program will have increasing difficulties obtaining positions upon graduation. Job markets for Ph.D.s in many fields are rapidly becoming buyers' markets and the average holder of a baccalaureate degree will no longer be able to command the premiums in the job market which he was once able to command now that an ever greater percentage of our young people are attending colleges and universities.

Thus, in seeking policy development for the period ahead in higher education, we have some relatively certain findings to guide us. More difficult to assess will be the impact on the future development of higher education of many important uncertainties.

Part II

First of all is the attitude of the public toward higher education. Will we be able to avoid the "collision course" between the campus and society which some, including David Riesman, have predicted? The campus is increasing its demands on society through requests for increased financial support and for freedom from control by society at the same time that campus elements are urging the campus to take a more active role in attacking and changing society. It is difficult to predict at this time whether the crisis of public confidence which has intensified the growing financial stringency in higher education will continue. But there are some signs of growing public support. Many states have added to their commitment of funds to public higher education new commitments for funds to private institutions in their states. The federal government is now considering higher education legislation which would substantially increase the commitment of federal funds for students and institutional aid. In the legislative halls of the nation one finds continued deepseated support for higher education, but coupled with a growing desire for new types of accountability to the public for the manner in which higher education spends its resources.

A second and important uncertainty relates to the long-range potential impact of the growing importance of the senate concerns of students in higher education. In the survey of student attitudes mentioned earlier, 83 percent of the students believe that more attention should be placed by our colleges and universities on the emotional development of the student. Fifty-three percent felt that colleges should provide more opportunities for students to engage in creative activity, particularly the creative arts. There are other evidences of some turning away from the cognitive aspects of higher education and a movement toward experimental satisfaction. The strength of this movement is difficult to assess at this time.

Third, there are also evidences of growing politicalization of academic life.

A fourth factor of uncertainty is the technological revolution that seems to be waiting in the wings of higher education. Computers are becoming more useful and more readily available. The video cassette may turn every living room in the nation into a classroom. And it is possible that in the future computers and/or television may provide access to virtually unlimited information in regional or network-linked library and learning resource storage centers. How soon technology will show its mark on the structure and delivery of higher education is difficult to know. How much technology will become a substitute for present systems and how much it will simply augment existing systems is also difficult to predict.

The uncertainties of higher education today lead some people to ignore the certainties and to urge that we make only minimal plans for the future. But the future development of our colleges and universities is much too important to leave to fate or chance. We cannot afford to refuse to identify important objectives and effective ways of reaching them just because we are afraid we might upset some mystical natural evolution of our institutions and our society. We cannot hesitate to select a policy only because our choice might conflict with some ultimate, dark, and as yet unknown eventuality.

Part II

The Carnegie Commission was established because it seemed clear that American higher education could not prosper on a "wait and see" basis. That philosophy ignores present realities and encourages preservation of myths and wishful thinking. It leads to unwarranted duplication of effort and to wasteful uses of resources that are in short supply.

The future can be determined by principles as well as by events, by men and women, no less than by the mere passage of time. But if men and women, guided by principles, are to make sound decisions, they must have available to them the results of an orderly examination of available important information and experience in higher education and reliable definitions of those principles that have proved useful in the past and may be promising in the future.

Perhaps the clearest way to demonstrate the roles policy can play in shaping the future of higher education is to review briefly seven policy areas that have been of special concern to us. In each case, I hope to outline some of the circumstances that have created the problems to be solved and to indicate what the Commission has said about them thus far. In some instances, I will suggest aspects of the problems that remain to be considered.

One policy concern of the Commission is as old as our nation itself. It involves applying the principle of social justice to higher education. It commands priority so long as we strive to achieve the dream of our nation's founders that all men should be guaranteed equal opportunities to seek and enjoy the benefits of the democratic society they created. In our very first report, <u>Quality and Equality: New</u>

The Future of Higher Education

Levels of Federal Responsibility for Higher Education, we noted the historic role educational institutions have played in building our society. We also set forth in that report recommendations of things the federal government could do to alleviate the financial barriers to higher education that confront many young people from low-income families. We urged the federal government to strengthen and expand current educational opportunity grants, providing $1,000 to undergraduates and $2,000 to graduate students found to be in financial need. We urged that the federal work-study program be continued and expanded and that institutions be given federal funds for scholarships to be awarded to students with financial need. We recommend that certain federal incentives be employed to encourage states, local governments, and private philanthropy to continue and increase their contributions to student assistance. We urged that student assistance be instituted to reward various forms of national service provided by youth. To further eliminate financial barriers to educational opportunity, we recommend creation of a National Student Loan Bank from which students could obtain loans to be paid back out of their earnings after leaving college. The total first-year expenditures for such programs would be about $2.4 billion. It would increase to about $5 billion within ten years.

Through such measures, we believe that all economic barriers to education could be eliminated by 1976, the 200th anniversary of the Declaration of Independence.

We have recommended that the federal funds given to students should be considered an entitlement, similar to that given to G.I.'s. Students should re-

Part II

ceive the assistance we recommended regardless of where they reside or which institutions they choose to attend. Moreover, the students entitlements should be accompanied by federal grants--cost of education supplements--paid directly to the institutions in which they enroll. We estimate that such grants to institutions would total about $1 billion in the first year in which they were made and should increase to about $3.6 billion by 1980.

Unlike other proposals for giving financial assistance to institutions--particularly those based on across-the-board support tied to enrollment or degrees awarded--the proposals of the Commission are rooted deeply in the principle of social justice. They extend educational opportunity to those who would be deprived of it without federal assistance or if there were not enough college doors open to them. This form of support is clearly appropriate to the federal government because it serves the cause of equality of opportunity for all people that is so deeply imbedded in our national purpose.

The second report of the Commission, A Chance to Learn: An Action Agenda for Equal Opportunity in Higher Education, reiterated our proposals for increased financial aid to students, again underscoring the importance of the financial barrier to educational opportunity for many Americans. It also pointed out, however, that educational opportunity in America is unequally available for other reasons--including ethnic origin, location of higher educational facilities, age, and quality of early schooling. In response to these inequities, we have made recommendations concerning the improvement of the education in elementary and secondary schools that is available to children who live in disadvantaged or ethnically segregated neighborhoods. In this and subsequent reports we have also stressed the importance of having some kind of higher education available within commuting distance of 95 percent of the people in the country, as means of improving accessibility of institutions to prospective students.

To overcome inequalities of educational opportunity that are the result of age, we recommend both in our second report, and in a subsequent report, Less Time, More Options: Education Beyond the High School, that there be greater flexibility in the patterns of college attendance, so that people could attend throughout their lifetime.

To assure that educational opportunities would remain open at available institutions, we recommended that each state plan to provide universal access to its total system--though not necessarily to each of its institutions. We also proposed various types of programs designed to assist the adjustment of persons who did not have adequate college preparation, to education at the postsecondary level.

By the year 2000, opportunities can and must be totally free of all limitations imposed by ethnic grouping, or geographic location, or age, or prior schooling.

We are currently considering another item on the agenda for improving social justice--the equal participation of women in higher education. Thoughtful observers have long acknowledged that women have not enjoyed the same degree and quality of participation in higher education that has been available to men. Evidence that the time has come for important changes in this matter has pressed itself on the national

Part II

consciousness and conscience with increasing impact in recent years. Our Commission now has the question under study and we hope to offer a statement and recommendations on it before very long.

A second concern that requires study and policy formation involves the question of whether or not American higher education is producing the <u>trained manpower</u> the nation needs. In the past, our record has been generally good. Our colleges and universities deserve a large share of the credit for providing the skill and leadership the American nation has needed for its dynamic growth. But we now have information that indicates that we may be in trouble on two manpower fronts. The first is that we are geared up to train many more teachers than American society is going to need. The U.S. Department of Labor and the Bureau of the Census estimate that if our colleges continue to produce teachers at the current rate, we will, by the end of the 1970's, have produced 1, 2, or even 3 million more teachers than can be placed in the American school system. Primary registrations are already down; high school registrations are going down; and higher education enrollment in the 1980's, as an average, will be absolutely level. So we are geared up to produce more teachers than can be absorbed. In health services, on the other hand, we face serious shortage. During the present decade, through either private or public auspices, there will be some form of health insurance, we assume, available to all Americans. This will give rise to a demand for health service that is much greater than anything we have seen before--even during the years when Medicare was introduced. We need at least a million people trained in the health manpower fields than we are now prepared to train.

Before the end of the current academic year, the Commission hopes to have completed a fairly comprehensive review of the relationship between the nation's manpower needs and higher education.

We have already given considerable attention to the problems of training health service manpower. With the help of leaders in this field from all over the country, we have compiled data and experiences that have been highly instructive. Of particular importance in these deliberations was a study on Financing Medical Education done for the Commission by Rashi Fein of the Harvard Medical School and Gerald Weber of the Brookings Institution. It will probably be a classic in its field for a long time to come. We were also helped considerably by an analysis of Trends and Projections of Physicians in the United States made by Mark S. Blumberg, who is now a planning advisor for Kaiser Foundation Health Plan. The Commission's own report on this subject, entitled Higher Education and the Nation's Health: Policies for Medical and Dental Education, has recommended that the number of medical school entrants be significantly increased, that all university health science centers consider developing training programs for physicians' and dentists' associates and assistants, and that the instruction programs leading to the M. D. and D. D. S. degrees be accelerated so that they might take three years instead of four beyond the B. A. degree. Beyond these measures for increasing the supply of health care personnel, we recommended that health manpower research programs in the Department of Health, Education and Welfare be strengthened and expanded.

Of all the reports issued by the Commission thus far,

Part II

this one on medical education has been the most completely accepted. Almost all of its recommendations that require federal implementation are reflected in legislation that was passed by Congress during the current session and signed by the President into law.

A third area of policy conern is broadly described by the phrase academic reform. One of the consequences of rapid growth in higher education in this country, with its increasing diversity of institutions and its increasing accessibility to students from more varied sectors in our society, has been an erosion of consensus about what constitutes a good education. Between the two World Wars, colleges in this country were known the world over for their general education for undergraduates--for the idea that a core of knowledge in several subject fields could be taught in ways adequate to the needs of an "educated" man or woman. Today, if I were to pick one real disaster area in higher education, it would be general education. The failure of general education in America has been described with great insight in essays written for the Commission by such informed foreign observers as Sir Eric Ashby of Great Britain, and Joseph Ben-David of the Hebrew University of Jerusalem. They attribute the failure mainly to the fact that there is no longer agreement in America on what ought to be taught to college undergraduates. Other factors in the failure are the unwillingness of many first-rank professors to teach undergraduate courses, and a lack of consensus about the kind of person an "educated" man or woman ought to be. A consequence of the failure of general education is that at some institutions, there are no longer any requirements at all, and students are allowed to take virtually anything they want.

Another concern subject to policy influence involves the general structure of the college experience. In many respects it has changed very little since the mid-nineteenth century. Until very recently, four years was almost inevitably the norm required for earning a bachelor's degree, and these years were usually spent uninterruptedly beginning three months after graduation from high school. The modes of instruction, including lectures, discussion groups, and seminars, have varied little from institution to institution. Testing, grading, and certification for accomplishment were greatly standardized.

Effecting change in such matters has proved to be extremely difficult. Few guilds remain as strong as the academic guild and few other guilds have been as unreceptive to altering their ways of doing things. These observations were confirmed for the Commission in Dwight Ladd's down-to-earth review of the efforts of many institutions to effect significant academic change through self-studies conducted by their own faculties. His book, Change in Educational Policy, is sobering reading for anyone disposed to regard the task of institutional reform as involving no more than putting the influence of distinguished and respected colleagues behind rational solutions to identifiable problems.

Despite these difficulties, I believe the Commission is now having significant influence on efforts to achieve desirable changes. Stephen Spurr's study for us on Academic Degree Structures, and Alden Dunham's "Radical Recommendation" in his profile of the nation's state colleges and regional universities, helped to crystallize the Commission's rec-

Part II

ommendations in its report, <u>Less Time, More Options</u> that:

-- a degree or some other form of credit be made available to students every two years during their college career

-- the time required to earn a degree be shortened by one year to the B. A. and by one to two additional years to the Ph. D. and M. D.

-- two new degrees, the Master of Philosophy and the Doctor of Arts, be widely accepted throughout our colleges and universities.

The latter degree would be designed to recognize training to a level comparable to that of the Ph. D., but would be designed to prepare people primarily to engage in teaching rather than research.

This same report, in many ways the most controversial of the reports we have issued thus far, generally urges that there be greater flexibility in higher learning. Among its recommendations are that there be more opportunities created for students to "stop-out" at appropriate points in their educational career for work experience, national service, travel, or some other alternative activity. We also urged expansion of opportunities for students to pursue education while they hold part-time or full-time jobs, or to alternate periods of employment with periods of education. To reduce the pressure on young people to enter college immediately after graduating from high school, we recommend that, after high school graduation, every person in the United States have two years of postsecondary education put "in the bank" for them for use at any time during their lives.

But many unanswered questions of academic policy remain. How do we define the basic core of undergraduate education? What kind of flexibility and alternatives are desirable in development of a general curriculum? What styles of instruction are to be encouraged? What are the roles of the emerging technologies in the teaching and learning process? How should academic achievement be evaluated and certified? What are the most desirable academic environments for students at different stages in their education? How do we reward good teaching? These and other tough questions are now being considered by the Commission.

Easily as difficult as questions involving academic reform are those that concern governance. There has been an almost invariable sequence of battles between the trustees of institutions and the agencies that chartered their colleges. One development in this contest has been the addition of lay alumni to the board of trustees of church-related colleges in an effort to dilute the influence of the clergy. The second contest occurred when presidents demanded and, to a considerable extent, won from trustees greater authority in administrative matters. The third contest was between the faculties of many institutions and their presidents. The result was considerable new power for faculties. The fourth one, now in progress, and with an outcome still to be decided is between students and everyone else. Many institutions have experiences all four contests. And they have learned that after each one, the powers of contending forces may be altered but no segment has yet lost as much power as it has gained in

Part II

previous redistributions of authority.

One result of these contests is that there is no clear-cut vertical power-structure on most American campuses. Instead, there tend to be elaborate veto systems through which every important policy must be filtered before it can be enacted.

In this state of affairs--which is absolutely bewildering to students of political or business organizations--many questions must be answered if we are going to plan effectively for the future. Three of them are of special importance today:

- -- The first is the degree to which students are to be granted participation in the decision-making processes on our campuses.

- -- The second is how much autonomy our systems of education are to have from state and federal government, and from the growing number of coordinating agencies being created to plan educational development at state and local levels. This question will acquire increasing importance as government financial support for all institutions--public and private--becomes more commonplace.

- -- Finally, when it becomes necessary for someone to act promptly to meet an emergency, how can he break through the relatively cumbersome governmental procedures of the average campus?

We have begun to formulate answers to questions of this kind and hope to issue a report on our conclusions in the near future.

A fifth area of major policy involves the number and variety of <u>institutions</u> that ought to be available as we enter the 21st century. We do not believe we will need more new Ph.D.'s granting universities. Higher education and our society cannot absorb all of the Ph.D.'s we are producing now, and existing institutions have the capacity to produce all of the Ph.D.'s we will need in the foreseeable future. But in our report <u>New Students and New Places: Policies for the Future Growth and Development of American Higher Education,</u> issued last October, we recommended that between 175 and 235 new community colleges be built by 1980 with between 80 and 125 of them located in metropolitan areas with populations of 500,000 or more. We also recommended that between 80 and 105 new comprehensive colleges should be built by 1980 and that between 60 and 70 of these should be in large metropolitan areas.

To preserve the diversity of institutions that has been a hallmark of American higher education, it is particularly important that we assist the private colleges in their fight for survival. In many respects, private institutions have been those hardest hit by the hard times now confronting all of higher education. The problem is particularly acute for some of the smallest of these institutions. The nature of the challenges facing about 500 of these colleges has just been outlined for us in a profile by Alexander Astin and Calvin Lee. They say that many of them are plagued by inefficient size, apparent ceilings on tuition charges, and inadequate recognition for their educational con-

Part II

tributions. Our report on The Capitol and the Campus: State Responsibility for Postsecondary Education urged that states contribute or increase support of private colleges and universities, noting that "their graduates and the graduates of public institutions benefit society equally, that they provide diversity, innovative opportunities, models of interest in the individual student, and standards of autonomy useful to all higher education." Specifically, we have supported state subsidy of tuition costs at private colleges for students who cannot meet them. We also favor state support for special endeavors, such as medical schools, and assistance through grants or loans for construction. Of course, the financial aid we have urged the federal government to provide should also be given without differentiation between public and private institutions.

The colleges founded for Negroes constitute a rather special group of institutions, though they are only a small part of the total resources of the country employed to meet increasing student demand. These institutions are unique in terms of their history and will continue for the foreseeable future to have certain missions that other institutions cannot serve as well as they can. They are the subject of a Commission profile, entitled Between Two Worlds, written by Frank Bowles and Frank DeCosta, which is one of the most thorough historical and descriptive profiles of these institutions yet written. It clearly describes the problems of transition faced by these colleges as they lose their roles as the only institutions giving higher education to blacks in a segregated society and are led to compete with all other institutions in the country not only for financial support but also for students and faculty members. In our own Commission report on them, <u>From Isolation to Mainstream: Problems of the Colleges Founded for Negroes</u>, we stress the past contributions of these institutions, note the role they will play in providing educational opportunity for students in the coming years, encourage them to grow to the point where they double their enrollments, reaching an aggregate of 300,000 by year 2000, and then propose special federal expenditures of some $41 million annually through the 1970's to assist them with their problems of transition. These funds would be in addition to the approximately $315 million in federal financing to which these institutions would be entitled under other Commission recommendations. In all, the Commission urges federal expenditures for black institutions that are more than 5 times as great as the amount of funds actually expended on them in 1968-69. At a time when many were doubting the continued vitality of the black colleges, we concluded that they should be viewed as a "national asset."

A sixth area of the Commission's interest that is susceptible to analysis and policy recommendations relates to the probability that much of the higher education available on the nation's traditional campuses. We in higher education often ignore the fact that considerable postsecondary education is already available in some 7,000 private and trade and technical

Part II

schools, and in hundreds of apprenticeship programs, adult public schools and correspondence schools that are not now regarded as part of the nation's higher education system. The Carnegie Commission has already urged that these institutions be taken into consideration in future planning of higher education facilities at state and local levels.

In addition to these existing facilities, however, new kinds of programs within traditional colleges and totally new kinds of externally based institutions are being established. It is still difficult to tell what the full impact of such extended education programs will be. But a few impacts now seem highly probable. The first is that extended learning, will encourage people over a wide range of ages and in many walks of life, people not served well by existing colleges and universities, to take advantage of greater access to postsecondary education of considerable variety. Secondly, as has been the case in Great Britain, these programs will also attract many students who would normally go to traditional colleges. The reason for this is that individuals' tastes and needs for different kinds of education vary. For certain young people, the alternative systems will be the preferred ones. Thirdly, it is likely that these institutions will become the "proving ground" for some of the emerging instructional technologies. To the degree that they are successful in these endeavors, they will accelerate the use of such technologies within traditional institutions.

The Commission is already on record as advocating further experiment with degrees-by-examinations, open university-type programs, and increased opportunities for people to obtain higher education throughout their lifetime. In future reports we intend to elaborate on these proposals, and place the traditional systems of higher education more realistically within the full context of educational opportunities available in our country.

The seventh--and last--policy concern I want to discuss is the whole question of where the responsibility lies for financing higher education.

It is quite possible that Earl Cheit's report on The New Depression in Higher Education did as much as any single prior effort to open the eyes of the public and of policy makers throughout the country to the seriousness of the financial problems facing colleges and universities in 1971. By analyzing specific institutions, and recording the experience and expectations of presidents and administrators across the country, Cheit demonstrated that the financial problems were pervasive. Seventy-one percent of the institutions in his sample were either headed for financial difficulty or in financial difficulty. And the financial problems he encountered afflicted institutions across the board, public and private, large and small. Moreover, he found the fundamental problem to be universal--costs are rising faster than income.

The obvious question suggested by these findings

Part II

is "Where is the additional money going to come from to close the gap?"

We naturally look to the federal government for funds, partly out of habit, but also because it collects the largest portion of the tax dollar in the country. We also look to the federal government with some justifiable reservations. The experience of nations that have become heavily dependent upon national subsidies for their higher education has generally not been good. They have found that regardless of how they try to avoid it, national centralized support invites controls that significantly threaten institutional independence. This is one reason why the Carnegie Commission has consistently urged that, although federal support for higher education should increase from about one-fifth of total institutional support to about one-quarter, it should not become the basic component of financial support. Moreover, we have urged that federal funding, whenever possible, should support endeavors that are clearly in the national interest. Thus, as I mentioned previously, we believe that student assistance and aid to institutions tied to educational opportunity grants are in appropriate form of assistance to higher education. Funds thus provided obviously advance the principle of social justice, a national concern. We similarly urge continued federal support of research, medical education, and other special programs that are clearly in the national interest.

In our report on The Capitol and the Campus, we recommended that the major responsibility

The Future of Higher Education

for maintaining, expanding and improving post-secondary education in the United States should reside in the state governments in cooperation with local governments and private institutions. We believe that the state share of funding for higher education, like the federal share, should be about one-quarter of the total expenditures.

That leaves half of the total expenditures to be made by private sector. It is to be provided through fees and tuition and gifts and grants. By far the largest portion of the total amount from the private sector will be in the form of tuition and fees. Unless we are to abandon the principle of equal opportunity, if tuitions are to continue to increase, there must also be made available adequate loan funds for students from low-or modest-income families. For this purpose, the Commission favors creation of a National Student Loan Bank, a private nonprofit corporation financed by the sale of governmentally guaranteed bonds.

Predictions and prescriptions are much easier to make when we have fairly clear trends and definite information about what effects those trends. In higher education, the many uncertainties make predictions hazardous at the present time. Nonetheless, we must make our best efforts to develop wise policy to meet existing and future needs. It is hoped that the work of the Carnegie Commission, which is but one of many groups currently studying higher education, will be a meaningful addition to the ongoing discussions on the future

Part II

of American higher education.

Clark Kerr is the former President of the University of California. He now is Chairman of the Carnegie Commission on Higher Education, Berkely, California.

Space-Free/Time-Free Higher Learning: New Programs, New Institutions, and New Questions

Michael Marien

.....NEW RELATIONSHIPS BETWEEN EDUCATIONAL INSTITUTIONS AND VARIOUS COMMUNITY AGENCIES--LIBRARIES AND MUSEUMS, MUSIC AND THEATRE ORGANIZATIONS, BUSINESS, INDUSTRY, LABOR, SOCIAL SERVICE--SHOULD AND WILL BE CREATED AS NON-TRADITIONAL STUDY TAKES A FIRMER HOLD ON THE PUBLIC CONSCIOUSNESS.

Until very recently, virtually all forecasts of higher education, as well as proposals for its reform, dealt solely with campus-bound, fixed-time programs. A college or university was seen as a locatable place where students and teachers assemble, and a college education was defined by four years of courses (or three years, as recently recommended by the Carnegie Commission on Higher Education). This unconscious assumption of space and time has obscured a vision of the future that may not only be plausible, but also more desirable.

In 1970, several plans and proposals served to erode the traditional space/time assumption. In 1971, the collective impact of more plans and proposals, as well as the operationalization of several projects, has led not only to an abandonment of the space/time assumption, but to a "gold rush" stampede toward

Reprinted from Notes on the Future, Educational Policy Research Center at Syracuse, Winter, 1972.

Part II

open universities, universities-without-walls, external credit, and external degrees. However, despite ostensible similarities, there is a considerable variation in the administrative organizations, flexibility of programs and motivations for initiating these new arrangements for learning. Indeed, the only similarity is that all of the programs and institutions seek to promote learning beyond campus classrooms, while many of them are flexible as to when and how a student learns and the time required to meet degree requirements. And thus these programs, plans and proposals are collectively referred to here as space-free/time-free (SF/TF) higher learning.

With the acceptance of new SF/TF possibilities, an entirely new set of questions must be asked as to the future evolution of institutions for higher learning. But before raising these questions, a brief survey is required, not only of present developments, but of future possibilities that may accelerate them.

VARIATION IN ORGANIZATIONS

One approach to an overview of SF/TF higher learning is to make a distinction between single campus programs, multi-campus programs and non campus organizations.

Individual institutions have yet to sponsor a program for "college-age" students that allows all credited work to take place off-campus. However, there are an increasing number of colleges and universities that allow degree credit for some SF/TF work through campus abroad programs, independent study, or credit for community work or other "real-life" experience. This trend is complemented by non-residential adult degree programs at 18 institutions, as reported in an ongoing survey by John R. Valley of the Educational Testing Service.

Multi-Campus programs, sponsored by state, university systems or a consortium of institutions which may or may not be geographically proximate, have the potential for a far greater impact than the programs at individual institutions, in that more resources can be made available to learners. The State University of New York's Empire State College, which opened in September 1971, encourages students to utilize the resources of the entire SUNY system. Nine additional states-- California, Connecticutt, Illinois, Maine, Maryland, Massachusetts, New Jersey, Oklahoma, and Wisconsin--are presently considering external credit plans that will utilize the resources of public systems to some degree.

The best known consortium of institutions is the Antioch-based University-Without-Walls, also opened in September 1971, which coordinates local UWW programs at 20 widely differing institutions throughout the United States. Another consortium is being formed by the Policy Institute of the Syracuse University, Research Corporation, involving institutions in five upstate New York counties in a program that will prepare students for the external degree examinations to be offered by the state education department in Fall 1972.

New organizations independent of existing institutions have the greatest potential for profound impact

Part II

on higher learning. These non-campus organizations can be differentiated between those offering educational services and degree credit, those offering only courses, and those offering only credit.

England's Open University, starting in January 1971 with an initial enrollment of 25,000 (and planning to enroll 100,000 by 1976) is an entirely new and independent institution, utilizing weekly BBC programs on TV and radio, correspondence packages, and the services of 3000 part-time tutors and counselors at 250 study centers throughout the nation. Although presently limited to students aged 21 and over, the British government is increasingly interested in services for the college-age population in that the cost per student is about one-third of conventional campus-based education. Little wonder, then, that inquiries have been received from more than 100 nations!

In the United States, where education is still organized state by state, most of the Open University-inspired proposals have been made at the state level. Fifty different programs would result in considerable duplication, and proposals for regional cooperation, if not a national system, will surely occur. The Open University of North America, a small planning group in Washington, D.C., is exploring the possibility of utilizing the materials of the British Open University in the United States. A separate proposal for a University of North America has been made by Lawrence E. Dennis, provost and director of the Massachusetts State College System. An international University for Independent Study has been proposed by the Academy for Educational Development, and Alexander

M. Mood of the University of California at Irvine has proposed a national "Video University."

The only independent national programs in operation at this writing are quite small. The National College, Inc., sponsored by Rollins College of Winter Park, Florida and designed "to recognize learning whenever, wherever, and however acquired," initiated registration in Fall 1971. At the same time, Campus-Free College, perhaps the most radical of all SF/TF institutions, also began to enroll students. The basic concept of CFC is a national network of Program Advisors who work intensely with students to create an individualized learning program that may employ any combination of formal or informal learning experiences. Although CFC offers evaluation and a degree, it is similar in other respects to the degree-free learning webs advocated by Ivan Illich in "Deschooling Society."

Several organizations in the U.S., such as Future Resources and Development, Inc., are developing course packages that may be used as a cost-saving device on traditional campuses, or by individual students in external degree programs. In contrast to the course-only programs, there are several credit-only programs that provide legitimation for designated areas of knowledge that have already been learned, regardless of where, how, or when. The New York State Education Department's College Proficiency Examination Program has been administering examinations for course credit since 1963. On the national level, the College-level Examination Program, sponsored by the College Entrance Examination Board was

Part II

quietly introduced in 1967. In the next two years, both CPEP and CLEP expect their workload to be more than double that of 1970 levels. The expansion of external courses and examinations will surely be furthered by many of the above-mentioned programs that will require legitimation for independent learning, as well as new credit-only institutions such as the regional examining universities proposed by the first Newman report (or, more formally, the HEW Report on Higher Education), the National Baccalaureate Examinations proposed by Bernhardt Lieberman and Deborah Wycoff of the University of Pittsburg, or the National University proposed by Jack Arbolino and John Valley of CLEP and the Educational Testing Service respectively.

In summation, the future structure of higher learning appears quite uncertain at this point. A scenario could be constructed of substantial adaptation by individual campuses and state systems, each offering a range of SF/TF options to all students. But a contrasting scenario could also be constructed whereby adaptation of existing institutions is inadequate or unimaginative, thereby encouraging the emergence of new and separate institutions such as the Open University and external degree programs on a state, regional, national, or international level. In any event, there will be considerable duplication and confusion during the 1970's.

VARIATION IN PROGRAMS

Another approach to understanding SF/TF opportunities is to locate each program along a standardized/non-standardized continuum.

The standardized programs are a modern updating of correspondence study, where a student assimilates a fixed package of knowledge. England's Open University is making a substantial improvement in the mass dissemination of knowledge by virtue of several hundred resident faculty members at the newly-constructed student-free campus at Bletchley who devote all of their energies to multimedia course design. The interdisciplinary courses that are being carefully developed (and offered for export throughout the world) may well be the best available--but they nevertheless constitute a standardized package.

In contrast to the Open University and the examinations for credit offered by CPEP and CLEP, many of the other programs are based on an entirely different concept of education and learning. The standardized programs perpetuate and undoubtedly improve upon the traditional notion of higher education as a package of courses and credits. The non-standardized programs, characterized by the University-Without-Walls, Empire State College, and (most notably) Campus-Free College, seek to individualize programs, place much (but not all) of the determination of "an education" in the hands of the student, and therefore encourage independent learning in the deepest sense. Whereas the Open University continues the notion that higher learning can only result from credentialled teachers in academic disciplines, the non-standardized programs also recognize instructional expertise outside of the academy, personal experience as a valid source of knowledge, and evaluation criteria other than examinations.

The statewide proposals presently under construction,

Part II

as well as the single-campus adult degree programs already in operation, are well distributed over the standardized/non-standardized spectrum. Oklahoma's Talkback Television network, or TBT System, extends the same course-credit-exam system that exists in its universities. On the other hand, the adult external degree program at SUNY Brockport, and the Open Education System proposed for Wisconsin, can be located at the non-standardized and flexible end of the program spectrum.

VARIATION IN GOALS

The variation in programs, which appears to be seldom if ever analyzed, in part reflects the various goal mixes of individuals and organizations, which are also rarely analyzed. New programs and institutions can be proposed or authorized for any or all of the following reasons:

--extending equality of opportunity among age groups
--extending equality of opportunity to adults (between age groups)
--promoting equity in crediting individual learning
--increasing options available to students
--reforming the curriculum
--individualizing student programs
--humanizing the learning process
--promoting independent learning behavior as a desirable trait for lifelong learners
--utilizing instructional technology and team teaching techniques
--promoting an institutional revolution throughout society
--breaking the four-year lockstep by enabling easy re-entry into academic programs

There is a clear possibility that programs initiated to satisfy one set of goals may result in attaining different purposes. The Open University was created in class-conscious England as an opportunity for working class advancement. Present enrollments are predominently middle class, however, while the Open University is distinguishing itself for curriculum reform and mass applications of instructional technology. Programs in the United States tend to be more concerned with individualizing and humanizing learning, and promoting independent behavior. However, in an era of financial crisis, many SF/TF programs may become most notable (especially in the eyes of legislators) as cost-cutting panaceas, with a possible sacrifice to all other goals.

FURTHER DEVELOPMENTS IN THE 1970'S

Both social and technological developments during the next decade point to a rapid growth and acceptance of SF/TF higher learning.

Massive demands for public expenditure to salvage the urban and natural environment, and to renew obsolescing transportation, health, and judicial systems will continue to create a scarcity of funds for education. At the same time, there is a rising demand for higher learning. In part, this reflects the desire for equality of opportunity to obtain a college diploma, but there is also a desire among many to learn--and a patent necessity for doing so in a complex and dynamic knowledge-based society where brainpower is rapidly becoming a primary resource. At the same time, there is also a growing demand for flexibility, independence and self-determination in higher education, especially among the

Part II

"forerunner culture" largely composed of upper middle-class youth.

In five or ten years, the more affluent families (at least) will enjoy a situation that could be described as the "multi-screen home information center." Not only will there be a television screen with an expanded variety of source options (cable, videocassette, satellite), but also a picturephone, computer terminal, ultramicrofiche reader, and/or some multi-purpose screen, such as a mass information utility available through cable television. Video playback devices will encourage the individual's control of time, and increasing miniaturization will enhance portability and control of space. Instant access to the world's information may thus be possible, although the problem still remains as to whether individuals desire this option, and whether they are capable of dealing with it. Furthermore, the inevitable hoopla over hardware capacity will continue to obscure the software problems of the structure and quality of knowledge. In any event, children reared on Sesame Street will be acclimated to learning in the multi-screen home information center, whereas their parents, reared under the space/time assumption that learning occurs only in schools and colleges, will suffer the pains of unlearning old habits.

In New Dimensions for the Learner, a "first look" by the Commission on Non-Traditional Study (established by the College Entrance Examination Board in March 1971), it is concluded that non-traditional study will continue to develop whether or not it is carefully planned.

The Commission is certain that new relationships

between educational institutions and various community agencies--libraries, and museums, music and theatre organizations, business, industry, labor, social service--should and will be created as non-traditional study takes a firmer hold on the public consciousness. This suggests the exploration of new kinds of coordination and cooperation; it suggests a major move toward what has been termed a total learning society.

Not only will there be new forms of cooperation at the local level, but also at the international level. The United Nations itself is planning a space-free multi-learning center university, and many other proposals, such as that for an Electronic World University, are presently being circulated. There are several possible pathways to the creation of a global institution or institutions. State and regional open universities may ultimately consolidate to national and continental universities, which in turn would ultimately evolve to a global university. Or one or more global universities might cancel many of the plans for electronically-based universities on a more modest spatial scale. Or there may be a wide assortment of open universities organized on various spatial levels, which co-exist, if not interlock, with similar and/or traditional campuses.

The Commission on Non-Traditional Study also found "a general lack of communication and a consequent duplication of effort among those individuals, agencies or institutions engaged in or planning for non-traditional education." This situation cannot and should not continue. A national or international association or associations of SF/TF

Part II

institutions, open universities, off-campus degree programs, and/or personalized learning networks will surely appear in the next few years to join with the scores of educational associations that already exist. And a Bureau of External Degree Programs will surely arise in the U.S. Office of Education.

INITIAL QUESTIONS FOR THE 1970'S

There are no experts, including this writer, on SF/TF learning. There are no books on the subject. There appears to be no program that has planned ahead with a horizon of more than several years. There is no research study or even a popular article that suggests any of the consequences of SF/TF learning. A broad new arena for educational research has been opened up, and it is patently necessary to begin a self-generating cycle of questions and tentative replies. As a guide to resolving the major questions of educational policy that will surely arise, an initial set of questions is presented here.

1. What will be the magnitude of SF/TF higher learning by 1980?

Projections of enrollment in higher education are still based on the traditional "baby body count," or the percentage of "college age" people that are expected to enroll in space-bound institutions. But the new SF/TF institutions open up the "market" for post-college age students, and there has been no serious consideration as to how big this audience might be. Furthermore, will a greater proportion of the college age group be encouraged to participate in higher education as a result of SF/TF institutions? Finally, will the 4-5 million additional enrollments projected for the 1970's be accommodated completely, or in part, by SF/TF institutions? If this can be done with no sacrifice to quality, then serious questions must be raised over the recent recommendations of the Carnegie Commission on Higher Education for adding 175-235 community colleges and 80-105 comprehensive colleges by 1980.

2. Will SF/TF institutions improve the quality of higher learning?

The prospect of SF/TF learning will inevitably encourage fears from established interests that standards will be lowered. But existing standards are based on superficial criteria, rather than valid scientific measures. The 6 regional and 31 specialized accrediting agencies are controlled by prestigious representatives of conventional colleges and universities, rather than impartial representatives of the public interest. Thus, the judgments of quality by established accrediting agencies may be biased and inappropriate. There is no solid research to serve as a guide, but, ostensibly, the new SF/TF programs and institutions--whether structured or unstructured--may significantly improve the quality of learning. If existing accreditors are incapable of expressing fair judgment, there may be a crisis in accreditation, rather than in the legitimacy of SF/TF learning.

3. What will be the impact on traditional higher education?

The answers to the first two questions are obviously relevant to answering the question of impact on existing institutions. An immediate reaction, especially from traditional academicians, will be an

Part II

apocalyptic vision of SF/TF learning destroying traditional campuses. But this is not necessarily so. Televised sporting events did not lead to a decline in live audiences, as initially anticipated two decades ago. Similarly SF/TF higher learning may cultivate an audience for campus-bound activities that could be greater than the number of students drawn away from the classroom by the availability of new options.

As for the quality of impact, a scenario could be written of SF/TF higher learning transforming all existing institutions. But the opposite scenario might be equally plausible: SF/TF learning opportunities could preserve the status quo by attracting dissident students who would otherwise pressure institutions for change.

4. Will equality of Opportunity be enhanced?

One of the major motivations for initiating SF/TF learning opportunities is to enhance quality of access to higher learning and to the credentials that increasingly serve as passports to job opportunities. But, similar to the noble redistributive intentions of the Head Start program, the outcomes may serve to widen rather than narrow class differences. If the middle and upper classes prove to be both more interested in SF/TF programs and more capable of benefiting from them, a solution to the problems of the lower classes will have to be found elsewhere--if it can be found at all. Of SF/TF programs may prove to be second rate, but nevertheless promoted by cost-conscious legislators as a "solution" to problems of equal access.

5. Will the problems of "credentialism" be mitigated?

A final question to ponder is the impact of SF/TF opportunities on "credentialism" or the social practice of evaluating people on the basis of their diplomas. By making degree--credit more widely available among and between age groups, SF/TF programs will alleviate many of the injustices that presently exist in recognizing individual skills and knowledge. If more people are able to receive diplomas for what they know, the worth of diplomas to holders is lessened. But the disadvantages of not having a diploma are increased. The ready access to degree-credit programs may create an even greater emphasis on credentials than at present.

These questions, and many others, must be seriously addressed during the 1970's. A structural revolution is taking place in higher education. By acting on the right questions at the right time, the new framework for higher learning can be accomodated to humane purposes. But the consequences for our future society may be grim if mindlessness continues as it has.

Michael Marien is a Research Fellow at the Syracuse University Research Center, engaged in a study of emerging modes of non-traditional higher education. He has also recently organized a Futures information Network, whose goal is to identify and promote futures documentation projects throughout the world.

Toward an Unknown Station: Planning for the Seventies

Lewis B. Mayhew

.... THE FUTURE (OF CURRICULAR REFORM) IS IMPOSSIBLE TO PREDICT BECAUSE FACULTIES HAVE IN THE PAST BEEN SO DISINCLINED TO CHANGE.

The future until 1980 can be reasonably well predicted by extrapolation from existing tendencies and developments. Kahn and Wiener have listed 100 likely technical innovations, a sampling of which is indicative. [1]

New superperformance fabrics such as papers, fibers, and plastics will be available. There will be new forms of airborne vehicles of the superhelicopter, giant supersonic jet sort. It is quite possible that rockets will carry people from New York to London in 20 to 30 minutes. Beyond doubt there will come major reduction in hereditary and congenital defects as well as extensive use of substitutes for human limbs, organs, and senses. Homes will be automated and mechanized, and automation and cybernetics will be generally used in management and production. Weather prediction will have become quite precise, and there will be some actual control of weather. In spite of the conservatism of educators, there will be available

Reprinted with the copyright permission of the Journal of NAWDC and the author, Summer 1969.

quite reliable educational and propaganda techniques for modifying human behavior, including direct electronic communication with and stimulation of the brain. Before the year 2000, it should be possible to choose the sex of unborn children, and it will be much easier to change the sex of an individual. Computers, which will be generally available for homes and businesses, will, among other things, make possible automated credit, audit, and banking systems. For those now forced to travel a great deal, conference television should provide some relief, but travel itself will become quite inexpensive and quick because of such means as road-and facility-free transportation. Home education via video and computerized learning may ease the overcrowding of schools and colleges.

These specific predictions derive logically and directly from several basic trends in Western society. Western culture is and will increasingly be sensate and bureaucratic, based on accumulation of scientific and technological knowledge. As present research and development techniques are perfected, change will be even more institutionalized, resulting in worldwide industrialization and modernization, with increasing affluence and leisure as natural results. In spite of the pill, continued population growth will likely continue, and the added population will typically live in the megalopoles. The constant race between increased literacy and level of education will be paralleled by a greater capability for mass destruction.

The emerging shape of higher education can also be anticipated. By 1980, every state will have some form of suprainstitutional control of institutions of higher education, and, consistent with the increased

Part II

centralization of power and source of support, the federal government will be even more deeply involved than it presently is, probably even maintaining cabinet rank for the chief education officer. There will be such an expansion of graduate education that by 1980 undergraduate enrollments will be as large as were all enrollments in higher education in 1952. While private higher education will continue to be influential, it will be changed by being forced to depend on public funds for survival. In spite of official dogma, junior colleges will not be the main source of lower division education for those who receive bachelor's degrees but will instead provide much general, technical, and adult education for those who do not obtain the bachelor's degree. Four-year institutions simply cannot release the endowment which lower division tuition or full-time equivalent support comprises. Although small institutions will always be desired, the typical student in 1980 will attend a college with an enrollment of more than 20,000 located in a city of over 100,000 population. Higher education will cost the society about 3 percent of the Gross National Product--an increase over the 2 percent current figure. Faculty salaries will continue to rise at least until the mid-1970's, and costs of operation generally will increase until 1980, after which they may decrease because of improved technologies.

These broad extrapolations leave the future quite uncertain, especially when one considers the number of central issues which remain unresolved. But planners cannot wait for the future, and must make assumptions as to the probable outcomes of these unresolved issues.

The Future of Higher Education

The first, if not in importance, at least in visibility, is the matter of student protest, activism, and direct involvement in academic governance. No one knows how long the present unrest will continue or how students may change the nature of the university. The more militant youth, of course, feel they are cresting with the wave of the future, and some of their middle-aged apologists welcome them as full colleagues in university reformation. And certainly students have demonstrated power, not only to disrupt institutions but also to alter national policy and politics as well. However, this is nothing new. German student protest in 1814 retarded evolution of constitutional government in the German states. Russian student militancy, resulting in the death of Czar Alexander II, destroyed constitutionalism, and thus paved the road for the Revolution of 1917. Serbian student protest produced the assassination of the Austrian Archduke, which, of course, sparked World War I. And it was militant German youth who welcomed Hitler and joined his ranks in order to purify the German soul and state. But in the past, when the conditions which led to a conflict of generations changed, students returned to their roles of being inducted into a stable society through formal courses at a college or university.[2] If institutions of higher education, through the actions of their professors and administrators, can attend in a professional way to the educational needs of youth, it is likely that the present unrest will recede and student involvement in governance will become no more widespread than it currently is. Of course, student needs must be met and student opinion must be considered, but youthful spirit will, in the long run, find governing too time-consuming to attract its continued interest.

Part II

The second issue involves black militancy and black separatism. This is a particularly uncertain matter. The civil rights movement, or the revolt of colonial people, is one of the half dozen profound revolutions of the post-World-War-II period. The demands for justice, equality, and human respect on the part of Negroes must and will be met. There is no question that institutions of higher education have, in the past, been reluctant participants in bringing Negroes into the mainstream of American life. Their staffing, admissions, curricular, and grading policies have all been restrictive. But this is changing. White America is beginning to acknowledge its guilt over its treatment of Negroes, and from this acknowledgement is coming, and will come, steady progress. The issue is, however, whether campus protest will continue, as it has this past year, to be sparked by Negro students' confrontation efforts to obtain instant rectification of accumulated wrongs. Beyond doubt, black militancy on campus will continue for several years, and demands for black studies and black separatism will be made to gain a symbolic recognition of human uniqueness. But this trend is not likely to continue long for several reasons. First, there is simply not enough basic scholarship or enough qualified professors in the country to make black studies a regular curricular element. Until the research and staffing problems are solved, black studies are likely to remain a fad just as courses in personal adjustment programs for the gifted and non-Western studies for all students were fads which could not survive the paucity of fundamental knowledge. Black separatism and black militancy must also diminish, for they both run counter to strong underlying themes in America. Even if it were

The Future of Higher Education

ideologically desirable to consider a distinct black subculture, the high concentration of people, the transportation and communication networks, and the centralization of power for the resolution of problems make assimilation of all people, into a common culture inevitable. This is not to deny the value of subcultural differences, but it does suggest that powerful traditions of language, religion, jurisprudence, family structure, and ethical principles (no matter how imperfectly applied) have operated, and will operate, on all. Africa will be studied and African art will be appreciated, just as jazz has eventually found even academic respectability. But this will be a gradual infiltration of the total civilization just as oriental influences have gradually made themselves a part of the American fabric.

The third imponderable is the nature of statewide governance, control, or coordination. Higher education has become much too expensive and potentially much too important to be left to single institutions. At present, the concept of some coordinating agency has currency. In 1957, 10 states had a statewide coordinating council or commission; in 1968, only 10 states did not. But the achievement record of these states has not been particularly outstanding. Proliferation of expensive programs has not been contained, diversion of students to different appropriate levels of education has not been accomplished, and economic benefits have not been established. The question then is: Can coordination be made to function? Or will coordination give way to some form of statewide control? At this point, it appears that future control will be in the form of boards of regents of the senior institutions assuming

Part II

responsibility for all institutions in the state or new supra boards, with power to control, actually being created. This will not happen without incident, for individual boards or boards for different types of institutions will fight for their identity. But eventually public pressure for better organization and greater economy, and failure of existing agencies will probably prevail. This move is consistent with the earlier noted drift toward higher and higher levels of centralization of power and source of support.

A related matter is direct political involvement and intervention in the practice of higher education. In theory, the American tradition has been that the political arm should not control education directly. Behind the creation of the constitutional universities in Michigan, Minnesota, California, Colorado, and Oklahoma lay the belief that if universities were to function effectively they had to be protected from political vagaries. One motivation for the creation of statewide coordinating agencies was the belief that such bodies could mediate between state governments and universities, thus preventing direct political intervention. However, as costs of higher education have mounted and in recent years as student protests have convulsed campuses, political leaders have been more and more tempted to intervene directly in the affairs of individual campuses. In the spring of 1969 legislatures throughout the country were considering punitive legislation to prevent campus disturbances. Now, the question is, will this drift toward intervention continue, or will means be developed to leave institutions their needed freedom while at the same time safeguarding the interests and concerns

The Future of Higher Education

of the society? Very probably, if past experiences are at all indicative, political interference will increase for several years, then, as some of the irritations such as student protest recede and emotion gives way once again to reason, direct political involvement will decrease. However, unless institutions, particularly public institutions, attend more closely to public interests and needs, it will not disappear completely. For almost a decade, higher education has experienced the greatest support and esteem in its history and has been allowed freedom to achieve what Riesman and Jencks have called the "academic revolution." That revolution allowed faculty members in some institutions to achieve virtual autonomy, and faculties in all others aspire to similar achievement. Light teaching loads, higher salaries, opportunities for research and consultation, and scant concern for undergraduate students were the spoils for the victorious revolutionaries. If faculties will now exercise self-restraint, e. g. , not demand teaching loads of one course, not reject service in favor of research, not place consultation above teaching, political intervention will be slight. But if faculties continue to strive toward autonomy, the state will move in, and the state will win.

In a sense the resolution of the political intervention issue and the matter of continued student unrest and protest depend on the progress of the academic revolution. Because of a host of things (e. g. , success of the Manhattan Project, social demands for technically trained and proficient people, popular belief that a college education is the key to a high prestige and economic comfort, and general affluence), college professors and officials have convinced

Part II

society that what they did was of great personal and social worth deserving of ever-increasing levels of support. Parents have been persuaded to pay high costs, even for daughters, and to send their children to college without any real knowledge that a college education changed or helped them at all. Congressmen, legislators, and private donors have been persuaded to make larger and larger contributions to colleges and universities in the expectation, but without real evidence, that higher education was positively related to economic prosperity and the good life. States were persuaded that sound public policy should provide every student access to higher education. From approximately 1957 to 1967, higher education was the darling of the American public--a darling from which much was expected but to which even more would be given, and on its own terms. By 1968, however, it seemed clear that the honeymoon was over and that other needs of society and other problems would receive the attention and support previously given colleges and universities. Now, in 1969, a crossroads is approaching. If public criticisms of higher education and the competition of the other social institutions slow the academic revolution by forcing those in the academy to become more responsive to those they would serve and to present evidence as to how they have cared for their trust, then the twin dangers of political intervention and student revolt may be averted. But if the public once again entrusts professors with full autonomy over what they do and how they do it and if professors respond as they have previously, then the mandarins will have isolated themselves and set the stage for their own ultimate destruction.

The sixth issue (and the failure thus far to resolve

it) is one of the reasons for a somewhat pessimistic view of the responsiveness of higher education to the needs of students and of society: By the mid-1950's, reformers and researchers had been able to establish that colleges and universities were not very effective in achieving their objectives. Jacob, Sanford, Dressel and Mayhew, Pace, Newcomb, and Goldsen were all convinced that most colleges did not change the students who attended them in any lasting way. The curriculum was not generally regarded as a real significance in the lives of students, and grades, which served as legal tender, were unrelated to anything other than previous or subsequent grades. Now, during a decade in which the society lavished unprecedented support for higher education and after repeated demonstrations that prior educational practices were ineffective, one might have presumed massive curricular and instructional changes. But this did not happen. Undergraduate curriculums changed but little in that critical decade from 1957 to 1967, and innovation was not widespread. There has been a slight reduction in requirements, a slight increase in foreign language study, and a mild strengthening of the position of science and mathematics, "but the overall pattern of general and concentration requirements has changed but slightly."[3] The need for future curricular reform can be well documented, the directions reform might take clearly indicated through recourse to developmental studies of college-aged youth, but the future is impossible to predict because faculties have in the past been so disinclined to change.

Another issue also involves clearly expressed need but absent or ineffective college response. This has

Part II

to do with institutional involvement with America's increasingly urban condition. Most college students will attend urban institutions. An urban condition creates problems of the quality of life, use of resources, transportation, and politics. Universities could presumably make a contribution to the solution of these problems. Yet, the results have been generally paltry and frequently hurtful. Pleas have been made for urban-grant institutions to do for the city what the land-grant institutions earlier did for agriculture and rural America. Yet sustained funding has neither been requested nor supplied. Junior colleges have been suggested as institutions well suited to the segment of the population not previously affected by higher education. Yet when these new campuses are created, they are located away from the central city in the suburbs and foothills where upper-middle-class America abides. A few new universities have been deliberately located to serve large urban areas, but the faculties motivated by the promises of the academic revolution, have rejected service to the city in favor of spending time on orthodox research which enhances their national reputations. It is almost impossible to predict the outcomes. It is, however, certain that urbanization and urban problems will not disappear. If existing institutions don't respond society will eventually create new ones which will.

A last unknown is the future nature of campus governance. The administrator-centered style which has prevailed in the past will no longer work. The question is whether faculty and administration can cooperate and share power or whether they will become adversaries and adopt the techniques of management and trade unionism. There are strong pressures in both directions, but the advocates of antagonism have a slight advantage. Teachers' unions have forced confrontations on campuses, but even more significant, they have forced other organizations such as the National Education Association and the American Association of University Professors to assume a more militant stand and even to drive out those elements which still believed in professionalism and shared responsibility. Here it should be indicated that AAUP leadership has striven to withstand pressures toward trade unionism, but its stance has gradually changed because it must satisfy its membership.

Each of these issues could be resolved in several different ways. Student protests may intensify, or black separatism may become institutionalized as it once was previously, or assimilation may proceed. Laissez-faire, cooperation, coordination, or control are each possible options for statewide higher education. It is possible to conceive of higher education becoming another part of state government just as it is possible to visualize all state institutions as constitutional entities, a fourth and truly independent branch of government. And campus governance can also go either the adversary or shared responsibility route. However, if several values, long influential in or implied by the American tradition, are reaffirmed and acted on, then the direction of resolution will be indicated.

In spite of frequent deviations, distortions, and incomplete realizations of the ideal, these values seem pervasive in the society and, over a period of time, governing for policy and practice.

> 1. A widespread acceptance of, respect for and sympathy with, youth and its needs. Permissive parental behavior, educational efforts to identify developmental needs, and a national

Part II

resolve to provide educational opportunity for all are the manifestations of this regard. While in 1969 there is some momentary regression and a growing distrust of youth and its needs (The Chicago Tribune blacked out all news about youth for one day in the belief that people were tired of its antics), the prevailing faith is in the perfectability of youth and a resolve to aid its development. This value, of course, does lead to dysfunctions, child tyranny, parental neuroses, and the like, too, but it's the healthy side which allows the potentiality for great human openness.

2. A widespread acceptance of constitutionalism and a belief that consensus is not only preferable to polarization but is the only way a democratic society can handle pluralism and diversity through political checks and balances, informal interraction among pressure groups, operation of a two-party system accommodating all but the most extreme minority subgroups, and the historical tendency for the society to seek equilibrium when one element expands too rapidly or expresses its power too vigorouly. As Max Lerner remarks, "The problem of reaching a consensus has always been hard in America, yet it has always had to be solved. Otherwise government would be deadlocked and society stagnant and the carving out of a line of direction for American growth would be frustrated."[4]

Consistent with constitutionalism and reliance on formal systems of checks and balances is America's pervasive pragmatism. While the pendulum has swung on occasion to idealism, transcendentalism, and mysticism, such notions have not taken deep root in American soil. Pragmatism has determined the most influential court decisions, the style of education, the combinations and recombinations of political groupings, and the continuous efforts of reformers to achieve the socially possible as quickly as possible. Through American intellectual life has run the theme of revolt against formalism, fixed principles, rules, and absolute or mechanical formulas, but the great intellectual tradition in America has always been close to the concerns of social reality and what an individual can do about them. [5]

Materialism stands with pragmatism as a significant cultural value. De Tocqueville could observe: "In America the passion for physical well-being is not always exclusive, but it is general; and if all do not feel it in the same manner, yet it is felt by all. The effort to satisfy even the least wants of the body and to provide the little conveniences of life is uppermost in every mind."[6] And critics have been commenting on the phenomenon ever since. Some would regard American materialism as almost lethal, and would caricature it as a preoccupation with things to disguise or conceal impoverished spirit. But a more realistic and healthy interpretation is that this very materialism, which has provided America with an incredible proportion of the material goods of this world, has enabled the society to mount a Marshall Plan, a Point Four Plan to motivate science and technology to unprecedented achievements, and even to provide the leisure and comfort from which critics can speak and protest. In this connenction Robert McAfee Brown says:

> It is interesting that in Jesus' parable about the Last Judgment, the questions that are asked are not--Have you had a religious experience? Did

Part II

> you go to church regularly? Were you baptized?
> Can you recite the creed? But quite simply--
> Did you feed the hungry? Did you clothe the
> naked? Did you care for the sick? Did you visit
> the imprisoned? Did you, in other words, concern
> yourself with the neighbor in need? That is the
> criterion for the life acceptable to God. Our
> neighbors' material concerns, if we may so put
> it, are our religious obligations. [7]

The last cultural value of especial significance for a resolution of educational issues is the attempt within the American polity to maintain, and when necessary, reconcile the twin ideals of egalitarianism and excellence or even elegance. It is the attempt to accept the Jacksonism notion that "every man is as good as any other--and a damned sight better," while still recognizing that the individual excellence of political leaders, generals, artists, scientists, teachers, and doctors upholds the notion that one man is sometimes better than another. The public polity reconciliation is, of course, the demand, not that everyone should receive the same education, but that everyone is entitled to the same opportunity, while at the same time expecting that "individuals at many levels of ability accept the need for high standards of performance and strive to achieve those standards of performance within the limits available to them."[8] So now we have the values of high regard for youth and an attempt to meet its developmental needs; dedication to constitutionalism and the need for consensus; pragmatism as a generalized approach to life; materialism, which can provide the resources all humans need; and a pragmatic reconciliation of egalitarianism and excellence. It is now necessary to see how acceptance of those values can, not predict, but rather bring about a reasonable and responsible resolution of the issues. If these cultural values are valid and if decisions are made consistent with them, what will be the form and practice of higher education during the 1970's?

Colleges and universities will probably reduce the variety of prescriptions or regulations of individuals but for those matters about which the institution must take cognizance, prescription will be expressed in highly specific and contractual terms. While students will be given greater freedom in their private lives, institutions will find it necessary to create a limited list of specific acts for which specific sanctions will be imposed through clearly delineated processes of adjudication. Increasingly, faculty and administrative rights and responsibilities will also be specified through written constitutions, bylaws, and policy statements which will attend as much to process and procedure as to substance. This tendency is most clearly exemplified in union demands for a contract but is also illustrated by the growing number of faculty senates operating with expressly delegated powers and responsibilities. As state systems of higher education emerge with suprainstitutional boards and bureaucracies, this same specification of procedures will develop there. Since it seems likely that both public and private institutions will be joined together in suprainstitutional organizations, this observation holds for both sectors.

The revolutionary fervor presently gripping college and university campuses will gradually recede. This, in part, will be forced as militant and protesting youth come to realize that a revolution like the

Part II

English, French, Russian, or American revolutions is virtually impossible in a post-industrial society. The powers of bureaucracy, the powers of wealth, and the influence of centrally controlled media are simply too great to be overcome by small dissident groups. This is not to say that radical dissent has not altered important elements in the national life, but the results have been and will be of transitory significance, and militant and protesting youth will gradually see this. For example, though Berkeley was the scene of the initial student disturbances the changes in the governance of that institution since 1964 have been scant if not completely nonexistent. Constitutionalism does provide ways for reform--virtually every concern expressed by militant youth in 1969 can be resolved through constitutional (using this term in a generic sense) means. This decline in revolutionary fervor will also be intensified as the Depression-born generation begins to yield its leadership because of death, retirement, or occasionally even senility. There is strong reason to suspect that the Depression of the 1930's left an indelible scar on those who grew up at that time which distinguishes them from those born and reared after World War II. The actiona of leadership which recalls severe economic privation are incomprehensible to the youth who throughout their lives have experienced nothing but relative affluence and ease of satisfying personal desires. Within a few years that Depression-born leadership will give way to leaders born after World War II, which once again may restore legitimacy to those responsible for families or for the major institutions in society. Last, in this regard (and this may be more of a pious hope) institutions may reform themselves somewhat more rapidly than they have in the past. As reform comes about, so reasons for militancy will lessen.

A part of this reform may be reflected in colleges and universities in which the developmental needs and concerns of students are gradually accepted. Partly this may happen because of the psychological sophistication and even the psychological preoccupation of the Amercian society. It is no accident that Vienna-created psychoanalysis found its most fertile ground in the United States, which became the center for the expansion of psychoanalytic psychology. Harold Taylor has remarked that the present generation of youth is the "first understood generation" in the history of the world. Particularly middle-class families have sought to be permissive and understanding of the developmental needs of the children, and these insights are gradually becoming available to those in the academy. Through the work of Joseph Katz, Kenneth Keniston, Paul Heist, and others, important reports dealing with developmental needs of youth are being made available for the professoriat. This acceptance of developmental needs of people on the part of professors may also be encouraged by the sheer fact that the society is becoming an educating one in which most people will spend much of their lives being educated. Concurrently will come the demand that that education be effective.

Colleges and universities will also be affected and will reflect a return to liberalism in the entire society. This prediction is made in part because the liberal tradition in the American society is stronger, more pervasive, and has deeper roots than the

Part II

countervailing conservative tradition. The conservative tradition has really never spoken to the needs of all people and hence stands in sharp opposition to the historic egalitarianism in the society. It is no accident that John Kenneth Galbraith's books attract much wider attention and seem much more influential than the books of William F. Buckley or Russell Kirk. If this observation is valid, the return of liberalism will be reflected on campuses through such things as greater safeguards to individual liberties, greater use of the university in solving human problems increased attention to the service role of the university (expressly in urban situations), and an intensified search for ways to meet the needs of minority group students. A parallel development is the gradual acceptance within the academy of a psychology, sociology, and economics of affluence rather than of poverty. Much of past practice in such things as college admissions, grading, expansion of college programs, and debate over who shall be educated has been based on the assumption that abilities and resources were clearly finite. However, in 1969 advocated reforms in the testing movement, generally accepted public policy of the need for universal higher education, and a gradually accepted assumption that even the central city can be restored suggest this more optimistic approach. In the 1930's urban sociology stressed the inevitability of the steady deterioration of the core of the central city with the rot moving outward on the heels of the expanding suburbs. No one assumed that this process could be reversed, yet fundamental to pleas in 1969 for attention to the urban conditions is the belief that somehow the central city can become self-renewing. The brilliant example of Atlanta, Georgia, provides impressive evidence.

Such, at least, is the silhouette of the unknown station toward which this society is moving so rapidly. These are hopefully responsible predictions based, in spite of some pessimistic overtones, on a deep faith in the power of America as civilization to be a renewing society. American history has been spotty, but a renewing society it has been in the relatively short 300 years of its existence.

Dr. Mayhew is professor of education, Stanford University, California. He made the keynote address for the 53rd Annual NAWDC Convention on April 10, 1969.

Notes and References

1. Kahn, Herman, and Wiener, Anthony J. "A Frame Work for Speculation." Toward the Year 2000. Cambridge: American Academy of Arts and Sciences, 1967.
2. These ideas are based on Feuer, Lewis S. The Conflict of Generations. New York: Basic Books, 1969.
3. Dressel, Paul L., and DeLisle, Frances H. Undergraduate Curriculum Trends. Washington D. C.: American Council on Education.
4. Lerner, Max. America as a Civilization. New York: Simon & Schuster, 1957.
5. Lerner, op. cit.
6. De Tocqueville, Alexis, Democracy in America. New York: Vintage Books, 1955.
7. Brown, Robert McAfee, America: No Promise Without Agony. Unpublished paper given at the 24th National Conference on Higher Education, March, 1969.
8. Gerdner, John W. Excellence. New York: Harper & Brothers, 1961.

Utopian Perspectives on the University

John S. Brubacher

A GLANCE AT HISTORY DISCLOSES THAT UTOPIAN THINKING IN ONE AGE MAY BECOME IDEOLOGY IN ANOTHER. SO CLOSE, IN FACT, DO CONTEMPORARY EDUCATIONAL UTOPIAS SEEM THAT THERE IS THE QUESTION OF WHERE TO DRAW THE LINE BETWEEN UTOPIAN AND PROGRESSIVE THOUGHT. DR. BRUBACHER, IN A COMPARISON OF OLDER AND PRESENT-DAY UTOPIAN THINKING ON HIGHER EDUCATION, REVEALS THE CHANGE IN DIRECTION OF UTOPIAN THOUGHT WHICH HAS MADE POSSIBLE MODERN UTOPIAS THAT ARE NOT SO MUCH "NO WHERE" AS "NOT YET."

With two-thirds of the twentieth century already spent and the end in sight, it is appropriate to focus on what we can expect vis-a-vis the university by the year 2000. Nor are we alone in lifting our sights to this fin de siecle. The American Academy of Arts and Sciences not long ago appointed a Commission on the Year 2000, whose first deliberations have been published.[1]

Notable, also, among those who have addressed themselves to higher education in the year 2000, is Sir Eric Ashby, the master of Clare College at Cambridge University.[2] Although fixing his gaze on a point more than a quarter of a century off, Sir

Reprinted with the copyright permission of the <u>Educational Record</u>, Spring, 1969 and the American Council on Education

The Future of Higher Education

Eric disavowed any attempt to take a utopian view of things; this he left to the writers of fiction. Rather he drew a remarkable analogy between the university and living organisms in that both had a heredity and an environment. What the heredity of the university would be in the year 2000 he could easily predict from the history of universities. Certainly its DNA would include academic freedom, autonomous government, and the like. But concerning the forms the university would take as a result of its environment, he made no prediction.

It is regrettable that Sir Eric was so cautious, for if ever we needed imaginative thinking about the university, it is now. We have plenty of forward-looking Five Year Plans, but we also need people who are willing to take risks in envisioning the future. As the Hebrew prophet warned, where there is no vision the people will perish. And even if the university does not perish, without vision it will become emaciated and anemic. We venture, therefore, to examine some utopian thinking about the university and to see what possible conclusions can be drawn.

UTOPIAS OF HIGHER EDUCATION

In spite of much writing over the centuries on utopia and in spite of the fact that most utopias rely heavily on education to achieve their objectives, there has been comparatively little utopian thinking about education itself. And that little has generally been concerned with mass education in the lower schools. Higher education has been relatively neglected.[3]

Edward Bellamy, who had his eye on the year 2000 as early as 1887, employed the device of <u>Looking</u>

Part II

Backward[4] to describe a higher education to which all were entitled, whether it cost half or nearly all of the nation's revenue. Such generous provision was necessary on three grounds, he thought: First, everyone needed education for self-enjoyment-- indeed, higher education was necessary just for living, to say nothing of vocational or professional training; second, everyone's self-enjoyment diminished in proportion to the lack of development of his peers; and third, such an education was owing so that children might have the best possible parents. Of course, even in utopia, not all would be able to profit equally from their higher education, but all would appreciate their education even though some fell short of its full enjoyment. Exposure to as much higher education as they could absorb would give everyone protection against failure of communication between classes and consequent class antagonism.

Bellamy was not the first American to project a utopia of higher education. William Smith, one-time provost of the University of Pennsylvania, preceded him by more than a century. The fledgling United States had not yet been born when in 1753 he published his College of Mirania.[5] There, in the argot of utopias, he described higher education in Mirania, a place not too distant from Pennsylvania or New York. It was the curriculum of Mirania's college which, if anything, justified its utopian pretensions. Smith noted its inclusion of modern languages and modern history, politics, and even agriculture. Such a curriculum was certainly quite beyond the imagination of colonial colleges, which still concentrated on Latin, Greek, mathematics, and natural philosophy, but it did find lodgment in Jefferson's University of Virginia in the nineteenth century.

Before Smith, perhaps the most notable idealization of higher education was found in Sir Francis Bacon's <u>New Atlantis</u>.[6] There, in the seventeenth century, he proposed a "college called Salomon's Home," where a self-perpetuating group of capable scholars would devote themselves to enlarging human knowledge of the "causes and secret motions of things." In fact, he hoped to realize this then-utopian scheme if he could but persuade King James to make him master of a college at Oxford or Cambridge. But the king was too shortsighted to comprehend the worth of such a project.

Two utopias of higher education were perhaps paradoxically, conservative, because they idealized a form of the university which was already past history. Most notable was Thorstein Veblen's <u>The Higher Learning in America</u>.[7] Here he presented as an idyll the university as conceived at Johns Hopkins, which derived its inspiration from the University of Berlin. Veblen imagined that we must go back to a university exclusively dedicated to basic or pure research. So strictly did Veblen adhere to this historical ideal that he did not consider as a proper part of the higher learning undergraduate instruction, professional education, or technological training. Indeed, harking as far back as Immanuel Kant's <u>Streit der Facultat</u> for inspiration. Veblen would have completely divorced the university from any utilitarian purpose. To be sure, utility had its role, in some institute off campus, but "idle curiosity" and the "instinct for workmanship" would be warped if subjected to the influence of the pecuniary culture, especially as practiced by captains

Part II

of industry on university boards of control. The only teaching in the ideal university was incidental to research and the only students wanted were those who were self-motivating.

'NEW' REPUBLIC OF SCHOLARS

A more recent utopia based on the past is that of Paul Goodman. In The Community of Scholars[8] he goes even farther back into history to idealize the medieval guild of scholars. After faulting conventional universities, Goodman suggests two remedies for the defects. First, the university might seek self-renewal, as it has done frequently in the past, But contemporary proposals for reform do not seem to him sufficiently radical. He therefore suggests, secondly, that the only solution is through succession from the conventional mould and the creation of a different model. This model, this utopia (though he does not call it such), he finds in the ancient community or republic of scholars. He returns to this ancient body to recapture the early spirit of higher education, the free informal play of mind on mind found in the medieval guild of scholars and, before that, in Plato's academy and Aristotle's lyceum.

To this end he proposes an unchartered university of less than 200 students and less than a score of faculty. Emphasizing the personal relationship between teachers and students, this university would be completely autonomous in its government, a true republic of scholars. Not only that, but it would sharply curb the stifling impact of administration. This spirit of "anti-Establishment" is nowhere better caught than in Goodman's preface, where he describes The Community of Scholars as a "treatise in anarchistic theory."[9]

Perhaps the most complete examination of the university in utopian perspective is Robert M. Hutchins' description of The University of Utopia,[10] which describes a liberal rather than a conservative utopia. Not only do Hutchins' utopian ideas spring from the soil of discontent, as in most utopias, but his utopia is made to seem not too far away, nor too incongruous with the hard realities of the present. In fact, the University of Utopia is surprisingly similar to the University of Chicago during the time Hutchins was president. So great is the similarity that it is difficult to escape the conclusion that Hutchins' notion of a university became utopian when he found it difficult to initiate and sustain at Chicago. He wrote The Higher Learning in America[11] as an ideology; when it did not work, he rewrote it as a utopia.

The university as a center for independent thought and criticism is basic to Hutchins' utopian thinking. He asserts this independence by reserving to the university the right to make decisions concerning its curriculum. His utopian university exemplifies the biblical text

> Do not be conformed to this age but be transformed by the renewal of your mind.[12]

Thus the university is not to be at the beck and call of society to perform whatever chores the public wishes. It only includes disciplines which have intellectual content and that in their own right.

Part II

UNIVERSITY AS PROTOTYPE

While conventional universities must conform to social pressures to gain public or private financial support utopians are enlightened enough to support their university generously without strings attached. This does not mean that the university in utopia is unrelated to the daily life of utopians. In fact, it provides invaluable service to society but as a by-product not as a chief end, of its existence. So autonomous is the university as a republic of scholars that it provides a prototype for the larger political republic itself.

An independent university naturally has independent students and independence, of course goes hand in hand with diversity and diversity with controversy. The University of Utopia, however, is not dismayed by this; on the contrary, it holds that a university without diversity and controversy is not a university. Specialization in such a university could be a block to communication, but the University of Utopia guards against that by prescribing a curriculum which insures that all have acquaintance with the main fields of culture as a common universe of discourse. Moreover, both faculty and students constantly endeavor to clarify and reinterpret ideas through discussions and investigations. Unlike the conventional university, where professors lecture annually on the same themes, professors in the University of Utopia lecture only on research in progress and then only once. The visitor to the University of Utopia will notice that the preoccupation of everyone with ideas does not foreclose having convictions. On the contrary, faculty and students at this university are activists.

There is an echo of this emphasis on student independence in B. F. Skinner's Walden II.[13] Skinner is expansive on education below the university level but cryptic about education above it. In fact, his utopia plays down distinctions between all levels of schooling; as there are no natural breaks in a child's development so, too, there are no breaks in his educational ladder. Walden II emphasizes learning over teaching, giving its students an excellent survey of methods and techniques of thinking drawn from logic, mathematics, psychology, and scientific method. It then turns these students loose in libraries and laboratories, confident that that is all the "college education" they need.

An echo of Hutchins' emphasis on communication is found in the brief reference Father Courtney Murray makes to utopian, or "post-modern," thinking. The modern university has been characterized by its pluralism. But pluralism is so rampant that an almost irreconcilable conflict has resulted on the so-called "ultimate questions" of our culture. To date pluralism has been welcomed in the modern university on the theory that truth will be assured if there is uninhibited competition in the market place of ideas. Thus, the encouragement of pluralism was seen as a protection against stagnation and a warranty for progress.

But what did it profit a civilization to have the utmost variety of thought if men could not understand each other? In that event pluralism ultimately led to the decay of argument, because controversy can only be successful if men share a common universe of discourse. According to Murray, such a common

Part II

universe of discourse will distinguish the university of "post-modern" times.[14] When the modern era is behind us we will have a university with a common denominator by which the plurality of our cultural numerators can be compared.

CITIES OF EDUCATION

Moving in the same direction, perhaps, is Stephen R. Graubard's "University Cities in the Year 2000."[15] By that year Graubard conceives of cities whose main business will be education, just as the main business of Washington is government or Miami recreation. These university cities will differ from contemporary cities as the latter differ from the cathedral towns of medieval or renaissance Europe. The university city will be a vast cooperative enterprise with both public and private higher educational facilities, hospitals, museums, research laboratories for business enterprises, and the like. Whereas conventional universities are populated principally by prebaccalaureate and predoctoral students, the university city will have a large number of postdoctoral students seeking something more than what goes by the name of "continuing education" today. In the year 2000 business men may take a sabbatical in the university city, where today they vacation by traveling. Indeed, it may become common for people to train for and pursue several different careers in a lifetime.

We may look now at one final imaginative concept of the university--that of Walter Lippmann.[16] In writing of the university and the human condition

Lippmann divorces himself from such practical pressures as alumni, trustees, legislatures, and chambers of commerce. Though he does not call the results of this emancipated state of mind utopia, it obviously is found nowhere in reality. What the university might be under such circumstances, Lippmann suggests by noting that already the conventional university has become society's leading arbiter of fact. While formerly priests, kings, tycoons, and commissars have been guardians of truth, none would likely contradict the university as heir to that role today. To be sure it has not inherited the mantle of infallibility, but it is nevertheless the most dependable agency we now possess for adjudicating the truth.

But this exalted position is not enough, says Lippmann. The university must become not only a repository of truth but a laboratory where, by a subtle alchemy, knowledge can be transmuted into wisdom--wisdom being the selection and shaping of knowledge to human values. To this end the university must transcend the sterile dualism of C. P. Snow's "two cultures" and compose a curriculum in the history and practice of judging rightly in the choice of ends and means. If Lippmann is right, then will his university have found an answer to the question raised as far back as the Greeks: Can virtue(wisdom) be taught? Yet, it remains quite utopian to think that the laymen, from whom Lippmann has cut loose in his thinking, will ever concede to the university the preeminence in wisdom they now concede to it in knowledge.

SIGNIFICANCE OF UTOPIAN THINKING

A glance at history serves notice at once that

Part II

utopian thinking about higher education has not been in vain. In some instances what was utopian in one age has become ideology in another. Not everyone attends college today, as Bellamy predicted for the year 2000, but such a large number do that we may still achieve this goal by the end of the century. Again, Bacon's vision of a higher learning devoted to research, for instance, did not die aborning for the Royal Society, when it subsequently came into existence, owed much of its conceptualization to Bacon's idea of a collegiate foundation for research. Even later, Diderot ascribed the success of the French Enclyclopedie in part to Bacon's foresight:

> That extraordinary genius, when it was impossible to write a history of what was known, wrote one of what it was necessary to learn.[17]

And, of course, the University of Berlin took Bacon's idea as a point of departure in the next century, to be followed by Johns Hopkins and others.

It is really small wonder that utopian thinking about the university has yielded such a harvest. After all, the seed of most utopian thinking has been sown in the soil of discontent with existing conditions. Smith took off from the inadequacies of colonial higher education and Hutchins prefaces each chapter of his University of Utopia with a discussion of the shortcomings of contemporary higher education. Goodman, too, starts from the malaise that has beset the overgrown, impersonal university of the latter twentieth century.

The Future of Higher Education

Taking as their point of departure dissatisfaction with current ideology about higher education, modern utopias, far from being "way out," often seem right around the corner. Skinner's college in <u>Walden</u> II seems within reach, if not already in the grasp, of many colleges and universities. So, too, Goodman's secessionist community of scholars was embodied in Black Mountain College and the present struggling Free Universities emblazoned on the banners of many student activists as they march against the Establishment.

In fact, so close do utopias seem that the question arises as to where to draw the line between utopian and any progressive thought.[18] In Utopian thought our concern is with grand strategies of higher education. The perplexing question of tactics does not inhibit our imagination when we are concerned with what ought to be in spite of present obstacles. Lippmann shows the way: he clears his approach by sidestepping such practical restraints on his thinking as alumni, trustees, and legislatures. Utopians are not concerned with short-range, merely "eutopian" thinking: or if it be "eutopian" thinking. Yet the range must not be so long as to be impossible. Those in the vanguard are looking to utopia, not as an escape from present reality, but as a means of ultimately reconstructing present ideologies. Perhaps utopia is not so much a place or a time as a frame of mind.

Modern utopian writers seem to be more successful than classical ones in keeping utopia in that tantalizing position of being in view and yet just beyond reach. Earlier utopias seemed out of reach because they were closed and perfected systems

Part II

and, therefore, static. Such utopias tended to be millenial in character and authoritarian in organization and rule; only divine grace could have brought them into being. Perhaps there are church-related colleges that take millenialism as their model, but none of the utopias reviewed here has been of this sort.

OPEN-ENDED UNIVERSITY

Recent utopias have been open systems, expecting the unexpected, seeking perfectibility rather than perfection. They admit of change, variety, even conflict and strife. Note that Hutchins reports that the University of Utopia has only one educational philosophy, but that one is very hospitable to controversy. Remember, indeed, that Hutchins says a university that does not welcome controversy is not a university in the first place. The open-ended utopian university is, moreover, distinguished by freedom and autonomy. Consequently, one can bring this kind of university into being, as Goodman points out, by just wishing to do so.

Undoubtedly open-ended utopias owe a debt to Darwin. This direction in utopian thinking is very significant. Paying attention to continuity in evolution reveals an inclination to think of utopia, although distant, as an extrapolation of history, as somewhere on a line of continuity with the present.[19] The classical meaning of utopia as "no where" underscored the idea of the geographical location of utopia. One thinks of modern utopias, however, not so much as "no where" but as "not yet." One cannot get to "no where" under any circumstances but, given enough time, one's imagination may well realize itself.

There are those who think a utopian university is impossible unless society, too, is redesigned along utopian lines, that there cannot be a utopian university without utopians to harbor it.[20] But Hutchins regards this as no insuperable obstacle, for we can all become utopians just by taking the first step in that direction.

In spite of that encouragement a word of caution is in order. Some eager utopians shortsightedly mistake the means (tactics) for the end (strategy). This kind of utopia can become the tail that wags the dog e.g., it was the Industrial Revolution that led some to expect that in utopia man could be standardized. Bellamy, for example, deduced that the many could receive higher education more cheaply than the few from the fact that **costs** could be reduced through mass production. Needless to say, the analogy is false. We must guard against a similar danger in the twentieth century, with its tremendous promise for higher education, from the technology of instruction offered by teaching machines and computers. These may be fantastic means, but they must not become confused as ends. In his Erewhon Samuel Butler was already frightened that machines might take over, while Aldous Huxley's Brave New World[21] gave us a view of cacatopia rather than eutopia.

Also noxious to utopian thinking is a body of openly and aggressively anti-utopian thought located among certain student activists. Many of these students, like existentialists, place existence ahead of essence. Capable of immediate intuitions, they want to treat

Part II

controversial issues by adversary procedures rather than by protracted re-examination of conceptualizations. In this they betray not only their anti-intellectualism but also their impatience with remote ideals and utopias.

UTOPIAN CONFUSION

The chief opposition to utopian thinking about the university, however, is the great majority of university idealogues who pride themselves on being realists and, therefore, tend to deride utopian schemes of higher education as, at best, impractical. To transcend time and place in thinking about the university might cause one to become dislocated, as well as confused by road signs to utopia pointing in different directions.

A notable instance of such confusion can be found in several utopias. Those of Veblen and Hutchins hold the involvement in public affairs at arm's length from the university. They do not think that the university should do chores for either government or private industry and commerce. Lippmann, on the contrary, envisions a university that concerns itself with wisdom as well as knowledge. And what is wisdom but an admixture of knowledge with values, both moral and political? What are those responsible for policy in higher education to do in the face of such a contradiction? They must have recourse to the theory of higher education in its broadest terms, and if utopian thinking does no more than provide this, it may well have justified itself. Unfortunately, the general run of administrators in higher education is not noted for this kind of intellectual exercise. Indeed, Hutchins at one time remarked that he could count on the fingers of one hand the university presidents capable of thinking about the university in terms of fundamental theory.[22]

It is misfortune to speak, as so many do, pejoratively of utopia as a kind of dilettante daydreaming. As Kant said, it does no harm to have a noble educational ideal even if we are not in a position to realize it immediately. If our ideal is right, its realization is not at all impossible in spite of current hindrances. Much earlier, of course, Plato constructed just such an educational ideal in his Republic. Though it failed to save Athens from decadence, it has provided future centuries with a critique by which to judge educational systems from kindergarten to university.

This conclusion is of special import for the custodians of the university--the corporation, regents, trustees, and the like. When the administration proposes new directions for university development, how are the custodians to evaluate the proposals? For that matter, how is the administration itself to be self-critical of the plans sent up from the bureau for institutional research, if it is fortunate enough to have one? If the only criterion they have is tactical feasibility, they may be very shortsighted. The Roman poet Juvenal put the issue very pointedly when he asked, "Who takes custody of the custodians?" The custodians can save themselves in part if they have a utopia up their intellectual sleeve. This does not mean that starry-eyed utopians have final answers--far from it. But it does mean that this type of thinking, this habit of mind, performs a useful--in fact, indispensable--function

Part II

in decision-making in the university.

John S. Brubacher is professor of higher education at the Center for the Study of Higher Education, University of Michigan, Ann Arbor. While responsibility for this article belongs to the author, he wishes to acknowledge the influence of many exchanges of thought with Dr. James Doi, professor of higher education, at Michigan.

Notes and References

1. Stephen R. Graubard, "University Cities in the Year 2000," Daedalus, Summer 1967, pp. 117-22.
2. "Ivory Towers in Tomorrow's World," Journal of Higher Education, November 1967, pp. 117-27.
3. Theodore Brameld, who considers his "reconstructionist" educational philosophy utopian-oriented gives a brief survey of all levels of education in utopia in Toward a Reconstructionist Philosophy of Education (New York: Dryden Press, 1956), pp. 24-37, 149-65, and 254-57.
4. Boston: Houghton Mifflin, 1926, chap. 21.
5. Works (Philadelphia: Hugh Maxwell & William Fry, 1803) pp. 173-226.
6. Oxford Clarendon Press 1915.
7. New York: B. W. Huebsch, 1918.
8. New York: Random House, 1962.
9. Ibid. p. 8.
10. Chicago: University of Chicago Press, 1952
11. New Haven Yale University Press, 1936.
12. Romans, 12:2 a.
13. New York: Macmillan Co., 1948.
14. John Courtney Murray, "The Making of a Pluralistic Society--a Catholic View," in Religion and the State University, ed. Erich A. Walker (Ann Arbor: University of Michigan Press, 1958), chap. 1.

Notes and References (cont'd)

15. Op, cit., pp. 817-22.
16. "The University." New Republic, May 28, 1966 pp. 17-20.
17. Joyce O. Hertzler, The History of Utopian Thought (New York: Macmillan Co., 1923), p. 295.
18. Karl Mannheim, Ideology and Utopia (New York: Harcourt, Brace Co., 1953), p. 176.
19. Ibid., p. 222.
20. Cf. Harold Laski, "A New Education Needs a New World," Social Frontier, February, 1936, pp. 144-47.
21. New York: Doubleday, Doran, 1932.
22. The University (Santa Barbara: Center for the Study of Democratic Institutions, 1961), p. 29.

The Alberta Academy

Commission on Educational Planning

WHILE...(THE ALBERTA ACADEMY) WOULD HAVE SOME OF THE CHARACTERISTICS OF THE BRITISH OPEN UNIVERSITY AND CERTAIN CAMPUS OUTREACH PROGRAMS...ITS STRUCTURAL DYNAMICS COULD NOT EASILY BE COMPARED WITH THOSE OF ANY (OTHER) INSTITUTION...

Essentially the whole question of access to higher education is a moral one. Can our society continue to offer the benefits of improved knowledge only to those who can afford it? Surely, we must respect the right of each Albertan to enjoy this opportunity regardless of socio-economic status just as we respect his personal imperative for greater self-fulfillment. If we were to employ certain incentive devices to overcome the current under-representation in higher education of females and persons from low-income families and smaller centres, enrollments would quickly increase. And if we could deliver higher education to people where they want it--and when they want it--in the ways that they want it--the increase in enrollments would be dramatic. The very thrust of this report is at orchestrating greatly increased participation in recurrent education. If the Commission's call for a structure and resources to support lifelong learning

Reprinted from A Choice of Futures, a report of the Commission on Educational Planning for the Cabinet Committee on Education, Edmonton, Alberta, Canada.

The Future of Higher Education

is heeded at all, we may expect much larger enrollments of both full and part-time students in the years ahead.

All these conditions suggest the need for a new approach to higher education in Alberta: one that can offer socially relevant programs on a part-time basis, at less cost and with assured transfer of credits to higher education institutions across the province; one that would be flexible enough to meet sudden changes in enrollment; one that would operate close to the student's home and place of employment. But how could we possibly finance education for such large numbers of geographically-dispersed, new and different clients? How could we assess the readiness and upgrade the qualifications of large numbers of new and differently prepared clients for education? How could we readily respond to sporadic, sometimes unforeseen, fluctuations in demand? How could we take education to these new and different clients or, alternatively bring them to education? These are the challenges of a system of recurrent education based on lifelong learning. Confronted by these challenges, our present institutions and financial bases--while capable of some extension through longer operation, shift systems, imaginative programming and prudent fiscal policy--are not likely to be equal to the task. Therefore, one way of helping meet these challenges is to establish a completely different type of institution: the Alberta Academy.

The Alberta Academy would be aimed at the distinctive needs of lifelong learning in Alberta. It would represent a break with the institutional

Part II

tradition of a central place of learning.

Students would not be required to go to the academy, for the academy would go to them. While it would have some of the characteristics of the British Open University and certain campus outreach programs offered in Newfoundland, Prince Edward Island, New Brunswick, Ontario and Quebec, its structural dynamics could not easily be compared with those of any institution the Commission has encountered.

The academy would employ a wide variety of learning media, including televison and radio broadcasts, cable-vision, correspondence, telephone and tape technologies. It would also place equal stress on interpersonal communications, including tutorials, group learning, peer learning, community support and social activities. The emphasis will not be on mass education through mass media, but on individual instruction through the efficient management of technology and human resources.

The academy would employ personalized learning systems in much the same way that they have been envisioned by Athabasca University and by the University of Calgary's Learning Technology Unit. In fact, these systems could be jointly developed by all three bodies--and by others, such as Mount Royal College, now actively investigating the learning system method. At its heart, a learning system consists of learning modules, such as a combination of books and other print materials, audio and video tapes, slides and tutorial and/or seminar sessions which systemize a single topic--often along lines similar to the inquiry method of teaching.

The Future of Higher Education

These modules are capable of many combinations, in sum or in part, so that each institution might create a course to its own distinctive requirements. In fact, so might each user.

The academy, too, is like a learning system. Its whole concept is based upon extreme flexibility so that response to social and economic change can be immediate. Its services may be combined and permutated in endless ways--full-to serve thousands or tens of thousands in traditional ways or in radically different ways.

While the Commission may talk of courses and credits and degrees and classes in order to introduce the academy concept, the future may not tolerate such traditional notions at all--indeed, these notions are being questioned in reputable quarters right now. No matter. The academy has the innate capacity to be higher education's all-terrain vehicle.

While the academy would have no campus and be neither a university, nor a college, nor a technical institute, it would act as a staging agency for, and provide entrance to, all of these institutions- or to others, as they are created. In fact, it might be thought of as a concept rather than as a place. While it would grant no degrees itself, the academy could offer an individualized diploma program of its own. And it is reasonable to expect that there are now thousands of people in our province waiting for the kinds of opportunities that could be provided by the Alberta Academy.

What really counts in education is what is built inside a student--not what is studied inside a building.

Part II

The campus of the Alberta Academy would be under no particular roof. Its location would be in air waves, telephone lines, mail routes, living rooms, businesses, community buildings, learning resource centers and tutorial offices spread across the province. The Commission believes that the individual's own motivation, his desire to learn and grow, should play a more central role in the formulation of educational policy. Ideally, the attainment of higher education should represent a positive act of individual will, rather than passive acceptance of an institution's routines and requirements. The academy would strive for a closer approximation of this ideal. One of the ways in which this can be achieved is by developing course content that would stimulate individual inquiry.

The academy would occupy a position of considerable leverage in the Alberta educational system. It would offer a new road to higher education--a road with a bridge at the end. Registration in the academy would be open to all, regardless of their educational credentials. Not only would those mature students seeking greater educational opportunity be able to use this road, but so would those students coming out of Alberta's newly-flexible schools. The term newly-flexible is used for good reason: secure in the knowledge that there was a road to higher education other than the matriculant diploma mill, students could undertake different, and more individually relevant, basic education programs. And educators would not be afraid to structure and promote these new programs. Nor would parents be reluctant to have their children take them.

From the standpoint of quality, the academy would

not be satisfied with equivalent standards: it would seek improvement in the general level of higher education. Its courses would be developed by the very best talent available, using worldwide resources and sophisticated methods which would assure high quality materials of tested educational validity. Already such materials are being developed in other parts of the world and the opportunity now exists for Alberta to join Ontario and other provinces in joint Canadian production. Generally, the academy's core-program would be patterned along the lines of the foundation year recommended by the U.S. Carnegie Commission, with built-in remedial opportunities for those who come to the program without sufficient preparation. The foundation year would be interdisciplinary--an ideal often attempted but seldom achieved by established institutions, where discipline boundaries can be like armed borders and not enough resources are available to mount an invasion.

The diploma program of the academy could begin once four courses from the foundation year had been completed. We can think of no better words to describe this diploma program than Community Life and Self Development. If this description sounds gauche, then so be it. The point is, people want what these words suggest--personal growth, good friends and a better place to live. These courses would include research projects and mini-courses aimed at improving rural life, the local environment, the economic climate and cultural development. They would also include optional study topics such as child development, small business management, agricultural extension, human rights, group leadership, recreation management and community plan-

Part II

ning. Finally, there would be many opportunities for the development of personal insights and attributes--in both the arts and the sciences.

At its outset, the academy would offer only a limited number of courses, but certain of these would provide wide individual option. Courses would really be of two kinds: those that form the foundation year would constitute the equivalent of first year in an Alberta university or college--and would be transferable; those that form the diploma year would constittute a self-development framework with considerable room for the student to tailor his own program--probably these courses would not be transferable.

Because the Alberta Academy would cover such wide ground, the Commission recommended that it be established and operated by the Department of Advanced Education, in close consultation with all of Alberta's higher education institutions, public and private. It will be no small matter to link the academy's course offerings with those of existing institutions. Historically, it has been difficult to transfer credits between higher education institutions, even where two institutions were offering courses of identical description. Since the academy's foundation courses will be unlike others currently offered, it is likely that the Department of Advanced Education will wish to assist in the establishment of a transfer agreement.

Surely a beginning agreement can be reached whereby other institutions would accept the academy's foundation year program for transfer as a single unit, thus honoring the integrity of a fellow institution. For students not completing the foundation year, it follows that institutions would also be willing to accept say, three-fifths of a year of academy work as a unit, for entry and advanced credit toward their own first year programs. Further, the institutions should be willing to acknowledge the transfer of individual courses within that unit.

The core segments of the academy's foundation year would be developed as a series of radio and television programs. Given the financing suggested, these programs could combine the best audio-visual materials available from outside sources with the best materials we are capable of producing in this province. The transferability problem might be eased, and the full social and economic benefits realized, if the use of these programs does not end with the academy's students. The programs would be freely available for closed circuit use by all other educational institutions. Obviously, the use of these programs in or as first year courses at the universities and colleges would greatly facilitate the transfer of course credits between all institutions, including the academy.

Further, other Alberta institutions utilizing the academy's audio-visual materials could realize some worthwhile financial benefits. It was demonstrated in a recent Ontario study on televised university teaching that substantial cost savings could be obtained in situations where the number of students taking a given course was reasonably large and the average class size was sufficiently small. Cost comparisons in the study provided for a major investment in TV production and for the expense of tutors to supplement the televised lec-

Part II

tures. The employment of the academy's media materials in other Alberta institutions would compare even more favorably because these materials would be supplied at no cost to the institution. Freed of the high cost of media production, participating institutions would have to finance only the complementary tutorial expenses.

The foregoing draws attention to the fact that the creation of the Alberta Academy, which is valuable in itself, would have a second benefit--its existence would be an important pressure for change in the existing institutions for higher education. While the scope of the academy concept is wide, its activities have been purposefully aimed at a single critical stage in our educational system--that stage in our educational system--that stage of emergence from basic education and the beginning of higher education. The academy would develop a delivery system for this stage using the ACCESS network described in Section VI; once it is developed, other institutions should be encouraged to use it--to offer courses for second and third year students enrolled in their programs. Eventually, it should be possible to earn a degree by this route.

As will be shown later in the sub-section on cost benefits, the Alberta Academy would be committed to the provision of higher education on a more cost-effective basis than is currently evident in this province. Not only would the academy be intended as a more economical means of providing higher education from the public purse; it would also serve as a pilot model for Alberta in the application of technology to education--an application with total commitment to the belief that technology and humanist values can, and must, advance together--an application that can bring us one step closer to the person-centered society.

ADDITIONAL LEARNING STRATEGIES

Some of the principles advocated by Ivan Illich in The Deschooling of Society are, in fact, operative in the academy concept. Therefore, some of Illich's strategies might also be worth consideration. Each registrant in an academy course could receive the names, addresses and phone numbers of others in his community who are taking, or have taken, the same course. Peer learning consultation would provide an additional support system, both to the student and the academy. Tutors could assist in the orchestration of these peer support systems. Some of Illich's ideas concerning the identification of teaching masters within a deschooled society are also worth investigating.

In certain geographic instances, and with certain courses, mobile campus trailers should be employed to bring learning support services to academy students. Their use would be similar to that envisioned by George Brown College in Ontario.

In the 1830's, hunger for knowledge led to the grass roots establishment of the Lyceum Movement in the United States. It developed into a North American network of more than 3,000 town study groups. During the first third of the 20th century the Chautauqua movement, half reading circle and half tent show, became even more popular and at its zenith in 1924 was bringing educational motivation to millions, including many Canadians. In the '30's and '40's, CBC's Farm Forum and Citizens' Forum

Part II

radio programs became community events with discussion groups meeting in living rooms, schools and community halls across the country. Farm Forum was the most popular single radio program on the prairies. The Department of Extension at the University of Alberta helped to organize these programs and supplemented them with locally relevant follow-up activities, which were eagerly joined by tens of thousands of Albertans. After the Canadian experience, similar programs were developed with great success in India and Africa.

While television and other mass media may have satisfied part of the hunger for knowledge, and the academy program may satisfy more of it, the social dynamic of the movements we have described still awaits our use in the last third of the 20th century. Indeed, 15 years of research in adult ETV programming has shown us that the most effective programs were those employing community listening and viewing groups, volunteer teachers and social interaction. The Commission sees distinct possibilities for endowing the academy programs with similar grass-roots popular support. Why not Academy Clubs as well as Toastmasters' Clubs and Lions' Clubs? Why not community corporations as foreseen in the mosaic campus being planned by Conestega College in Ontario, which would enable local citizens to participate in the planning of academy activities? Indeed, why not academy travel tours, academy fairs and academy communes?

Recently the Royal Canadian Legion has been speculating on its role in the future. There is feeling within this closely-knit organization that its original purposes have now been largely served. It is suggested, in all earnestness, that the Alberta outposts of the Royal Canadian Legion consider turning their facilities over to higher education to be managed by the academy, or by other institutions such as Athabasca University, who have envisaged community outposts as part of their academic concept. Further, there is no reason why the social nature of these legion outposts should change. It can be convincingly argued that darts, shuffleboards, beer and billiards, together with the warm atmosphere of comradeship, have long made significant contributions to higher education-indeed, to all forms of education.

Also intriguing are a variety of strategies that might be best described as people helping people. For instance, there would be some academy students who would freely wish to help other students enrolled in the academy program, or in the Early Ed or basic education broadcast programs--just for the sake of personal fulfillment. Still others would welcome employment as part-time tutorial assistants while enrolled in the academy program. Certain of the academy courses might even include experience as a learning helper as a study requirement; for instance, help in a day-care center as requisite for completion of a unit in child development. These strategies for providing significant life experiences warrant closer investigation within the academy concept.

Finally, some specific mention of the correspondence component in academy programs must be made. It may be fairly stated that Alberta is already one of the world's leaders in the quality of its grade school correspondence instruction. Some of Alberta's

Part II

correspondence courses have been adopted internationally--most recently by the United Arab Republic. At the same time, the Correspondence School Branch has just launched credit courses on MEETA (Channel 11) in Edmonton that combine written work with television viewing and phone-in discussion on radio station CKUA. This evidence of Alberta's reputation in correspondence work, and of the innovative methods currently underway, is given to demonstrate further that the academy concept really is attainable. The Department of Advanced Education, therefore, already has available some well-oiled machinery that could assist the academy's implementation. And, of course, another source of strength for this endeavor is some of the planning which has been done in connection with Athabasca University.

ILLUSTRATIVE ORGANIZATION

How might the program of the Alberta Academy be organized? What kinds of people, places and things would be required to offer it? Only illustrative and partial answers to questions like these can be given at this time, their purpose being merely to aid in understanding the concept and demonstrating its feasibility. Implementation must await the preparation of a full-scale development plan by the Department of Advanced Education. However, it is worth mentioning here that Alberta does not presently have the population base to support a full academy degree program. Degree programs require a wide range of optional subjects in their senior years; this would entail the development of many courses, each of which would serve relatively few registrants. Such a move would imperil the economic feasibility of the academy, which is based upon few courses and large registrations.

It is suggested that 12 courses might be developed: six interdisciplinary first-year foundation courses; six diploma courses in Community Life and Self Development. As an example, only the foundation courses will be referred to, and in very broad-brush and conventional terms:

(1) Man and mankind (history, religion, and the arts)
(2) Communications (writing, oral and visual literacy)
(3) Modes of Reasoning (logic, philosophy, mathematics)
(4) Technological Man and His Environment (science, technology and natural law)
(5) The Human Community (psychology, sociology, anthropology)
(6) Man and Country (Canadian studies in geography, ecology, economics and politics)

During its first year, the academy would offer courses 1, 2, 3, and 4. Registrants would be restricted to carrying no more than three courses. The completion of courses 1, 2 and 3 would allow entrance to any college or university in the province, with three-fifths of a year's credit. Completion of courses 2 and 4 would offer entrance and advanced credit at any technical institute. Completion of course 2 and any four other courses would constitute a full year's work at any university or college. Completion of course 2 and any three other courses would allow entry into the academy's diploma program. Course offerings during the academy's second and subse-

Part II

quent years of operation would likely rise to six or seven and would be staggered so that certain courses would be offered every year, others once every two years.

Each course would consist of 30 correspondence papers, 30 half-hours of television programming, one half-hour per week repeated at varying times on both broadcast and CATV systems, supplemented by radio presentations and talk-back opportunities, and at least one two-hour tutorial per month. Tutors would be available for more frequent consultation and would be stationed in as many as 20 different regional locations, hopefully none more than 50 miles distant from any client. In addition to being located in cities and towns having institutions of higher and further education both public and private, tutors would also be at the regional learning centers. Probably, still others would be required in places like Athabasca, Brooks, Cardston, High Prairie, Lac La Biche, Oyen, Rocky Mountain House and Wainwright with access to local learning resource units, as well as to the entire provincial learning resource network.

Frequent telephone communications, initiated by both tutor and student would be provided for. In addition, where living room groups could be congregated, blackboard by wire systems, which use telephone lines, might be employed. The tutors would be competent in at least two courses, and some in four. Initially, each tutor would run 100 course registrants, and tutorials would be set for 10 participants. Since 112 teachers now run 18,000 course registrants at the Correspondence School Branch, and still devote much of their time to course development, this tentative ratio should provide a comfortable margin for both marking assignments and tutorials.

When economically feasible EVR (electronic video recording), and other television cartridge systems (be they tape, foil or film), and CAI (computer assisted instruction) could be easily integrated into the total learning package.

Part III
SCENARIOS: FACTS OR FANCIES ABOUT THE FUTURE?

*To the extent that particular scenarios
may be divorced from reality,
the proper criticism would seem to be of particular scenarios
rather than of the method.
And of course unrealistic scenarios
are often useful aids to discussion, if only to point out
that the particular possibilities are unrealistic.*

HERMAN KAHN

ANTHONY J. WIENER

"The Use of Scenarios"

Uncritical Lovers, Unloving Critics

John W. Gardner

THE TWENTY-THIRD-CENTURY SCHOLARS UNDERSTOOD THAT WHERE HUMAN INSTITUTIONS WERE CONCERNED, LOVE WITHOUT CRITICISM BRINGS STAGNATION, AND CRITICISM WITHOUT LOVE BRINGS DESTRUCTION.

This one hundredth commencement is an occasion so rich in history that it has administered a strong stimulus, perhaps too strong, to my sense of the past and future. Had it been a milder stimulus, I could have contented myself with the nostalgia, congratulations, and rosy prognosis traditional to centennial celebrations. To look back reverently, to applaud present vitality, to predict an upward path ahead would have been particularly easy in the case of this great institution--so vital, so full of promise, so worthy of our admiration.

But this is not a year in the life of American universities, or in the life of the nation, that invites such a traditional approach. So I am going to broaden the focus beyond Cornell and beyond universities to human institutions generally. I am going to take you on a 600-year tour of history, beginning some three centuries ago and stretching three centuries into the future. Such a tour might present some difficulties for a qualified historian, but it is a mere finger exercise for the practiced commencement speaker.

John W. Gardner's 1968 Commencement address reprinted with the permission of Cornell University.

Part III

In the seventeenth and eighteenth centuries, increasing numbers of people began to believe that men could determine their own fate, shape their own institutions, and gain command of the social forces that buffeted them. Before then, from the beginning, men had believed that all the major features of their lives were determined by immemorial custom or fate or the will of God. It was one of the Copernican turns of history that brought man gradually over two or three centuries to the firm conviction that he could have a hand in shaping his institutions.

No one really knows all the ingredients that went into the change, but we can identify some major elements. One was the emergence with the scientific revolution of a way of thinking that sought objectively identifiable cause-and-effect relationships. People trained in that way of thinking about the physical world were bound to note that the social world, too, had its causes and effects. And with that discovery came, inevitably, the idea that one might manipulate the cause to alter the effect.

At the same time, people became less and less inclined to explain their daily lives and institutions in terms of God's will. And that trend has continued to this day. Less and less do men suppose, even those who believe devoutly in a Supreme Being, that God busies himself with the day-to-day microadministration of the world.

While all of this was happening, new modes of transportation and communication were breaking down parochial attitudes all over the world. As men discovered that human institutions and customs

Scenarios: Facts or Fancies About the Future?

varied enormously from one society to the next, it became increasingly difficult to think of one's own institutions as unalterable and increasingly easy to conceive of a society in which men consciously shaped their institutions and customs.

The result is that today any bright high school student can discourse on social forces and institutional change. A few centuries ago, even for learned men, such matters were "given," ordained not subject to analysis, fixed in the great design of things.

Up to a point the new views were immensely exhilarating. In the writings of our founding fathers, for example, one encounters a mood approaching exaltation as they proceeded to shape a new nation. But more recently another consequence has become apparent: the new views place an enormous--in some instances, an unbearable--burden on the social structures that man has evolved over the centuries. Those structures have become the sole target and receptacle for all man's hope and hostility. He has replaced his fervent prayer to God with a shrill cry of anger against his own institutions. I claim no special insight into the unknowable Deity, but He must be chuckling.

Men can tolerate extraordinary hardship if they think it is an unalterable part of life's travail. But an adminstered frustration--unsanctioned by religion or custom or deeply rooted values--is more than the spirit can bear. So increasingly men rage at their institutions. All kinds of men rage at all kinds of institutions, here and around the world. Most of them have no clear vision of the kind of world they

Part III

want to build; they only know they don't want the kind of world they have.

So much for the past and present.

I told you I would take you three centuries into the future. I am able to do this thanks to a Cornell scientist who recently discovered how man may step off the time dimension and visit the past or future at will. You may be surprised you haven't heard about this, but he's finding his capacity to know the future rather profitable. He doesn't want to publicize his findings until he has won a few more horse races.

At any rate he gave me a few pills, and since I'm not interested in horse races, I decided to find out what the future holds in the struggle between man and his institutions. I cannot guarantee the results. I do not offer what follows as a prediction. Perhaps the pill just gave me bad dreams.

The first thing I learned is that in the last third of the twentieth century the rage to demolish succeeded beyond the fondest dreams of the dismantlers. They brought everything tumbling down. Since the hostility to institutions was a product of modern minds, the demolition was most thorough in the most advanced nations.

You will be pleased to know that unlike the fall of Rome, this decline was not followed by hundreds of years of darkness. In fact, there followed less than a century of chaos and disorder. In the latter part of the twenty-first century the rebuilding began. Since chaos is always followed by authoritarianism,

Scenarios: Facts or Fancies About the Future?

this was a period of iron rule, worldwide--a world society rigidly organized and controlled. I don't think I shall tell you what language was spoken.

But tyrannies tend to grow lax, even under futuristic methods of thought control. By the end of the twenty-second century, the sternly disciplined institutions of the world society had grown relatively tolerant, and the old human impulse to be free had begun to reassert itself.

In the new, more permissive atmosphere, men were again allowed to study history, which had been under a ban for two centuries. The effect was electric. To those austere and antiseptic minds, conditioned to the requirements of a technically advanced authoritarianism, the rediscovery of man's history was intoxicating. It generated an intellectual excitement that dominated the whole twenty-third century. Scholars were entranced by the variety of human experience, shocked by the violence and barbarism, saddened by the stupidities, and exalted by the achievements of their forebears. And as they searched that history, excitedly, sadly, lovingly, they returned increasingly to the twentieth century as a moment of curious and critical importance in the long pageant.

All the evidence available to them indicated that the preceding centuries had seen a vast and impressive movement in the direction of institutions that were responsive to the will of men. There were setbacks, to be sure, and trouble and hypocrisy and failures, but over the years the trend was unmistakable. Why then in the late twentieth century did men turn on their institutions and destroy them in a fit of impatience? As one twenty-third-century scholar put it,

Part III

"Until we answer that question we shall never be sure that we are not preparing the same fate for ourselves."

As they studied the history of the twentieth century, they discovered that human expectations had risen sharply in the middle years of the century. They observed that men came to demand more and more of their institutions and to demand it with greater intransigence. And they noted that the demands for instant performance led to instant disillusionment, for while aspirations leapt ahead, human institutions remained sluggish--less sluggish, to be sure, than at any previous time in history, but still inadequately responsive to human need.

Twenty-third-century scholars agreed on these facts but they disagreed as to the implications. One school of thought said the big mistake had been to let aspirations loose in the first place. Human aspirations, they said, should be kept under tight control. The opposing school of thought argued that human aspirations were a dynamic force that held enormous potential for good. They insisted that the main requirement was to make human institutions less sluggish. The only error of the mid-twentieth century, they said, was to release aspirations without designing institutions responsive enough to satisfy those aspirations.

After years of debate, the two schools of thought began to come together, and a common doctrine began to emerge. The first thing they agreed upon was that human aspirations were capable of contributing enormously to the dynamism of the society and therefore should not be tightly bottled up. But

Scenarios: Facts or Fancies About the Future?

they also agreed that there must be procedural bounds within which the aspirations could express themselves.

Some were quick to point out that in the mid-twentieth century such procedural bounds did exist and functioned quite well, permitting extraordinary scope and variety of dissent until the last third of the century, when the bounds were increasingly rejected and the dissolution of the society began. Back of the rejection was the impatient hostility that late-twentieth century man felt toward his institutions. Those who consciously sought the destruction of their society were never more than a small minority, but they found it easier to trigger the latent hostility of larger numbers of people. Many, of course, were ignorant of the long, painful evolution of procedures for the expression of dissent, for the protection of individual rights, for the maintenance of that framework of order without which freedom is impossible. Others were not ignorant but very angry. The result was the same.

The second thing twenty-third-century scholars came to agree upon was that if society is going to release aspirations for institutional change--which is precisely what many twentieth-century-societies deliberately did--then it had better be sure its institutions are capable of such change. In this respect they found the twentieth century sadly deficient.

Most institutions were designed to obstruct change rather than facilitate it. And that is not really surprising. The institutions were, after all, designed by human beings, and most men most of the time do not want the institutions in which they themselves have a vested interest to change. Professors were

Part III

often cited as an interesting example of this tendency, because they clearly favored innovation in other parts of the society but steadfastly refused to make universities into flexible, adaptive, self-renewing institutions.

There were, of course, a good many people in the twentieth century who did want change, but they were curiously indifferent to the task of redesigning their institutions so that change could be readily accomplished. Many of them were moral zealots who expended their total energy in headlong combat between themselves (whom they believed to be very, very good) and specified others (whom they believed to be very, very bad); and the object of the combat was to do in the bad ones, even if it meant doing in oneself. This led to endless hostilities, especially when those marked for assault had equally strong convictions about their own moral superiority. It was particularly difficult when the two groups spoke a different language or were separated by an ocean or thirty years of age.

There were other reformers who were considerably more discriminating and saw that to achieve their ends they must change human institutions. But even these often misconceived the fundamental task.

Each such reformer came to his task with a little bundle of desired changes. The society is intolerable, he would assert, because it has these specifiable defects: a, b, c, and so on. The implication was that if appropriate reforms a', b', and c' were carried through and the defects corrected, the society would be wholly satisfactory and the work

Scenarios: Facts or Fancies About the Future?

of the reformer done.

That, as twenty-third-century scholars plainly saw, was a primitive way of viewing social change. The true task, they saw, was to design a society (and institutions) capable of continuous change, continuous renewal, continuous responsiveness. They understood that this was entirely feasible; indeed, they noted that the twentieth century had hit upon a number of partial solutions to the problem of designing self-renewing institutions but had never pursued the task with adequate vigor. (I might add that I, myself, wrote a book on this subject, back in the twentieth century. It was entitled Self-Renewal. I won't review its findings here, because I wouldn't want to spoil your enjoyment of the book.)

Because of their failure to design institutions capable of continuous renewal, twentieth century societies showed astonishing sclerotic streaks. Even in the United States, which was then the most adaptable of all societies, the departments of the federal government were in grave need of renewal; state government was a waxwork of stiffly preserved anachronisms; the system of taxation was a tangle of dysfunctional measures; the courts were crippled by archaic organizational arrangements; the unions, the professions, the universities, the corporations--each had spun its own impenetrable web of vested interests.

Such a society could not respond to challenge. And it did not. But as one twenty-third-century scholar put it, "The reformers couldn't have been less interested in the basic adaptability of the society. That posed tough and complex tasks of institutional redesign that bored them to death. They preferred the

Part III

joys of combat, of villain hunting. As for the rest of society, it was dozing off in front of the television set."

The twenty-third-century scholars made another exceptionally interesting observation. They pointed out that twentieth-century institutions were caught in a savage crossfire between uncritical lovers and unloving critics. On the one side, those who loved their institutions tended to smother them in an embrace of death, loving their rigidities more than their promise, shielding them from life-giving criticism. On the other side, there arose a breed of critics without love, skilled in demolition but untutored in the arts by which human institutions are nurtured and strengthened and made to flourish. Between the two, the institutions perished.

The twenty-third-century scholars understood that where human institutions were concerned, love without criticism brings stagnation, and criticism without love brings destruction. And they emphasized that the swifter the pace of change, the more lovingly men had to care for and criticize their institutions to keep them intact through the turbulent passages.

In short, men must be discriminating appraisers of their society, knowing coolly and precisely what it is about the society that thwarts or limits them and therefore needs modification. And so must they be discriminating protectors of their institutions, preserving those features that nourish and strengthen them and make them more free. To fit themselves for such tasks, they must be sufficiently serious to study their institutions, sufficiently dedicated to

Scenarios: Facts or Fancies About the Future?

become expert in the art of modifying them.

Having arrived at these judgments, twenty-third-century leaders proceeded to redesign their own society for continuous renewal. Commenting on the debt they owed to the twentieth-century experience, one of them said: "It is not just that we have learned from twentieth-century insights. For in that troubled time there were men who were saying just what we are saying now. Had they been heeded, the solutions we have reached would have come 300 years earlier. But no one was listening."

Ladies and gentlemen, as I told you earlier, I cannot guarantee the glimpse of the future given me by my friend, the Cornell scientist. Come to think of it, he hasn't been winning his horse races consistently. So perhaps it's not too late to alter history's course.

John W. Gardner, former U.S. Commissioner of Education, is now Chairman of Common Cause.

Letter from Tomorrow

John Caffrey

....SINCE "AUTHORITY" IS SO SEVERELY QUESTIONED, DISPUTES ABOUT WHAT IS CONTEMPTUOUSLY REFERRED TO AS "TRUTH" ARE SETTLED BY VOTE OF THE STUDENTS.

May Day 1978

My Dear Colleague:

Having been in the United States for only ten days, it is premature to write my impressions of my first visit to the colleges and universities in this amazing country. However, the impressions are so vivid, and the conditions so extraordinary, that I hasten to write before my memory is blurred by an overcrowding of sensation. Although this is my first visit to America, I believe much has changed in the almost ten years since you were here in 1969.

The skyscrapers, the crowded corridors and escalators, the thousands of students carried on moving sidewalks through automatic cafeterias, the teeming libraries, lawns, and classrooms-- all seem to confirm that 2 out of every 3 persons under 25 are enrolled in a college or university.

On my first day, I was assigned a handsome and

Reprinted with the copyright permission of AAUP Bulletin, Vol. 54, No 3 (Autumn, 1968).

Scenarios: Facts or Fancies About the Future?

articulate guide, a young man with two golden braids hanging to his shoulders, pearl and gold earrings, a beard almost to his waist, and red thong sandals. In his white toga, one would have thought him to be one of the shepherds in our mountain country. The only "modern" touches were the radio strapped to his wrist and the identification badge, with his picture, fastened below his left shoulder. My own badge is of a color which at once identifies me as a guest and a **foreigner.**

I must at once discuss these badges. They are required for passage from any major area to another and symbolize the mode of governance. My guide, who is 25 and hopes to graduate this year was 16 in 1969 and vividly recalls the turbulence of that period. His oldest brother was almost killed in what is still called the Battle of Alumni House. The violent disturbances of that year, and the intervention of the National Guard in 1970 to prevent further bloodshed and the further burning of campus buildings, led to the reforms which marked a turning point in higher education and also the beginning of the present system of security regulations.

Although you and I are used to police supervision of our movements from province to province, we are at least used to moving freely on our campus. Here, although one quickly accommodates, it seems strange to have to show one's badge to armed guards as one leaves or enters the campus and its buildings. In the few large classes, most taught by television or film, guards are posted at the doors. In the few large-scale meetings now permitted, television cameras mounted on the walls perpetually scan the audience. In more modern institutions, automatic

Part III

controls may be activated to seal the doors of large rooms, which may be flooded with chemical sprays which quickly reduce all violence.

Important academic administrators have become used to these regulations and no longer seem to notice the guards who perpetually accompany them. In fact, most students are resigned to the security system, and many prefer it to the anarchy which flared up a decade ago. The administration is still resented, but the security measures of today, as my young guide points out, at least ensure that students will not have to hear the "garbage" and "immoral opinions" of those who still control the federal government under the emergency powers assumed during the escalation of the Cambodian conflict in 1970-71.

During my first days, I found it difficult to interview important administrators, largely because of concern with security violations. No matter how often I passed any exit or entry point, guards who had seen my face many times still compared it carefully with my picture before pressing the buttons to release the electrically locked doors.

You may wonder why I have not mentioned contacts with faculty. It is partly because I am never sure when I am speaking with one. That students and faculty dress, speak, and apparently think alike at first struck me as evidence of new, admirable harmony. I quickly sensed that no one is sure, at least on major campuses, who the members of the faculty are. No one admits to being a faculty member. Even in classroom discussions, led by students chosen in alphabetical order, any attempt

Scenarios: Facts or Fancies About the Future?

to assert something on the basis of "authority" or "experience" brings a visible stir to the group, and anyone who speaks too certainly may be accused of being a "spy" or a "subversive" or a "faculty stooge." Since "authority" is so severely questioned disputes about what is contemptuously referred to as "truth" are settled by vote of the students.

One of the most interesting activity groups is Authorities Anonymous, composed principally of those who at one time permitted themselves to be called Faculty, but also including students with too obvious ambitions, as evidenced by their willingness to concede to now obsolete "requirements." Members of AA must publicly confess their earlier errors in presuming to know more than their students, and they do further penance in periodic ceremonies in which they publicly burn old files of lecture notes and examinations.

The granting of degrees is determined by secret vote of the student body, closely supervised by the administration to ensure that only votes and no other kinds of "evidence" are used. Entrance to the institution is determined, not by examination or previous record but by ethnic quotas, which ensure that specified proportions of certain racial groups are given admittance and that there is proportionate representation of all social classes. Failure of an institution to observe this quota system may lead to reprisal blockades, strikes, or the burning of diplomas.

Leaders of the business and industrial community have established an internal educational program which substantially imitates the previous functions

Part III

of the university. Thus the burden of support has fallen on the business community, but this is cheerfully accepted as an alternative to the improvements in the former ostensible system of higher education.

Later I will deal with the curricular reforms introduced as the results of what, back in the 1960's was called the "Free University" system. The abandonment of the concept of "authority" was made clear to me on my second day when, temporarily deprived of my guide, I asked my way to a computer center. The first student I stopped looked at the ground and said, in a soft voice, "Well, man, I think it's that grey thing over there." Another student, passing by, overheard my informant, stopped, and angrily asked, "Who do you think you are, baby? Who are you to be passing our opinions?" My informant apologized and pointed out that it was only his opinion. The passerby replied, with evident asperity, "Well, don't go setting yourself up as a honky big-mouth faculty type. The important thing is Discovery. Let The Man find his own way. Like the rest of us. Who knows where or whether that Machine will be tomorrow?"

Well, my dear colleague, I must close. I have been warned to spend the next two days visiting museums. The campuses in New York have all agreed to close so that the election of next year's presidents of this city's colleges and universities can proceed without the violent incidents of last year, when several candidates were injured. The president of the university I visited today told me privately that he will be very happy to see the end of his one-year

Scenarios: Facts or Fancies About the Future?

term of office. He hopes that relief from the duties of office will enable him to graduate before his 24th birthday next year.

Best wishes until later

         Your friend,

          C

John Caffrey is Director of the Commission on Administrative Affairs of the American Council on Education.

The School System:
A Look into the Future

Robert T. Grant

TEACHERS SUDDENLY FOUND THEMSELVES
IN A COMPLETELY DIFFERENT MILIEU.....
(THEY) FOUND THEMSELVES SETTING THEIR
OWN FEES FOR SERVICES RENDERED....

The Federated Association of State Teachers (FAST), who negotiate for all of the teachers in the state, and the State Board of Trustees who speak for the "local" school districts in the state, were bogged down in a hopeless impasse. The issues were the same as always--salaries, fringe benefits, transfer policies, extra duty pay, assignment of students to classes, curriculum reforms, and something the State Board called "accountability."

It all took place a few years ago when local school boards found they were no longer able to bargain effectively with the teachers who had formed a power bloc, and were united on a statewide basis, with national affiliations. In fact, the legislature had even passed into law something called "The United Professions Act," which required that all teachers belong to FAST before they could be licensed to teach; somewhere back in history, it had been called a "closed shop." Finally, in self-defense, the local Boards of Education in the state

Reprinted with the copyright permission of
The Clearing House, May, 1971.

Scenarios: Facts or Fancies About the Future?

united under one Board (The State Board of Trustees), with local sub-groups serving in advisory capacities only; under this system all of the major issues were negotiated at the state level.

Statewide salary schedules and fringe benefit packages had long since been established, along with a statewide taxing base. The local community school district, that last bastion of local control, had fallen hard. The voters, especially in the rural areas, were still highly incensed and frustrated because the big communities had locked everyone into what amounted to one huge school district. No longer did the local boards deliberate over instructional programs, or the kinds of buildings they would build, or even where to build a fence. Secretly, some of the local board members (now called school representatives) were rather pleased that they no longer had to make some of these "minor" decisions, let alone those issues relating to teacher salaries, sex education, tenure or grievances. It was much easier to "pass the buck" to the State Board. The local citizens no longer came to the old-fashioned school board meetings, now called "advisory sessions," for it was only a "forum in futility" since none of the important decisions were made there anyway.

There was however, one last vestige of local control--the good citizens of the state still had a vote on any major increase in the statewide tax base. To meet the current demands of FAST, the citizens would need to increase the existing rate by 25 per cent. The issue was overwhelmingly defeated, and FAST "withheld their services" as they were tired of subsidizing the educational programs of the state.

Part III

The legislature, in desperation, submitted a referendum to the voters of the state, a plan popularly called the POP Act--Professional Opportunities for Pedagogues. This act, in essence, abolished both the State Board of Trustees and the school system as it currently existed and set up regional contracting agencies composed of local representatives (formerly the Trustees), whose job it was to administer the existing school property and the funds generated from the current statewide tax base. Students were to be issued an educational credit voucher that could be applied towards any "approved" educational enterprise operated by a licensed professional. The referendum was over-whelmingly approved, in spite of the fact, as FAST informed the parents, that the vouchers would only cover about two-thirds of the child's educational costs and that they, the parents, would need to make up the difference.

Teachers suddenly found themselves in a completely different milieu (some even dared to call it "a more professional one.") FAST also found itself in a new role, one whose major function now seemed to be in "policing its membership" and sitting as a licensing and examining board for the professional education graduates of the universities. The professional educators (no longer called teachers) found themselves setting their own fees for services rendered. They also decided upon which clients (students) they would accept. (Of course, this also worked in reverse; if the client was not satisfied with the results, he could choose another professional.) Office or classroom space was rented or leased from the regional contracting agency representatives at fair rates. Supplies and auxiliary services were arranged for by

Scenarios: Facts or Fancies About the Future?

each professional. There were a considerable number of referrals to various specialists. The school integration problem suddenly disappeared, as did, the sex education controversy, and a host of other problems, not the least of which was the "Phonics" vs. the "Look-Say method." Some "professionals" found themselves looking for other lines of work because they could not make a living this way. Others formed Professional Groups "emphasizing various skills such as reading, early childhood education, physics, mathematics, psychology, speech, learning disabilities, ad infinitum. (Some clients, however, did not like the idea of a clinic and continued with the general practitioner who maintained his own office.) Billing procedures, retirement plans, supplies, administrative costs, insurance, and other overhead costs were handled much more conveniently by a business manager. Each professional was responsible for his own actions and, of course, results. Although licensed by the state, and policed by his own professional ethics group, the educator continued to set his own standards and used his best professional knowledge in working with his clients. The results were simple to measure: the child either learned or he didn't; he took what was relevant for him and couldn't blame anyone if it was wrong because the choice was his. (Some counselors were having a tough financial struggle.)

Many administrators were aghast at what appeared to be the loss of their functions and services, but it wasn't long before some of them were administering the business operation of the clinics for groups of professionals, running bus systems, arranging for building leases and maintenance services for providing mobile food services. Some

Part III

became outstanding professionals in their own right. The more enterprising became the head residents of clinics. A few head residents felt that a group of these clinics operating cooperatively would be more efficient. So they formed a corporation and elected a board of trustees to oversee the services and functions of these clinics, which soon were called schools, and, by and by, they appointed one of the head residents to become the chief, and they called him Superintendent. Then the professionals began to demand rules and regulations to operate these schools because.... well, where do we go from here?

Robert T. Grant is an associate professor of educational administration at The University of Arizona in Tucson.

Leave the Teaching to Us!

Stephen Dobbs

.....MANY (PARENTS) RECEIVED PROMOTIONS FOR SENDING THEIR YOUNGSTERS TO THEIR EMPLOYERS' SCHOOLS.

First it happened in a city in Ohio, then in other communities across the nation. The schools were broke. The decades-old buildings were inefficient and costly to maintain; inflation had moved the prices of educational services almost out of reach. Like the disappearance of the night stars in the dawn sky, the lights in American classrooms flickered briefly across the land and finally went out altogether.

Government could no longer afford to operate the schools, and therefore the private sector had to take over. Leaders of top corporations announced that plans had been in preparation for some time in the event of financial collapse of the public schools. Washington pledged to maintain close watch from the day the doors reopened, exercising the same quality controls as had been applied to business in other areas of consumer protection.

Not that the schools were to be handed over on a silver platter. Many stipulations were attached to thousands of contracts negotiated between local

Reprinted with copyright permission of Phi Delta Kappan, June, 1972.

Part III

districts and the National Business Council. New physical plants were demanded; up-to-date equipment and materials were promised; and substantial wages and personnel benefits were arranged. A vision of handsome new buildings and of classrooms humming with efficient teaching gadgetry began to take hold of the public consciousness.

Referenda in thousands of cities revealed the overwhelming popular sentiment favoring the surrender of the schools to business. Plans were devised to abolish school taxes, as parents would henceforth pay tuitions for their children at the institution of their choice. Newspapers and television explained the new free market philosophy, and one exuberant Detroit executive proclaimed, "What's Good for General Motors Is Good for the Country."

Corporations began a massive Madison Avenue effort to recruit students for their schools. Greyhound kicked off with the slogan, "Leave the Teaching to Us!" The automobile companies chimed in with "Wouldn't You Really Rather Attend Buick?" and "Ford Teaches Better Ideas." Some firms indicated their commitment to a particular educational philosophy, such as "General Electric, Where Process Is Our Most Important Product."

Competition was fierce; everyone wanted a piece of the action in the new education market. Owning schools replaced building art collections as a corporate status symbol. As expected, the largest companies constructed and stocked the most elaborate facilities. International Business Machines for example, quipped their network of 400 branches with sophisticated computers that far exceeded the

Scenarios: Facts or Fancies About the Future?

teaching machine systems other schools provided. Likewise, the McGraw-Hill schools had the best libraries, the Kodak schools the widest variety of audio-visual equipment, and the Wilson and Spalding schools the top athletic facilities. (All of these schools also charged the most tuition.)

The curriculum also began to reflect the interests of individual industries. Rand McNally placed heavy emphasis on its geography courses, requiring students to take geo-politics, geo-math, geo-history, and geo-economics. The National Broadcasting Company developed its studies around communications theory, and Xerox repeated this pattern. Encyclopaedia Britannica brought back memories of the pre-corporate days with its Great Books program.

Methodological strategies, also demonstrated the influence of the business managers. Standard Oil, for instance, chose a depth rather than breadth approach. The Bell Telephone System emphasized discussion groups, while Rand Corporation schools tapped inquiry skills. Southern Pacific developed the piggyback idea, in which the students built concepts upon ones they had previously acquired.

Morale among the student population was high from the inception of the free market school system. A new pride accompanied the business takeover. Each company had a distinctive name, philosophy, method of operation, and set of products around which students could develop their self-image (often with free "product patches" for jackets and binders). Business was now obliged to provide summer employment, and vocational counseling reached a new

Part III

peak of efficiency. Also, most schools offered their students substantial discounts on the company's products, which made parents happy in the knowledge that their kids were "getting it wholesale."

For the business world things couldn't be better. The credit for rescuing public education rested on corporate shoulders. Executives basked in the limelight of double professionalism as industrialists and educators. Some were pictured on a series of bubble-gum trading cards given out for good behavior in the Wrigley schools. Operating the schools brought the under-20 market to the corporation doorstep; not only were young people buying more than ever before, but their purchasing habits could be studied at close quarters so that techniques for developing enlightened adult consumers could be implemented.

The takeover of the schools seemed to be a progressive and popular move. The nation's children were being instructed in bright, modern classrooms filled with educational materials. The rise in teachers' salaries suddenly made the profession one of the most sought after in the universities. Parents were pleased with the lowering of taxes and the range of choice of schools. Many received promotions for sending their youngsters to their employers' schools. The government was relieved to have the educational monkey off its back. Critics of the free market system and of the schools in general were mollified by the rapid achievement of so many long-called-for reforms.

The economic establishment savored its triumph.

Scenario: Facts and Fancies About the Future?

Prestige and import attached to their management of public education, and future cadres of loyal consumers were being trained to assure the continuing success of capitalism. In short, everyone was happy and everything was going well in American education.

It wasn't until 1990 that Ralph Nader, Jr., made his first attack on the "bureaucratic, monopolistic, blood-sucking private schools." Then the first of the neo-romantics began to say that the system was mindless and inhuman, distorting and demeaning the best in human nature....

Stephen Dobbs is a graduate student at the Institute of American History, Stanford University.

1996: Where You May Go When You Can Go Anywhere

Frank K. Kelly

SO THE GREAT ISSUES OF 1996 COULD BE SUMMED UP IN THE GREAT ISSUES THAT TROUBLED PEOPLE IN THE YEAR 96 AND WOULD CONFRONT PEOPLE IN 2096 AND ALL THE CENTURIES TO COME....

In the 1990's, there were no big wars. The 300 billion dollars which had been spent annually on arms became available for the recycling of waste, the production of food for all, the reduction of pollution, the clearing of the air. With plenty for everybody, the absurdity of wars became apparent. Conflicts and confrontations continued, but the people of the world refused to participate in mass slaughters.

Astonished by peace, the leaders of the nations had to put their minds on other things--although few of them believed that peace could endure.

Lifelong learning was recognized as a fundamental human right. Each child at birth was issued a Certificate of Opportunity, an educational credit card renewed at three-year intervals with wider opportunities at each renewal. Grades were abolished, but each child was tested in a broad range of cate-

---

Reprinted with permission from the September, 1971 issue of College & University Business. Copyright 1971, McGraw-Hill Pubs., Inc., Chicago. All rights reserved.

Scenarios: Facts or Fancies About the Future?

gories to obtain Profiles of Possibilities.

Beginning at age two, each child had access to teaching machines geared to enable a child to learn at his own speed. Each child also had access to a cluster of counselors--persons with experience in a variety of activities. The principal qualifications of these counselors were attitudes of acceptance for people of all kinds--and a sense of warmth without a desire for dominion.

At age three, each child spent several hours a day at a learning center--formerly called a school. The buildings were used all year-round for classes, dances and art exhibitions, for gatherings of young and old, for celebrations and elections, for the training of peace patrol officers (formerly called policemen). The emphasis in every activity was upon the importance of participation by every person, and respect for the dignity of each person. No one was expected to be exactly like anyone else. People grew up at different rates and were not chided for not meeting the expectations of others.

After the age of 12, no one was required to attend any sessions at a learning center--but the excitement there was so high that few dropped out. Each person was encouraged to go through the stages of mental growth described by the philosopher Alfred North Whitehead--by stage of romance, uncovering the wonder and beauty of fresh life; the stage of precision, seeing the structures of languages and the arts and sciences, and the stage of generalization, when participation in university courses became available to all.

Part III

When discoveries in nutrition and the development of technics for removing genetic defects made it evident that the normal lifespan would range from 120 to 150 years, the pressures for immediate achievement fell off. The pace of technological change slowed, giving people more time to absorb the changes that did occur. There was an abundance of time for wandering in many avenues, for recognizing limitations without being crippled by frustrations or anxieties.

In 1996, an astonishing array of alternatives could be faced without fear. The ogre of efficiency for human beings had been banished. Efficiency was for machines, and machines took care of basic material needs. Human beings were expected to spend their lives as explorers, traveling through inner and outer space, swinging along the mysteries of time.

Counselors and teachers, as well as parents and all other adults, were asked to take bio-feedback training to develop their ability to control their brain waves. Bio-feedback (initiated in the 1970's) enabled people to regulate their own pulses, their blood pressure, and their anxieties. With personal control of their damaging emotions, teachers and counselors were less defensive with students and more open to the needs of their pupils. The pupils, also given bio-feedback training, were less afraid of one another and more ready to cooperate in projects.

Everywhere, emphasis was placed upon an awareness of life as a flowing process--a stream of

Scenarios: Facts or Fancies About the Future?

energy, taking many forms and then being transformed into streams flowing through many dimensions. New areas of the brain, areas not used in previous generations, were stimulated through the bio-feedback systems, and new visions of the past and future emerged.

Precognition, extrasensory perception, and glimpses of other beings in other worlds coexisting on several planes were reported fully by especially gifted persons. Studies carried on in many countries showed that man was far more than a collection of atoms and molecules: Man was shaped by energy fields within himself and outside himself.

Construction of permanent buildings had halted in the 1990's. Temporary structures--light in weight, easy to move, plastic as soft clay--were shifted from place to place to meet particular demands. Many courses of instruction were transmitted by picturephones and cable television. The number of channels for communications became almost limitless.

With the establishment of the guaranteed annual income and the increasing automation of production in all fields, the number of ordinary "jobs" shrank rapidly. Education was no longer linked to vocational training. Since most of the technical decisions in factories and on mechanized farms were made by sophisticated computers, the role of the human workers became more and more a matter of attendance at classes in the arts and crafts carried on for their own sake, and participation in encounter groups with other persons to overcome the frictions between the old and the

Part III

young, to understand the impact of incessant changes on the "family" and the ideas of "masculine" functions and "feminine" functions in a society where many distinctions were disappearing.

The rates of alcoholism and drug addiction were very low in 1996. Since careers in medicine, law, painting, sculpture, music, poetry, all the arts and crafts, were open to everybody, the number of people seeking escape from "reality" through intoxication became very small.

Crime rates also declined steeply. With a basic income available to each person, with an enormous scope of opportunities for travel around the earth and to other worlds through mental development, the incentives for crime were largely cut down.

With the virtual elimination of most of the fears and frustrations which drove men to violence, few human beings attacked one another or killed one another. Jealousies and rivalries, sex quarrels and rages, were brought under control through bio-feedback training.

The revival of faith in the immense potentialities of the human mind, combined with a resurgence of religion on a universal scale, relieved the spiritual depression which had plagued mankind in the era of wars. Men who could not compete effectively in the hard-driving culture of the old era could find satisfaction in the age of acceptance. Women who had believed themselves to be inferior in many ways were free to release a dazzling display of talents.

Scenarios: Facts or Fancies About the Future?

Those who had talents as administrators had to accept short terms in power and restrictions on authority. Everyone in learning centers and colleges participated in the decisions that were made. Continuing dialogs went on between students and teachers, administrators and students, teachers and administrators. No one could lay down a set of rules without being challenged.

Since credentials and special certificates--except for doctors of medicine and others in certain technical fields--were no longer regarded as necessary for teachers or administrators, the tests of practical experience were applied. Those who demonstrated wisdom in dialogs were elected by consensus to the posts of deans and presidents. Guarantees of tenure and formal contracts did not exist.

Students, teachers and administrators moved freely from college to college--seeking models best suited to their needs at different cycles of learning and different stages of life.

The whole range of talents available from women as well as men, kept up to date in computer banks, made it possible for administrators in industry, agriculture, government and the professions to find the skills needed at particular times to keep the flow of products and services running smoothly. In emergencies, people with certain knowledge and experience could be required to serve in particular places. Generally, however, a call for volunteers produced more people than were actually necessary for these crucial positions.

Part III

Late in 1996, human beings achieved the greatest breakthrough for education since the development of articulation through language. Electronic gloves--predicted by John Rader Platt and other scientists in the late 1970's--came into common use. People who wore those gloves and clasped hands could exchange ideas and feelings through 19 different channels.

The electronic gloves, along with bio-feedback control of brain waves, were used for important meetings when people with sharply different viewpoints could not agree on methods or steps to be taken. Representatives of each viewpoint were required to wear the gloves and to sit with hands clasped until everyone had a fairly thorough understanding of every position. This did not mean that minorities had to surrender themselves to majorities. It meant that each member of a group knew that all decisions were tentative and subject to revision with more understanding, but certain decisions had to be followed for the time being.

The adoption of laws requiring the use of the gloves stirred as much debate in the United States and other countries as the earlier laws specifying bio-feedback training for all persons. But these laws were gradually accepted. Freedom of conversation without wearing the gloves was guaranteed in the Declaration of Rights which accompanied the adoption of a World Constitution. In lawsuits, however, plaintiffs and defendants as well as the prosecutors and attorneys were required to use the gloves if one side or the other demanded such a procedure.

Disputes between teachers and administrators,

Scenarios: Facts or Fancies About the Future?

students and teachers, students and administrators, were usually settled quickly when the gloves were worn. Trials in courts became searches for truth rather than arenas for legal combat. The World Constitution was amended at annual meetings of representative of the earth's nations, who put on the gloves to deal with thorny questions involving allocation of the planet's resources and the control of pollution through a world monitoring system. The gloves made it possible for the International Court of Justice to issue rulings that were obeyed.

Thought helmets were being tested in 1996. Specially trained persons, wearing these helmets, were able to travel backward, and forward through time and multidimensional space, visiting other galaxies and communicating with minds far more intelligent than those of human beings as well as with minds of creatures on lower levels of evolution. Often these explorers had to be guarded by companions, who communicated with them through the electronic gloves and aided them in returning through invisible fields of energy to their own brains.

Awareness of millions of possible realities staggered students. Worlds within worlds, worlds beyond the imagined worlds of science fiction were opened with brilliance that blinded the inner eyes of many. The Bible's statement that man was made in the image of God was revealed as a scientific truth with smashing power.

Man began to decipher more and more messages from the distant stars, the songs that whales could sing, the voices of the dolphins, the cries of creatures on 10,000 planets. And yet man still did not know fully what he was or what he

Part III

should become.

The bright roses of wisdom bloomed in garden upon garden, but the thorns grew huge and threatening, too.

In the thorns man found a question: Where may you go when you can go anywhere?

With the opening of endless journeys through many worlds, the minds of many began to spin. The necessity of living with the unforeseen on many planes, in many dimensions, brought back eruptions of anxiety that could not be managed by the bio-feedback training systems.

There were sudden, senseless attacks on the computer headquarters, on the colleges and the learning centers. Among the very young and the very old--especially among those who approached the end of 150 year lifespans--there were aberrations, hallucinations, spasms of fury. When the electronic gloves were forced upon such persons, the doctors and nurses who held them received only chattering vibrations and chaotic signals through the open channels.

Philosophers tore the thought helmets from their heads, shouting: "Let us alone!" The presence of a cloud of witnesses, made over-whelmingly evident was too much for them. They preferred to speculate about the unknowable, rather than to plunge through the experience of world after world.

The arrival of "the learning society"--predicted so accurately by Robert Maynard Hutchins and other

Scenarios: Facts or Fancies About the Future?

leading educators of the Twentieth Century--was greeted with joy by many persons, but a sense of foreboding pervaded others. Some people turned to silly hobbies or frivolous pursuits and forthrightly refused to participate in the democratic dialogs through which decisions were determined.

Rejecting the synthetic food and synthetic garments which were produced in limitless quantities by machines, people returned to the land and began to use plows and gather wool from sheep. Tables and chairs made by human hands were regarded as far more precious than the glowing, changing, softly molded furniture shaped by molecular beams.

The more men soared through spaces and times, the more some people sank into apathy and perplexity. Their genetic defects were removed, their minds were flooded with encouraging thoughts, but they turned toward the depths of darkness, seeking escape and oblivion there.

Many people could not bear the knowledge that there was not a single reality, one universe to which they belonged, but many universes existing simultaneously spiraling up and spiraling down. The spells of sorcerers, the charms of medicine men, the warped ways of witches, the levitations of yogis, were revealed as aspects of many-sided universes, principalities and powers.

There were too many fountains playing, too many geysers spouting from holes in space, too many streams running under too many cascades of music. In the midst of a thousand orchestras playing at once, in the thunder and blaze of continuing fireworks, some fell apart--some people begged to

Part III

be taken to quiet hospital rooms, under restraints.

But the enormous journey of mankind went on--because the being called man could not exhaust the mystery of his own nature. Mankind could never stop, because there were worlds beyond worlds, horizons beyond horizons--and glimpses of God, calling from the future.

Even those who traveled back and forth through time, who claimed to have been on the other side of the mountain ahead and to have descended the slope behind, could do no more than give hints and intimations. The risks of life, the compulsion of choice, the need for courage, could never be removed.

So the great issues of education in 1996 could be summed up in the great issues that troubled people in the year 96 and would confront people in 2096 and all the centuries to come:

"What should a man or a woman know to be wise?

"What kind of wisdom could bring happiness--or keep open the pursuit of happiness?

"What kind of faith could bring, courage to step into the unknown--to keep men and women leaping, generation after generation, into the swirling darkness of uncertainty, into the clouds of change?"

Not to move was to make a choice. To move was to change the future. In 1996, man was moving faster and faster. He had chosen to be aware of

Scenarios: Facts or Fancies About the Future?

heights and depths--and he was becoming aware
of more and more.

Whether he is writing science fiction, working on
Capitol Hill, lecturing at colleges or serving as
a war correspondent, Frank K. Kelly combines
a practical understanding of what exists with a
vivid imagination for what could be. His present
position is vice-president of the Center for the
Study of Democratic Institutions.

Looking Back from 1999 —
The Noise and the Quiet of the Sixties

Louis Shores

THE INTELLECTUAL RENAISSANCE STARTED IN LIBRARIES WITH EARLY ASSISTANCE FROM THE QUIET PLURALITY.

It was a decade of noise, and of quiet, too. People marched and demonstrated, picketed and possessed facilities, and engaged in other forms of physical communication. But there were other people, too (although you couldn't prove it by our videotapes of network news), who studied in libraries quietly, communicated intellectually, and dared to experiment and innovate positively with prototypes for the good society.

There was no "silent majority" as one president of the United States had once claimed. The United States, as always, was composed of minorities. The difference in the sixties was the addition to the previous groupings by color, by faith, by national origin, by affluence, et al., of some new identifications on the basis of issues.

There was an attempt to divide the population by chronology. Mostly this was pushed by the mass media as good show business. Demagogues among the politicians sought to capitalize on alliances with the so-called "young people." It is amusing to

Reprinted with the copyright permission of <u>American Libraries</u>, April, 1972 and the author.

Scenarios: Facts or Fancies About the Future?

observe how many older people seemed to compensate for their own disappointments and frustrations by virtuously, vindictively, and self-righteously declaring, especially on TV, "We must listen to the young people." So many of these older folks appeared to be faculty members who had not received the recognition they wanted; columnists and commentators hoping for a wider audience; divorcees trying to be gay.

Investigation fails to disclose an adequate chronological definition of young people. The Republican Party, for example, divided at forty at one time; the women's clubs at thirty-five. Most polls favored thirty as the magical age. Yet when CBS staged its notorious "Generations Apart"[1] series, the statisticians found it necessary to lower the dividing line to twenty-six, to provide any kind of "gap." Even then, those below that age and those above revealed some startling agreements on major issues and on minor issues, such as topless dresses.

The real divisions of the sixties appear to have been on issues. For media "show business," a confrontation was promoted between the so-called "Establishment" and the "Protest." Ignored were any third positions. But even general investigation of that raucous decade will reveal the Quiet Plurality, the small group that has always been responsible for positive and lasting reform. To members of that quiet plurality, both establishments were equally repulsive. (And by 1970, the Protest had an establishment that ranged from male sideburns to party lines on contemporary culture.)

The divisions began on the top cause for town and

Part III

and gown disorders: Vietnam. If you were a hawk you presumably favored pushing the war to a military victory in the American history tradition. But if you were a dove you wanted the U.S. to get out of Vietnam, immediately. The Hawk Establishment was most often pictured by the opposition as imperialist, chauvinist, militarist munitions makers. Seldom were any of them credited with really believing that history might repeat, that a Chamberlain peace-at-any-cost in Vietnam might only postpone a Hitler-like confrontation, eventually, at Key West, Florida.

The doves insisted, rightly, that if war was ever a way to settle differences, it had certainly become outmoded in 1960. No one, not even the most militant hawks, really believed in the killing of human life. Where the Quiet Plurality departed from both was in its opposition to not just half a war, but to the whole war. Whereas the hawks opposed only Hanoi's Peking-Moscow backed attempt to impose the Viet Cong on Saigon, and the doves opposed only Saigon's Washington-backed effort to maintain a separate South Vietnam; the Quiet Plurality opposed both halves of the war, equally.

But the Quiet Plurality was too positive to confine itself to a negative opposition only. Tucked away in an inside-page Associated Press dispatch was a proposal by one member of the QP for a Vietnam solution. It suggested that if the marchers really wanted to accomplish something for mankind, the time had come not only to march in Washington, but to appeal in Hanoi, people to people, and in Peking and Moscow also:

Scenarios: Facts or Fancies About the Future?

Look here. We in the U.S. admit we have had some wrong on our side as well as some right. But we have stopped bombing Hanoi; when will you stop shelling Saigon? We did invade Cambodia. We asked our government why, quite demonstratively. When will you ask your Hanoi government why they violated Cambodia's frontier earlier? Your government is accused of violating the Geneva Conference on prisoners of war. When will your government release them, in view of Washington's proposal to return at least three times as many prisoners held by them, unilaterally, if necessary? Disparage as "imperialistic" if you will, but is it not worth saving the shedding of additional blood to accept the president's invitation to stop all military action at once, on both sides?

More positively, a Quiet Plurality in the United States proposes, daringly, to counterpart Quiet Pluralities in both North and South Vietnam, and in Peking as well as Moscow, that a new kind of competing societies, a competition that will involve no bloodshed but help all of mankind to discover the elements of the good society. Today, the whole world is divided by an "iron curtain" between the Communist and non-Communist nations. Since World War II we have all suffered from a cold war that has warmed up to bloodshed in Korea, in Vietnam, and in countless other places.

We invite the people of North Vietnam and South Vietnam to model for the rest of the world the two major social philosophies--Marxian Communism and Jeffersonian Democracy. Even Marxists have compared the Jefferson Declaration of Independence to the Marx-Engels Communist Manifesto as a

Part III

revolutionary guide to social reform. Why not compare their implementations in social prototypes? Let Washington contribute a portion of the money that has gone into South Vietnam military action; let Peking-Moscow likewise devote a fraction of the resources that have enabled the North Vietnamese and Viet Cong armies to wage war, to rebuilding and restoring both Vietnams, to demonstrate the best in the two ways of life. Let both sides and all of the world observe in free exchange the comparative advantages and disadvantages of Marxian and Jeffersonian applications, with a view to selecting the best from both theories of society for the individual nations' requirements. Would not this type of friendly competition do more for human progress than the senseless war both sides have been equally guilty of conducting?

Nearly as frequently as Vietnam, "racism" was responsible for the noisy violence of the sixties. Perhaps it was inevitable that such a melting pot as America should boil, many times, over prejudices. From time immemorial antisemitism has persecuted the Jews. When immigration from East European countries threatened to out-populate the predominantly Anglo-American country, prejudices mounted against the "wops" from slavic countries, from Italy, and from other non-English speaking nations. A "Roman plot" was created to protect Protestant America from the Catholics. Originally, the white man had robbed the red man of his land, and later relegated the yellow-skinned Chinese and Japanese immigrants to second-class citizenship. But none of these prejudices quite equalled the injustices to the black-skinned people who were forcibly emigrated to the United States from Africa by

Scenarios: Facts or Fancies About the Future?

greedy white men.

Alan Paton had put the case frighteningly in his great novel, Cry the Beloved Country: What if when the white man at last is overcome with remorse for the unspeakable injustices he has inflicted on the black man, and asks to be forgiven, the black man is no longer able to forgive? This appeared to be the situation in the United States toward the end of the 1960's. Militancy appears to have dominated black leadership by the end of the decade. The march and the demonstration seem to have appealed most to black mass media. Just as the Ku Klux Klan had led white segregationists, the Black Panthers appeared as a violent counterpart.

It was not until much later that the great sociologist of race relations--Charles Spurgeon Johnson--was rediscovered. Most disconcerting to the militants, at first, was the fact that Dr. Johnson had been a black. But all of the documentation clearly establishes he was one of the first of the great thinkers to write, speak, and work for only one race--the human race. A quiet, scholarly man who later became president of Fisk University, Dr. Johnson labored tirelessly in biracial meetings to reconcile, to bury the past, to construct a future in which "a man is a man for all that." It was the Quiet Plurality that rediscovered Charles Spurgeon Johnson and the one human race.

And then there was poverty, the chief cause for town marches, none of them particularly "nonviolent," as the protesters liked to claim on television. There had been some especially bloody communications like Watts in Los Angeles. There

Part III

was no question about the incongruity of slums in a nation of incomparable plenty. But in retrospect, the lack of comparative among the protesters is most difficult to show any more conscientious attempt to repudiate the ancient cliche "the poor are always with us" than was made in the United States under the leadership of presidents of the sixties, Democrats and Republicans.

A member of the Quiet Plurality had once proposed that instead of negative protest, positive "protowns" be undertaken that would model some urban communities of the future. Each of the fifty states still had some free land. It was proposed to develop some new cities on this land that would be self-supporting, and that would relieve, at once, the slum conditions in the antiquated metropolitan centers of the United States. It was proposed, also, that as nearly as possible the American Melting Pot be represented in these new cities in the approximate proportions then existing in the United States. In this way, the cities could also model relationships among minorities-- in race, faith, national origin, affluence, and all of the other artificialities by which American society divided humans in the Staccato Sixties.

Gown's counterpart to town's violence was billed by the national networks as "campus unrest." Despite claims of nonviolence and democratic action the videotapes record opposites. Campus buildings were occupied by force, libraries were burned at Purdue and Indiana universities, faculty and students who wanted to study were prevented from it. The loud minority insisted they were not being listened to; yet they were given the majority of space by newsprint, and the most time by news-

Scenarios: Facts or Fancies About the Future?

cast. When dissent with dissent undertook to state its case on campus it was usually interrupted by the noisy minority's disorder, or ignored by their walk-out, as an evidence of neodemocratic action.

All through the sixties, while the noisy minority was negatively protesting, self-righteously identifying problems, excoriating scapegoats, the Quiet Plurality was positively experimenting and innovating with prototypes for the higher education to come. In the Library-College Journal department Innova, descriptions of college reform ideas on over five hundred campuses, developed by the generations together--students and faculty jointly sketching some new dimensions in post-secondary school learning--were reported. Among these innovations was the library-college movement. The idea for a "college that is a library and a library that is a college" originated in Thomas Carlyls's Tuesday, May 19, 1840 lecture, "The Hero as Man of Letters." The library-college is the essence of our 1999 higher education, committed to student independent study under faculty bibliographic guidance. The mass media of the sixties, however, preferred to feature campus unrest rather than campus innovation.

Since the mass media are a considerable part of any study of the Staccato Sixties, it is necessary to indicate something of the communication and culture climate of 1960's. Intellectual freedom was fiercely advocated by those who claimed to be "liberal." But in retrospect, we know that the pendulum had swung so far in the direction of license that intellectual responsibility was much more to the point in the decade of the sixties. Indeed, one

Part III

member of the Quiet Plurality who had also been a member of the ALA Intellectual Freedom Committee for six years wrote "Dissent With Dissent" for a 1969 issue of the Intellectual Freedom Newsletter,[2] challenging the committee to accent responsibility more.

By the end of the 1960's almost all of the mass media were committed to exterminating the Puritan ethic. Not one of the noisy minority that extolled its own liberalism ever philosophically inquired into what had impelled mankind, or at least some of it, toward the Puritan ethic. Why had some liberal thinkers rejected the "new sex" that appeared to advocate "anything the animals can do on the street humans should be free to do on the Broadway stage." The Harvard math instructor turned comedian--Tom Lehrer--had indeed parodied the "sex freedom" position with his song Smut: "Of course, we liberals have to defend it on the basis of Intellectual Freedom. But you and I know what is really involved: Dirty Books Are Fun."[3]

Inevitably, the near-monopoly the noisy minority had gained over the mass media led to the library quiet reaction that followed. Above all, the powerful television networks of the sixties were committed to show business. Whatever else television insisted influenced their selection of news significance and entertainment, it is quite obvious that showmanship was dominant. There is no other way to account for the mass media commitment to loudness, to violence, to physical action, to change for change's sake. It is reflected in television's preference for loud, staccato music, exemplified by a phenomenon called the Beatles. Although their

Scenarios: Facts or Fancies About the Future?

music is now almost unknown, the beautiful and haunting works of their contemporary Anita Kerr still live today. Her masterpieces on The Sea have almost obscured the earlier Debussy La Mer. There was other soft, legato and lyrical music composed in the sixties, despite television's celebration of the foundry-like cacaphonies of what they called "rock." Indeed, the first reactions to the stentorian histrionics of the sixties came as early as 1971 when two of the leading exponents of popular music were quoted in an Associated Press feature on April 8.[4] Said Mary Travers of the Peter, Paul and Mary folk trio: "The marches didn't change anything... Out of that came an anti-intellectualism... no reason to reason. Let it be... Rock is supposed to go straight to the guts. Very anti-intellectual."

And Alice Cooper (a name taken by the young man leader of a hard rock group from Phoenix, Arizona, in that unisex decade of the sixties) was quoted: "The purpose of rock music is sex. It doesn't exactly hit you in the brain. The drum, that four-four beat is a sex feeling... We play hard which is very loud."

The combination of showbiz television and hard rock music produced such a din that after a while no one could hear anyone else. At first, librarians, especially some of them committed to more "public relations," attempted to compete with all of the noise by outshouting. But librarians were at a disadvantage in that kind of competition. Used to whispering on tiptoes, librarianship's feeble simulations of the swingers were ludicrously ineffective. Then some librarians began to rediscover the power of the library's traditional quiet. In all of the Parkin-

217

Part III

son disease-like bobbing of male coiffures and twitching of female anatomies, amidst all of the stentorian beats that had pulverized eardrums to early hearing aids (as warned by the medics), library quiet suddenly attracted a protest-weary population. The discotheques steadily gave way to the bibliotheques. Marshall McLuhan,[5] who had his television hour celebrating the decline of reading after the Frenchman Duhamel[6] had made this doomsday prediction a decade earlier, was all but forgotten as Americans returned to intellectualism with the generic book--not only in print, but all of the other formats, from graphics through projections and transmissions to computerized instructional aid.

The intellectual renaissance started in libraries with early assistance from the Quiet Plurality. Librarianship broke with the stereotyped futures of some librarians with the former ancillary complex which made a virtue out of belittling the profession. The symbols of the librarian ancillarians were a virtuous declaration, "There is no library literature, no library education, no library philosophy, no library discipline. We must support the classroom; we must service the substantive disciplines; we must accept the standards of the literary critics of the day," without a suggestion of reciprocity.

The Quiet Plurality among librarians soon changed this. Electrifyingly, in the middle 1970's, 30,000 American public libraries and their branches offered the people a more intellectual and effective medium of communications than the street demonstrations. Modeled on the old New England town meeting, the

Scenarios: Facts or Fancies About the Future?

public library meetings forced problem identifiers to become solution identifiers, through library documentation. Solutions approved by library meetings were advanced along constitutional channels of referendum, initiative, and recall, to orderly reforms of society.

Taking a cue from the public library, academic libraries, adopted the library-college proposal for a weekly SOTUDAY (state of the university day) when all academic work was suspended to consider campus problems and solutions. Out of these orderly deliberations, which soon put the disorderly out of business, emerged the independent study dimensions that comprise the dominant learning mode in 1999. As a result, the faculty who persisted in teaching without books in the classroom, exclusively were forced to fight for their faculty status. "College for all," formerly opposed by Ivy elitism, was proved not only feasible, but necessary if violent revolution was to be prevented. Parallel library reforms were accomplished by the other two library types in their respective communities. Schools became libraries when the high art of teaching evolved as the sensitive matching of individual differences in children with individual differences in library media. The special librarian modulated traditional reference into a more creative concept of information science, by replacing Fido-like retrieval of isolated facts with a gestalt for value interpretation, for selecting significance in the precedent of the encyclopedists as far back as Pliny and contemporaneously by the editors of the major English language encyclopedias.

The 1999 historian looking back upon the Staccato

Part III

Sixties might summarize with a paraphrase of Charles Dickens' opening for the Tale of Two Cities: That decade was the noisiest of times; but it was also a time of quiet. That the latter prevailed was in no small way due to library leadership. Without library quiet, mankind certainly would have been pushed over that brink the doomsday men of the sixties predicted.

Louis Shores is Dean Emeritus of the Library School, Florida State University and "Father" of the Library-College movement.

Notes and References

1. Columbia Broadcasting System telecast a series of three one-hour shows on "campus unrest." When members of the Quiet Plurality asked for equal time on campus experimentation and innovation by the generations together, CBS responded "not interested" at this time.
2. "Dissent with Dissent," ALA Intellectual Freedom Newsletter, July 1969.
3. Tom Lehrer, "Smut," That Was The Year That Was (Reprise, 1967, disc, side one, band four).
4. Associated Press feature article April 8, 1971, on Rock Music.
5. Marshall McLuhan, Understanding Media; The Gutenberg Galaxy, et. al.
6. George Duhamel, In Defense of Letters.

View from the Year 2001

Nell Eurich

.... THE MOST RADICAL DIFFERENCE BETWEEN TODAY'S COLLEGES AND THOSE 50 YEARS AGO IS IN THE USE OF LEARNING RESOURCES, AND THE RECOGNITION THAT INDIVIDUALS LEARN IN MANY DIFFERENT WAYS AND PLACES.

Great social and scientific developments have had a major impact on our colleges and universities -- indeed on the very definition of education itself. The most dramatic and drastic changes that led to our modern era really started in the late 1960's. Before that time the schools and education had been favorites of the American public; people believed strongly in their power to uplift the individual and the nation; there was plenty of money, new buildings, more teachers, and constantly more students.

Then--along with many other factors --came the financial crunch. And suddenly, in 1972, for the first time in nearly three decades, enrollment figures in the nation's schools from elementary through college showed an increase of only one-half of one per cent. What was more important was that elementary schools had a decline of 500,000 pupils. What had been the baby-boom after the second World War had ended; those students had finished college studies.

Reprinted with the permission of the author and <u>The Chronicle of Higher Education</u>, October 30, 1972.

Part III

By 1982 there was an absolute decline in college enrollment and "zero-hiring" of faculty--even as a man named Clark Kerr, chairman of the Carnegie Commission, had warned earlier. It was a tough period for Ph. D.'s, and many went to work in government and industry. Others adjusted to the new patterns in education which were emerging and with which we now live happily.

There were other cataclysmic changes that occurred in the last part of the century. The large public institutions continued their growth because of society's commitment to offer education for all. Now only about 10 percent of all college students are in private institutions. The result duplicated what happened earlier in the century when we shifted from private academies to public high schools. Just as those academies that survived became stronger, so too the colleges that survived greatly increased in strength.

Similarly, private two-year colleges have all but disappeared; their functions have been taken over by community colleges. Approximately one-half of our four-year private liberal arts colleges were closed or adapted to other purposes. Teachers' colleges are gone from the American scene and their place filled by multi-purpose institutions. Also, by eliminating duplication with high school work, all higher institutions have condensed their baccalaureate programs from four to three years.

Along with the reduction in the number of private institutions, we have seen a growing federal control of colleges and universities since the Higher Education Act passed in 1972. In addition, several

Scenarios: Facts or Fancies About the Future?

universities have become federal institutions, of which for many years Howard University was the only example. New York University forced the issue. When it became evident that this institution was about to declare financial bankruptcy and that the State of New York could not provide sufficient funds to keep it going, the federal government stepped in. It rescued NYU just as it had previously rescued Penn Central and Lockheed. Society could not afford to lose this educational facility.

Federal financing and control of New York University led to demands from other regional institutions for support from the federal government. George Washington University, University of Miami, Southern Methodist University, the University of Southern California, the University of Denver, and Washington University in St. Louis are now all federal institutions.

In addition, of course, all public and the remaining private institutions receive federal funds for operations and maintenance. Earlier, such institutions as the Massachusetts Institute of Technology, California Institute of Technology, the University of Chicago and Stanford, among others, had received more than 50 percent of their budgets from federal money, but essentially these funds were restricted to research rather than general support.

To us, many changes are more important than these which involved structure and financing. Today, we find it amusing and slightly droll that people thought there was a period in life for education-- that one was educated in blocks of time divisable by four: eight years for elementary, four years for

Part III

high school, and four for college. Apparently they thought that was it, and education was completed-- until adults started walking in and requesting further opportunity. It was an intrusion on the previous practices of some colleges, but those that welcomed it not only survived, but did a better job. They knew there was no biological function of age that prevented learning either for its own sake or for an exterior purpose. Certainly younger people are known to learn more quickly, but retention-- except for skills and facts used--is abysmally poor, and too frequently the younger people are not motivated to learn.

Our society today could not conceive the restrictions formerly placed on the educative process. Young people do not automatically go on to college. Congress enacted a program financed from public and private funds that provided for work experience for all youth. They gain life experience in a variety of ways; they serve as aides to teachers, doctors, nurses, lawyers, engineers, architects, public officials, and professionals of many types. It was like a rebirth of the apprenticeship in the Medieval Ages.

Also, and only after difficult negotiations with the labor unions, young people were apprenticed to carpenters, plumbers, electricians, steel workers, and other skilled craftsmen. Before this legislative act was passed, work experience was on a piecemeal basis and students had to "drop-out" in order to try other things. The program has given youths a chance to experiment with their interests and talents before settling on their educational course. They no longer wait until graduation from a college to experiment with their abilities.

Scenarios: Facts or Fancies About the Future?

Both the students and the nation have gained from this program. Many youths find the work experience satisfying, and remain with it. They no longer feel the same pressure to go on to college immediately, and they know they can study at any time in their lives. Industry and business corporations provide many opportunities, some of our best learning materials, and the technical means for their use. Career education--in which business cooperates with colleges and universities as well as communities--is the answer for many.

This has helped define the objectives for the liberal arts college. No one now expects that study in liberal arts will increase personal income or get you a better job. Instead, those studying in these fields realize that the purpose is thoughtful self-development, aesthetic pleasure, sensitivity toward others and man's goals, a greater understanding of institutions in society and how they work, and objective judgment developed to cope with crucial issues.

Probably the most radical difference between today's colleges and those 50 years ago is in the use of learning resources, and the recognition that individuals learn in many different ways and places. For a long time, people believed that what was learned in non-formal, out-of-classroom situations had no educational merit and consequently deserved no academic credit. They finally woke up to the fact that the greatest part of what a person learned throughout his lifetime, he learned outside the classroom or college. As George Bernard Shaw once quipped, "The only time my education was interrupted was when I went to school."

Part III

With this, people finally figured out that there was no one-to-one relationship between teaching and learning; that what was taught by one person was not necessarily learned by another. So, at long last, we discovered that teachers can motivate, inspire, guide and assist over difficulties, and present opinions on materials; but they cannot produce learning in the student.

It was wise of them to use all media at their command. For a long time before they started to use it, teachers saw the power of television and realized that it had become a major educational influence for that generation of youth. It occupied more of the student's time generally than schools did.

By 1972 some 30,000 courses were being given over TV in the United States, but several decades elapsed before colleges recognized its value in carrying the standard lecture course and the conventional laboratory demonstration.

We have also made enormous strides in teaching the individual student. Here the most exciting developments have been in independent study, honors work, language laboratories, work-study opportunities, foreign travel, video cassettes, programmed learning, and, more recently, the widespread use of computers.

These resources enabled us to break the ancient framework that for so long had held a college education to a rigid pattern. No longer do we have to divide the day into fixed 50-minute periods or the year into semesters or terms. No longer do we

Scenarios: Facts or Fancies About the Future?

measure the student's progress by the number of credit hours he has banked. No longer do we march all students through the same series of lectures and classes. We have finally applied to all fields of learning what a football coach has always known. He cares not how old the student is or how long he has gone to school. All he cares about is how he plays the game, how well he can handle the ball--perform--and what his potential is for further learning.

Today, flexibility, freedom to learn, and adjustment to individual differences are axiomatic. Each student progresses at his own rate. Much of the time he studies on his own or with fellow students who teach each other. Always he has instant access to a complete range of learning resources--taped lectures, programmed course materials with the computer, audio tapes, bibliography, and original documents on microfilm.

We also have libraries drastically different from those of the past. We revolutionalized the techniques of storing and transmitting information. Most of our documents are now reduced to pinpoint size and stored on film. We have established a national research library which, as President John Kemeny of Dartmouth predicted some years ago, has grown to more than 300 million volumes in miniaturized form. Through a multi-channel cable we can instantly transmit information from these volumes to reading units on campuses throughout the country. In addition, the Defense Department in the 70's set up a computer linking 30 campuses on which extensive investigations were being carried forward. This has now been extended to several hundred cam-

Part III

puses throughout the country.

One innovation, which developed later in the last century and which so profoundly affected all of higher education, stands out above all others. It does so because it united various trends--the emphasis on the student as an individual, the effort to provide self-motivating learning situations, the use of the entire community as an education resource, and the capability of modern means of communication to extend educational opportunities without a commensurate rise in costs.

It goes by various names--external degree programs, off-campus learning, university without walls, campus-free college. It has appeared in both the public and private sectors. It permits a student to pursue a program of study under the guidance of a faculty member, but not essentially in the classroom. It brings together experience, independent reading, observation and investigation, correspondence study, television, radio and cassette instruction, attendance in group discussion at various kinds of institutions, and special projects. In some cases, a student need never appear on the campus--indeed in some programs there are no campuses.

Under this program a student demonstrates his proficiency by a combination of examinations both oral and written, interviews, and personal evaluations. There are no rigid residence or time requirements. He can proceed at his own pace, according to his own schedule. Upon the successful completion of the examinations, he is awarded a college degree.

Scenarios: Facts or Fancies About the Future?

The "open university" idea also helped to internationalize higher education. The system of satellites offering instruction on a worldwide basis made possible an International Independent Study University which awards degrees wholly on examinations passed. Students can pursue this work anywhere and, when they feel qualified, can apply to take the necessary examinations that measure their achievement.

Partly because financial starvation of the colleges forced changes, and new alternative routes to education became available throughout man's life, the content of education changed dramatically. Major ideas are now central to all curricula--ideas that shape civilization, such as freedom and liberty vs. controls and responsibility, concepts of work, love for man and human dignity, aggression and competition as human traits.

Back in the 70's many people started to become dissatisfied with "cocktail" culture. Through such organizations as free universities and open colleges, and the various groups concerned with civil rights and the Vietnam War, a movement to redesign the content of higher education gathered strength. Graduate students rebelled against the narrow, sterile, and exhausting competition for degrees that meant little. A combination of these forces caused a revival of humanistic thought so that even our great technical institutions, led by M. I. T., sought a better balance in the curriculum through a renewed emphasis on the humanities.

University scholars began to take seriously Ortega y Gasset's insight set down years ago in his

Part III

<u>Mission of the University</u>: "The need to create sound syntheses and systematization of knowledge to be taught in the faculty of culture will call out a kind of scientific genius which hitherto has existed only as an aberration, the genius of integration." Major issues began to dominate learning, and many scholars came together to create answers and a better society.

Today our employment of knowledge, as of leisure, is much more satisfying than it was in the early days of the affluent society when men were consumed to the point of boredom with strictly materialistic pleasures. Many people reacted against rampant materialism on philosophical grounds. Many more were frightened by its ecological implications. Technology had gone too fast and too far; the demand was for human and humane values, for more consideration of people and less emphasis on knowledge as a product.

In essence we experienced a kind of spiritual renascence.

Now we stand at the dawn of another century. During the past 30 years colleges and universities, like society itself, have moved farther and faster than in our entire previous history. But as Oliver Wendell Holmes once said, "The great thing in the world is not so much where we stand as in what direction we are moving."

Nell Eurich is provost and dean of the faculty

Scenarios: Facts or Fancies About the Future?

of Manhattanville College. The game of prediction and foresight is one she has played through the years with her husband, Alvin C. Eurich. "It is hard to separate our thoughts," Mrs. Eurich says, " so I shall put down one large footnote to cover the entire paper."

2002: An Education Odyssey

M. Chester Nolte

LEARNING IS MORE EFFICIENT AND BETTER CONCEIVED, BUT CHURCH AND STATE ARE 'FUSED' AND THE STATE HAS GREATER AUTHORITY TO CONTROL DISSENT.

The scene is the Central Data Bankhouse of the Anytown Education Corporation, Unlimited, a privately-owned educational combine representing the merger of several hardware and software firms over the years. Time is 9:30 a. m. in early spring of the year 2002.

As the curtain rises, a long oblong table is seen at center stage around which sit the seven members of the 1972 Board of Education of the Anytown Public School District. Their presence is possible through an early experiment in cryogenics in which the seven board members volunteered to act as guinea pigs. As action begins, they are being "de-arrested," which translated into 1972 terms, means that their normal metabolisms are being restored after three decades in limbo. They are about to be brought up to date on educational events that have transpired during their 30 years in the deep-freeze.

A doctor with a stethoscope bends over each board member in turn, listens intently, checks the ther-

Reprinted with the copyright permission of The American School Board Journal, March, 1972.

Scenarios: Facts or Fancies About the Future?

mometer, then moves on to the next. Finally, he seems satisfied, and straightening up, nods to a young man in his early thirties who is wearing a white lab coat and stands near a podium at upper right. The board members cast sidelong glances at the shiny hardware and blinking lights visible through a glass partition separating the conference room at upper left. The Young Man whispers to the doctor, consults a small transistor-compulser on his wrist, then steps to the podium. He clears his throat, speaks:

YOUNG MAN: Good morning, ladies and gentlemen. Welcome to the 21st century. Our purpose is to bring you up to date on events of educational significance, then hear your questions as a means of checking our progress and philosophy against the motivational forces you used in your roles as board members in FY 1972. For your comfort, we have provided you with much the same physical boardroom furniture with which you were familiar in Anytown back in 1972, except for one feature which I will hasten to explain, since you won't be acquainted with it--your chair. You will notice on the arm of your chair several buttons, each in a different color. These buttons are for your use in changing position; some are for raising or lowering the chair, while others have other purposes. You will be using the green button by means of which we will be able in a few minutes to acquaint you quite rapidly with some of the educational changes during the past 30 years. Would you please all press the green button now?

(The board members find to their surprise that the green button makes the chair into a bed, from which

Part III

each has full view of the ceiling, on which now appear several animated areas containing moving pictures, charts, drawings, illustrations and similar electronic impressions, a multi-media screen using multi-sensory stimuli.) The Young Man speaks:

YOUNG MAN: This overview of intervening events between 1972 and 2002 is programmed to take $17\frac{1}{2}$ minutes, 11 seconds, after which we'll open the meeting to questions. In this presentation, I have dialed the search words School Governance; School Financing; Psychobiochemeducation; Sociology of Learning; and the Physiology of Learning. This automatically calls up such items as curriculum, teaching methods, scheduling, school buildings, and other more mundane titles by which you managed the schools back in 1972. You will therefore be able to see wholistically the major movements influencing education since you were... ah, living. The impressions you will register during this overview period on the Multi-Sensory Screen Aloft (MSSA) come from our huge data bank in the next room, and will be synchronized by means of our minor computer which thinks like a human being--the Human Evaluation and Logic Planner (HELP) connected with the major computer center in the basement of the state capitol. Please hold your questions until this presentation is completed. Are you comfortable?

(The board members indicate that, in spite of some lingering bewilderment, they are enjoying their experiences.)

YOUNG MAN: We will begin with a Tour of the De-

Scenarios: Facts or Fancies About the Future?

cades. Here we see the educational influences of the Roaring Twenties, in which the twin roots of the educational system you knew began to flourish, while the Root of Authoritarianism began to wither and die. I refer, of course, to the two roots feeding your system, the Root of Democratic Principles and the Root of Scientific Methodology. Through the Dirty Thirties these roots had tough going, but in the Fighting Forties they revived and grew large and strong.

During the Quantitative Fifties your generation became committed to the proposition that all children should be educated to the optimum of their abilities, regardless of race, color, mental capability, or country of origin. That was a big order, one which you found most difficult to fulfill during the Qualitative Sixties because of limited resources and the militancy of teachers and students alike. After Sputnik, fear of Russian domination and a public reaction against permissiveness caused a return to the fundamentals, and the progressive movement came to an end. This reaction served to perpetuate many indefensible practices of the Educational Establishment of your time, and, as you may recall from 1972, raised the question of what should be preserved and what needed to change as you entered the Scattered Seventies.

Oh, I beg your pardon. I forgot that you were unfamiliar with the sobriquet by which the Seventies were characterized. This decade was called by that name because education of the young, as well as of older adults, became highly decentralized during the Scattered Seventies. This was in direct conflict with the idea current to your time which

Part III

was to the effect that all learning must take place in a building called a school. When schools became rife, but it was not until the large hardware-software combines like mine, the Anytown Education Corporation, Unlimited came into the picture that decentralization was possible. (The Unlimited in our title means we are engaged in all sorts of educational activities, from the cradle to the grave.)

Through performance contracts, systems analysis and the use of tighter budgeting and accounting practices plus help from the computer, the school boards of the Seventies came to grips with the question of how to get more bang for the educational buck. In general, this was possible through a clarification of the desired OUTPUT, in contrast with the proclivity in the Sixties to tinker only with the INPUTS of education--pupils, teachers, time, space, methods and content, to be exact. When it became crystal clear (to borrow a cliche from your day) that fiddling with the established machine on inputs alone did little to make education more effective, concerted efforts by your colleagues to improve education brought on in the Seventies a proliferation of corporations all with certain performance criteria to sell in the marketplace. School boards like yours had little choice but to buy, and the electronic revolution became a reality. Pupils began learning through in-crib television and continued through senior citizen clinics and seminars on longevity--everybody got into the act. To say that education was "scattered" is perhaps the understatement of the decade.

(As the Young Man talks, dozens of visual "stills" and moving pictures are projected on the huge

Scenarios: Facts or Fancies About the Future?

overhead screen either supplementing or replacing entirely his narrative. The board members take notes on a device that allows each boardman to punch buttons related to the questions that occur to him as the visualization progresses. The Young Man can get the drift of their questions from the console at the podium, and he adjusts his lecture to answer many of their questions. He does this by dialing a number here, punching a button there to permit the computer to disgorge its data to fill in "holidays" in the understanding of the board members and answer their questions all within the scope of a few seconds' time.) The Young Man continues:

YOUNG MAN: While the 1970's were years of re-assessment and decentralization in education, the Eighties became the decade of focus on the product-- on the OUTPUT --the end and object of education in our schools. As you may recall from your service on the board, one dilemma was that of assessing measurable outputs, of determining in a quantitative way the measurable effects of learning, in contrast with an earlier emphasis on the means of education, the INPUTS. Thus, in the early Eighties considerable energy all around the country was given to defining for all time the end product. What kind of persons would be needed in the 21st Century? What would be their factual base, their attitudinal slants, their functional knowledge, their life style? This was not easy to determine, since times were changing so rapidly.

It was finally decided, after much debate, that the entire focus of the curriculum should be upon mankind as an object of study. The curriculum is man--

Part III

his problems, his needs, his relationships. One of your own contemporaries expressed this concept when he said, "A man bleeds, starves, suffers, despairs not as an American or a Russian, or a Negro or a Chinese, but in his innermost being as a member of single human race." That was Adlai E. Stevenson, once Ambassador to the United Nations. Within his vision of man's problems, the most important function of education is to give man the processes by means of which he can effectively deal with his environment. Therefore, based on this approach, the Humanistic Eighties were featured by a complete restructuring of the subject matter in the schools in order that the major focus might be on man himself as an object of study.

VOICE FROM SOUND TRACK: As you were aware, many of the so-called disciplines and educational concerns of your time were undergoing drastic changes which continued on after 1972 and are still changing. Here is a summary of each change:

ECONOMICS: It finally occurred to educators and the Congress that the wealth of this country is not so much in its natural resources as in its people. Laws penalizing families of more than two children were enacted in the 1980's, and the voucher plan was adopted in full. That raised the options available to parents while at the same time laws limited family size in the interests of both population control and improved educational opportunities for those children in the educational pattern.

RELIGION: With the voucher system, and the Supreme Court ruling that enabled the use of public funds for

Scenarios: Facts or Fancies About the Future?

private schools, the fusing of church and state began. Since parochial schools really perform a secular (government and social) function anyway, accepting this change was accomplished in the late Seventies to the surprise of nobody.

FINANCE: The cost per pupil of education was reduced considerably by the introduction of home learning centers composed of computer terminals responding to the tutorial needs of each child, and with both closed circuit and broadcast television in each home. This so reduced the cost of formal schooling that some school buildings and other facilities were sold and the money used to contract for home instruction with private firms such as ours.

The federal government is now involved to the tune of 50 percent of all educational costs, with the state picking up about 25 percent and the local property tax accounting for the remainder. This arrangement allows for control at the local level while obtaining support from all three levels in the educational partnership.

PERSONNEL: The Seventies saw the consummation of the bargaining process as a means of reaching agreement with faculty and staff. Today, teacher aides outnumber faculty by a ratio of two to one, and are organized for bargaining purposes just like teachers.

SOCIOLOGY: Biggest influence on man in groups was the power struggle which accompanied the Revolution of Rising Expectations, with which you are already familiar. Programs for the poor, the crippled, and the disadvantaged (not the same as the

Part III

poor) were introduced in the 1980's and seem to have evened the opportunities and reduced poverty and inequality, particularly in helping the recipients find means of education or vocational training easily and near their own homes. The Seventies saw a reduction in the strife accompanying integration/segregation, and the ecology studies instituted in the late Sixties succeeded in heading off complete chaos in the environment. We believe that the resulting emphasis on man and his environment in our educational pattern will tend to perpetuate the notion that man must be careful of nature, and spend time, effort and money to preserve it for future generations yet unborn. That really is the desired outcome of our educational pattern in the end.

YOUNG MAN: Mr. President of the Board, do you have a question?

BOARD PRESIDENT: Yes. Through all this, you've indicated nothing about the control of public schools, such as a board, or commission, or the like. Do you still have school boards to control the "educational pattern" as you call it?

YOUNG MAN: Yes, but they're not exactly like yours were in 1972. School boards today retain an important degree of local control, are far move involved in what we call the Total Education Pattern, but they work much more closely with other school boards and with The Committee of 100. This committee is selected every four years by competitive examinations. Its candidates are nominated by local school boards on a regional basis. The committee establishes national goals for education, which the school boards ratify through their nation-

Scenarios: Facts or Fancies About the Future?

al association.

SECOND BOARD MEMBER: But that sounds almost like a national curriculum and very little local controls. Is that the case?

YOUNG MAN: Yes and no. Local school boards still control most of the financial aspects of public education in their communities, and, as I've explained, they determine national goals through their own Committee of 100, but it is certainly true that a much more centralized approach to what children are to learn--and how they are to learn it--is now being used.

BOARD PRESIDENT: How did this come about?

YOUNG MAN: Continuing threats from foreign powers caused some of this trend, but it was really because of efficiency that the major changes to more centralization came about. Also, since about 80 percent of the people were not involved in school debates, they offered no objections when education went national, particularly since a lowering of local taxes went with the change.

THIRD BOARD MEMBER: What is the present cost of educating a pupil in your "total education pattern" for one year's time?

YOUNG MAN: We pay whatever it takes, since the alternatives are far too expensive to comprehend. Education starts at birth and continues till a person can no longer profit from formal instruction. The biggest payoff has been before age five, where the child is more impressionable and where he doesn't

Part III

have to "unlearn" bad habits. Then the costs go down as the child gets older, shrinking to less than 10 percent of what they were before age five. This way we get more leverage for our money, and allow the students in the upper years to earn as they learn.

FOURTH BOARD MEMBER: We were concerned in the 1970's with the great increase in constitutional freedoms which students were able to obtain. Is this still a problem?

YOUNG MAN: No, not really. Since the Constitution is, as Chief Justice Hughes said, what the Supreme Court says it is, we still have control centered pretty much in the highest court, but a conservative movement in the 1980's to counteract earlier permissiveness on the part of the Supreme Court did much to put student rights into balance. Also, many of the states as well as the Congress enacted legislation giving the state more power in controlling dissent and providing greater power to the police and constabulary of the nation. The revision of college and university curricula in line with the humanistic ideal also did much to make college "relevant" to students, and rebellious dissent subsided. We feel we have a balance now between student and faculty power in the universities and colleges. Also, since much of our education takes place in the world laboratory, there is less affinity for dissent in the form of campus violence and similar disturbances.

FIFTH BOARD MEMBER: If three R's are not emphasized, then what skills are taught in your educational "pattern"?

YOUNG MAN: Much of the drudgery of reading,

Scenarios: Facts or Fancies About the Future?

writing and ciphering has been taken over by technological advances not present in 1972, such as the hear-write machines, the automatic computers that deal with figures, and the rapid-scan machines which condense long articles into summary paragraphs at the press of a button. These devices made obsolete much of the drill and skill exercises present in your schools of the 1970's. For that matter, it changed many occupations, such as stenography, teaching, librarianship, and school administration. These new versions of older occupations you would hardly recognize today--they've been changed so much by technology.

SIXTH BOARD MEMBER: I am concerned about us as individuals. Could you tell us what our life expectancy might be after undergoing this experiment and finding ourselves in the 21st Century?

YOUNG MAN: Your life expectancy is your own age, less five years, added to 78. Age 78 was the life expectancy of a male in 1972. This would mean that most of you will be living from 20 to 40 years into the 21st Century. Does this excite you, or would you prefer to go back to your former condition before today? You may choose one or the other.

(The Board Members talk in whispers among themselves. Then the President of the Board calls for a vote on the resolution, and all vote Aye. The President turns to the Young Man.) In a voice heavy with emotion, he says:

PRESIDENT OF THE BOARD: Mr. Young Man, we have taken the consensus of this group, and it is to the effect that we appreciate all you have done for

Part III

us, but, sir, if you don't mind, we'd like to return to limbo for another 30 years. Since we cannot return to the year 1972, we think we'd much rather not compete at all than to flounder on the system you've just described to us. We regret this decision but believe it to be in the best interests of both yourselves and the schools. May we be again "arrested"?

M. Chester Nolte, professor of educational administration at the University of Denver and a school law authority, has an uncomfortable knack for drawing developments to logical conclusions.

Educational Plan for Atomia

John E. Tirrell and Albert A. Canfield

.....A FACULTY/STUDENT RATIO OF 1 TO 45 WOULD SUFFICE FOR 1980, A RATIO OF 1 TO 60 FOR 2000, AND A RATIO OF 1 TO 150 FOR 2020.

PHILOSOPHY

The accelerating requirements for education can best be met by an educational plan which recognizes the many different environments and circumstances under which differing aspects of the educational process can be achieved. If the objective of education is, at least in part, to prepare people for satisfying and productive lives in which they maintain gainful employment, participate in the many civic and community activities contributing to the welfare of the group, and live within the confines of accepted morality and legal limitations, then education must provide these contacts and experiences which will optimize the achievement of these goals.

Presentation at the School Facilities Conference July 19, 1967. The original material for this paper was developed by the authors for Rice University, School of Architecture, Design Fete IV, financed by the Educational Facilities Laboratory. This paper contains ideas from two educational plans for two new towns. Atomia is, of course, a fictional town.

Part III

The traditional practices of education, including the habitual utilization of "educational" facilities for the whole educational job, must yield to a wider cognizance of the educational process and to the great utility in spreading education among the community so that it, in fact as in fable, becomes an integral part of--rather than a super element of--community living and the personal growth of its citizens.

Modern technology permits the virtual instantaneous interchange of information between men on earth and devices on the moon and well beyond. Still, the transfer of information between teacher and student has been confined to the limits of normal unamplified sound transmission--the classroom. In this modern world and in these times, education as a social process must use technology in all its forms and potentials.

The recent educational evolution of programing instructional materials has given intense and sudden emphasis to possible improvements in the utilization of self-instructional devices such as textbooks, films, etc. The utilization of programing principles (small learning steps, frequent success, avoidance of failure, and repeated review) along with modern technology produces a remarkable climate for the extension of education in the home, the factory, the office, and the special facility for experiences designed to produce abilities, talents, and attitudes other than merely manipulative or cognitive.

The educational plan for Atomia, a modern city

Scenarios: Facts or Fancies About the Future?

limited only by its vision, combines the modern technology of telecommunications in all its forms, with programing instruction for use by learners in a wide variety of environments, and frequent opportunities for learners to assist in the learning process of others. Utilizing the backgrounds and talents of others, emphasis upon education as a continuing element in life, and maximum utilization of all community facilities (or the achievement of educational goals) characterizes the educational plan.

Utilizing home study through portable packages of learning materials, two-way communication terminals or consoles at the household level, specialized facilities for occupationally related training in most (if not all) major business institutions and service agencies, and the use of older groups to assist in the training of the younger -- the plan provides the model of a generalized educational process necessary to these times of knowledge explosion, changing job requirements, and world competition.

SCOPE

Because of and related to the relatively low group interdependency in the work environment, and the size and magnitude of industrial operations, feelings of personal meaningless are apt to develop -- particularly in the non-managerial or non-professional groups. This need, not met in the work environment, should be considered in the recreational, cultural activity of the city which will relate directly with and be related to the overall educational activity of the city. No differentiation

Part III

of the library, art museum, parks and recreation, from that of the overall educational activity of the community can be tolerated if the total social needs of the community can be met.

As the art and technology of automation develop, and as the applications are refined to fine tolerance activities, the need for highly skilled hands and eyes will diminish. A program to keep all employees and potential employees abreast and trained to the edge of the art will be necessary to avoid creeping obsolescence and/or labor shortages.

The intellectual pressures of work will create unusual requirements for non-intellectual or non-academic intellectual activity. The general lack of at-work contact and the high degree of interdependence which will exist may produce unusual unverbalized needs for group interaction in the non-work environment.

The backgrounds of the families are likely to be "beer and cheese" oriented. Recreational interests are likely to relate to participative active competitive sports such as baseball, golf, bowling.

The concern for production, inventories, and the general stature of the economy will be the primary producers of anxiety. Because of the general background of most of its citizens and the possibility of continuing defalcation between management and labor, it is anticipated that the upward thrust of most of the citizenry will be toward professional--rather than managerial--occupations.

College training will be pushed by parents. Educa-

Scenarios: Facts or Fancies About the Future?

tion will be viewed as something valuable in and of itself.

The continuing emphasis upon production, quality, costs, output, etc., will provide an essentially economically oriented environment within which strong pressures for selected cultural activities (such as bands) can be anticipated.

The educational plan proposed considers these requirements. It provides numerous opportunities for persons of varying ages and with varying interests and points of view to meet in discussion and in discovery. A great portion of the education process can be accomplished through home consoles and through self-study utilizing carefully and professionally developed sequences of lesson material.

AGES

The educational plan will provide material and activity for every age group from the first year until the last. The population distribution of ages would approximate that of any major suburb with an emphasis upon manufacture.

Since the population covers all ages, the educational plan must provide opportunity and equity for all of them.

> For the infant (below 3) educational-type toys will be produced and distributed through the media distribution center. This center, which provides the educational and media expertise for the whole educational-cultural program will be located near major transportation routes

Part III

of the city so that easy movement of the materials to and from major city sub-centers can be accomplished.

For the pre-school child in the conventional sense (3 to 5) the materials for the infant will be enriched with the supervised socializing experiences of a nursery or pre-school type handled at the city's cultural/recreation centers. These cultural/recreation centers will be located near hospitals, medical centers, media distribution centers, and convenient to major transportation areas.

For children in the age range of 5 to 16 many educational experiences will be handled in the home. The student will spend his play or recreational time in the cultural/recreation centers and in specialized facilities in the business and service agencies in the community. At these centers he will engage in a wide variety of discussions and activities designed to develop the affective and psychomotor aspects of his life. This will include the development of psychomotor skills related to occupations, as well as to those associated with lifelong recreational or survival behaviors--camping, swimming, etc.

For young adults, ages 17 through 22 or through the normal age of the baccalaureate degree, the student will spend most of his time in home study. Some time will be spent in developing specific occupational skills, depending upon his talents, interests and aptitudes. The training will vary from apprentice-related vocational/technical training to familiarization with professions such as medicine and law. Actual involvement (with lower skill and maturity level requirements) will be closely correlated with cooperating private and governmental agencies.

For the typical graduate school student, study will be undertaken at existing universities. No provisions for training at this level will be made in Atomia.

For the employed adult, continuing programs of home study and center activity will be provided to meet employer, community, and personal needs. Much of this will be handled via home study units and by special programing through the home consoles.

For the unemployed, the unemployable, the infirmed, the elderly, the availability of educational/recreational/cultural activity will no longer be dependent upon transportation, financing, and the programing of commercial television. Rather, a rich and wide variety of programs and materials will be presented on the home consoles. Evenings and mid-afternoon hours will be used extensively for programing materials to meet the interests and needs of this group.

Finally, an important and critical element in the whole developmental scheme of the educational plan, is the utilization of successively higher groups to assist in the real world development and processing of instructional materials for others.

Part III

Employed and retired adults, for example, will be used extensively in the training and development, and for the preparation and conduct of instructional materials and discussion seminars. The employed adult will be expected to contribute his experience and training to help make the work-time experiences of the young adult productive and meaningful in terms of today's world and today's problems--avoiding McLuhan's criticism that "..... Most present day schools may be lavishing vast and increasing amounts of energy preparing students for a world that no longer exists."

OCCUPATIONAL CHARACTERISTICS

Although the original occupational mix of the community will include a substantial proportion of people working in the semi-skilled and skilled occupational classifications, the continuing trend will be toward more and more semi-professional occupations as the automation of the manufacture and processing of steel increases.

The automation of the manufacturing activity will require elaborate and powerful systems for sensing manipulating, and forming. This continuing emphasis will make special demands on the physical science/mathematics discipline areas.

The highly competitive and commerical aspects of industry will continue to emphasize financial and manufacturing sophistication, including industrial engineering, financial control, cost-accounting, **machine** procedures, and the orderly and profitable utilization of the computer and related information processing technology. The **very** nature of the activity suggests a continuing dependence upon highly accurate and prompt reaction to business, economics, and manufacturing conditions.

A relatively small proportion of the jobs will require close or continuing physical effort in cooperation with others in a group. The contributions of the individuals will have impact upon others largely on the basis of their accuracy and timeliness. The need for social interaction in the work environment will be minimized, and occur largely within relatively small (15 or less) work groups.

POLITICAL

Atomia will be among those pioneering in the recognition that the educational process will function best when made an integral and independent part of the management of the city. A Superintendent of Educational Services will supervise all educational/recreational/cultural activities and events of the city --assuring their proper integration, utilization, and operation within the needs of all citizens of all ages and at all social-economic levels. No position of active participation in or supervision or any activity or element of the educational program shall be an elective office. All members of the administration and staff of the educational activities will be selected from among the professionals in the field, or from among these recognized as having the personal and professional qualifications necessary to provide intelligent and devoted service.

Part III

The Superintendent of Educational Services will serve under the City Manager in an appointive capacity. His term of office will not exceed five years, but will in all cases except for neglect or maleficence exceed that of the City Manager by at least two years. Their contracts shall not run concurrently except for a maximum of three years overlap.

Since a primary objective of the educational plan is to assure involvement by all the citizens in one or more phases of the educational program, the contribution of Parents-Teacher types of organizations will be minimal if needed. Rather, advisory groups representing differing occupations, age levels, cultural interests, etc., will be formed on numerous levels to involve persons of varying occupations, incomes, residential locations, etc., in meeting the overall needs of the community.

Faculty members will be hired on a contractual basis, but tenure will not be given any faculty member regardless of qualifications or achievement. The longest contract to be given any faculty member will be 10 years or half the years to retirement age whichever is shorter.

FINANCIAL

The greatest percentage of funds to support the educational plan will come from the Federal Government. These funds will be adminstered through the State Department of Education; they will pro-rate such funds depending upon the construction and instruction needs of its municipalities or counties.

Scenarios: Facts or Fancies About the Future?

Since a great portion of the States will have major population centers exceeding the populations of most of its rural or less densely settled urban areas, the needless duplication of County-City offices and facilities in urban areas will be eliminated. Federal legislation will provide that the State may and preferably will administer funds based on population centers or areas rather than on traditional notions of geographical units.

Atomia, with a population of 150,000, would qualify as a population center and receive financial support directly from the State. There would be no intermediate supervisory or advisory board between the City Manager and the State Department of Education.

The provision of educational services for governmental and private agencies, offices, factories, etc., would be optional but planned portion of the educational plan. Companies could utilize the services of the educational program for their employees to the extent of their participation in the training or re-training of non-employed and employed citizens.

A small local tax would be collected from all residents to support the enrichment of the educational program and the support of the cultural/recreation centers. All educational programs will be offered on a no cost basis, with the exception that highly specialized and costly programs operated to serve some particular interest group or agency would require fees to cover any expenses beyond normal.

Part III

The equipment necessary for home study, including the home console, would be supplied by the city. Its operation and maintenance would be handled by a special section reporting to the Director of Educational Services.

Educational television would occupy at least three UHF channels. Tuners for its reception, if needed, would be provided by the city. The maintenance of all television sets in the city would be handled by the city as a part of the training program of electronic technicians.

ADMINISTRATION

The whole educational/recreational/cultural program will be under the direction of the most qualified educational administrator available. His annual compensation should be nearly that of a Corporate Vice President or, in terms of 1967 salaries, approximately $50,000 to $75,000 per year.

The organization necessary for him to accomplish his objectives will have wide community involvement. All advisory committees to be appointed by the Superintendent with the concurrence of the City Manager at the level of any such boards or committees reporting directly to the Superintendent.

The community advisory panel, appointed by the Superintendent with the approval of the City Manager, would include approximately 50 members of the citizenry. Its size should reflect the various responsible and knowledgeable groups within the

Scenarios: Facts or Fancies About the Future?

community for which educational service is needed or provided. The youngest members should be no less than 12 years old. Care should be exercised to assure that all elements of the community receive adequate representation. The sub-committees of the advisory panel will be formed on an ad hoc basis to study selected aspects of community need, reaction or utilization as the particular circumstances suggested.

The four major branches of the educational services activity are briefly described below. They would be housed in a building located near the center of day time population of the city.

    The curriculum supervisor would have a division head for each of the major curriculum areas. Each of them would, in turn, have specialists for the development of content, media specification and media production.

    Each division head would have the responsibility for all educational services within his division. This responsibility would include the programs for all age groups and utilizing all media and methodology, including discussional and home study, both console and footlocker.

    The division head for career programs would have all technical/vocational programs for all age groups and covering all areas. Such an overlap is vital to the prevention of obsolescence in both subject matter and practice.

    The supervisor of the various facilities around

Part III

> the city and the central preparation facility would be responsible for the operation and maintenance of all educational equipment and facilities.

It would be the responsibility of the facility supervisor to assure that the materials designated for use in the many different elements of the educational program were available in appropriate quality and quantity, and that the facilities are well maintained, safe, and in good repair. The close integration of educational and cultural activities -- combining the conventional art museum and the school facility, the library and the school facility, etc., will make their overall supervision more consistent with generalized community needs and interests than under more conventional independent budget and administrative control.

Staff services will include supportive activities associated with the business office, the computer and related informational processing activities, and purchasing. In addition, it will contain a major element devoted to the preparation and distribution of reports, announcements, and other matters of concern to the community.

The research supervision would be responsible for special and on--going research activities to assure continuing examination and test of program effectiveness, cost, utility, use, and acceptenace. While the burden of research data would, in fact, be collected by others it would be the responsibility and authority of the research supervisor to direct the collection of information at such times and in such forms as considered prudent by the Director

Scenarios: Facts or Fancies About the Future?

of Educational Services. The expertise of this research office in matters of study design, data collection, data reduction, and data interpretation would be available to all members of the community.

FACULTY

The people associated with the educational program of the city will vary widely in kind. Rather than having teachers and administrators as the primary people involved, the faculty will include a wide range of specialists. The specialists will range from those responsible for the specification of programs, or courses of study to accomplish specific technical or vocational ends, to specialists who can best combine instructional content objectives and specific media. Within this group of specialists, there will be those responsible for pre-evolution of media packages for home study.

Since a substantial part of the educational program will involve adults in active participative roles, their training and supervision in fundamentals of human learning will be necessary. A major function of the academic faculty will be in the training of others to perform training within their fields.

Additional staff members will specialize in the development and production of a wide variety of media including ETV productions, computer programs, audio tapes, slides, and schematics. A great volume of paper will be neces-

Part III

sary to meet the specific material needs of a wide variety of people and disciplines.

A highly competent full-time faculty will be needed to work with the young in the discussional and affective developmental sessions in the cultural/recreation centers. These people will concentrate on accomplishing social maturity and growth as opposed to discipline excellence.

Since the subject-matter coverage will extend through the undergraduate level of college, the educational requirements of the faculty will vary from Ph. D. subject-matter and media specialists through the utilization of high school students to work with the children in the centers where they will assist in their socialization and maturing processes.

With increasing developments in information processing technology, automation, and the demands in many widely varying fields of employment, plans will have to be made to assure that every citizen can and will receive training through the sophomore college level. However, the majority of that training must be oriented toward specific occupational fields and employment upon graduation rather than continuing toward the baccalaureate degree or beyond.

As the efficacy of self-instructional materials increases through the years projected in this plan, the need for tutors in the nodes will progressively decrease. Similarly, the effect of curricula material development specialists will become increasingly effective, making the requirement for persons in all aspects of the educational establishment proportionately reduced.

It might be estimated that a faculty/student ratio of 1 to 45 would suffice for 1980, a ratio of 1 to 60 for 2000, and a ratio of 1 to 150 for 2020.

As the need for teachers and media specialists decreases, however, the need for recreational/ cultural activity supervisors and for monitors and leaders of discussions and social interaction activities will remain about the same or increase slightly as the workweek is shortened, the retirement age is lowered, and the amount of free time for such pursuits increases among the citizenry.

Further trends must be considered. First, the trend toward an earlier retirement age--there will be increasing demands on the cultural/recreation programing for the senior citizen. This trend will be heightened by the continuing life span of our citizenry. Their active involvement in the educational program of the community offers an attractive, useful, and productive outlet for much of their talent, experience, interest, and vitality.

FACILITIES

The basic facilities required will include the fol-

Part III

lowing:

1. An instructional materials development pre-test center.

2. An administration center-including the information data processing center.

3. A media preparation, production, storage, and circulation center.

4. An educational radio and UHF transmission center.

5. A cultural/recreation center to serve every 15,000 citizens.

6. Specialized educational facilities in business, industrial and governmental firms for the development of specialized job related skills, such as carpentry, machine operation, medical careers, etc.

7. Major recreational centers for outdoor and team sports.

Facility considerations should also extend to the home where a substantial proportion of total study will occur. Design recommendations for recommended or idealized home study centers would greatly facilitate the installations necessary to the achievement of the educational program.

As the city grows, it will be necessary to increase the number of centers, and to continue the design of specialized training and educational facilities

Scenarios: Facts or Fancies About the Future?

in the industrial and business enterprises.

The primary changes in the educational process will involve the gradual and continuing shift away from

>hand skills

>semi-skilled occupations, and

>narrow trade or vocational fields such as lathe operators, punch card operators, etc.,

and move toward

>intellectual/mental skills,

>semi-professional occupations, and

>generalized vocational fields such as metal forming, information processing, etc.

Additional emphasis will be necessary to cope with the continuing increase in the number of non-employed adults occasioned by the combined effects of increased life span and lower retirement ages.

As education is moved out of the school house into the home and the place of employment, the cultural/recreation centers will enhance and combine many of the cultural/educational/recreation activities formerly associated with the separate institutions of the ballpark, the art gallery, the library, the museum, the elementary school, the high school,

Part III

the college, and the factory.

Educational activities will more and more embrace the whole gamut of community activity, and inter-relate itself into a rapidly changing and challenging world.

John E. Terrel is the former President of Oakland Community College in Michigan. Albert A. Canfield is the former Director of Community Colleges for the state of Washington.

Part IV

ADVOCATES AND DISCLAIMERS OF FUTUROLOGY

We have learned the answers,
all the answers:
it is the question we do not know.

ARCHIBALD MacLEISH

"The Hamlet of A. MacLeish"

Is the Past Relevant?

William S. Banowsky

THOSE WHO CANNOT REMEMBER THE PAST ARE CONDEMNED TO REPEAT IT.

It is now the intellectual fashion in our country to disregard the importance of the past in meeting the challenges of a technological age. In fact, there is an open disdain for history to a degree never before known in America.

Many people believe in a radical discontinuity between our generation and all preceding ones. This sense of discontinuity grows from the feeling that our lives have undergone changes so cataclysmic--changes wrought by war; by the social and theological revolutions; and by explosions in population, scientific knowledge, and urban growth-- that we now face an entirely new experience in living. Life in the present, we are told, is so vastly different from the past and the challenges of the future are so fundamentally new that the experiences of our forefathers are simply not relevant.

Of course, there is nothing new or unusual about a teen-ager's saying to his parents, "Oh, you don't understand. You never faced the problems that I now face." Teen-agers have, no doubt, been

---

Reprinted with the copyright permission of <u>Today's Education</u> and the author, September, 1972.

Part IV

saying that for centuries.

What is new and alarming, however, is the widespread acceptance of the idea of discontinuity at a philosophical level. Peter Drucker's recent book is titled <u>The Age of Discontinuity</u>, Alvin Toffler's <u>Future Shock,</u> and Charles A Reich's <u>The Greening of America</u> are best sellers which make the same point. The respected historian, J. H. Plumb, has written a book called <u>The Death of the Past</u>. Professor Plumb is not saying that the past never happened. His thesis is that our previous perception of the past is no longer valid. And Walter Lippmann, who is clearly no teenager, holds the same view. He says, "The vast upheavals of the twentieth century have rendered the knowledge of the ages obsolete. The traditional wisdom is irrelevant for our time."

What we now confront, then, is a cult of contemporaneity. We hear constantly of a generation gap. People are being driven apart by an ugly process of polarization which demands a choice between the past and the present, the young and the old, the then and the now. "You can't trust anybody over thirty" was an early slogan of the cult. The test of validity is relevance, and only the contemporary is relevant.

Our institutions--the home, the church, the courts, the universities--have been shaken by our obeisance to the youth cult. Grandmothers wear miniskirts; middle-aged executives extend the length of their locks; and the worst of possible sins is to be thought old-fashioned.

Advocates and Disclaimers of Futurology

At a time when wise leadership is so desperately needed, we capitulate to our children. Thousands of teen-agers who have not lived long enough to acquire either judgment or wisdom become the sages of our time.

The existential movement is all that counts and the present is exalted because it is the now. Only those who are with it, who are tuned in, can cope with the new questions.

We hear of the now generation. While all of us want peace, some shout, "Peace now." At Los Angeles' Ambassador Hotel, the sedate and venerable Coconut Grove gets a face-lift and comes back as the Now Grove. And people in Fort Worth, Texas, known for more than a century as Cowtown, proudly display bumper stickers announcing they live in Now Town. (You can tell a lot about a culture by reading its bumper stickers.)

The old story about the airplane in trouble points up the almost irresistible appeal of the new. The captain asked some of the passengers to jettison themselves to lighten the load. A Frenchman leaped out first shouting, "Vive la France" An Englishman followed with "God save the Queen." But the American, next in line, turned pale and backed away from the door. At this point, the captain whispered something in his ear. Then the American promptly leaped out the door. A passenger asked the pilot, "What in the world did you whisper to him?" The captain replied, "I said, 'Go ahead and try it; it's new.'"

There is no reason to question whether our pre-

Part IV

occupation with the present is a good omen. Little wonder that ours is sometimes called the age of alienation and that young people, especially, feel cut adrift and depressed by a sense of impermanence, a rootlessness.

We are now in grave danger of becoming a cut-flower civilization. Beautiful as cut flowers may be and much as we use our ingenuity to keep them looking fresh for a while, they have already begun to wither and must eventually die. They die because they are severed from their sustaining roots. We are engaged in the frustrating attempt to keep alive the flower of America while separating ourselves from the roots which have produced America.

Every generation tends to believe that its circumstances are entirely novel, that it faces questions men have never confronted before. For instance, this comment:

> It is a gloomy moment in history. Not for many years--not in the lifetime of most men who read this paper--has there been so much grave and deep apprehension; never has the future seemed so incalculable as at this time... In France the political caldron seethes and bubbles with uncertainty; Russia hangs as usual, like a cloud, dark and silent upon the horizon of Europe; while all the energies, resources, and influences of the British Empire are sorely tried....
>
> It is a solemn moment, and no man can feel

an indifference.... in the issue of events. Of our own troubles no man can see the end.

That wasn't in yesterday's Times but in Harper's Weekly, October 10, 1857.

Even the generation gap is old hat. The Greek dramatist Menander, who lived 300 years before Christ, echoed the cry of his young generation when he wrote, "An old man is never welcome among the young." And Samuel Johnson was talking about the communication gap in the eighteenth century. He said, "The conversation of the old and the young ends generally with contempt or pity on either side."

Perhaps, there is, after all, some truth to the French adage that the more things change, the more they stay the same.

The time has come to challenge the idea of radical discontinuity between this and all preceding generations and to say that our progress in the future will depend, in part, upon a respectful regard for the lessons of history.

As we seek to nourish the roots of our culture, we must not engage in ancestor worship or seek a romantic escape from the demands of the present. We look back in search of direction. It is an act of suicide to live in the past. But if we are to live fully in the present and to face the future with hope, we must look to the past and profit from its light and from its lessons.

It is precisely because the changes in our society

Part IV

have been so great, and because we do, indeed, face a new and uncertain future, that we so obviously need the guidance of the past. When the waters are uncertain and the winds most severe, the chart and compass are most needed. Never in our national life have we been more in need of the stability, the coolheadedness, and the sense of humor which are products only of the historical perspective. This troubled hour would be the worst of possible times to grow disdainful of history.

A sense of history prevents cultural amnesia and furnishes mankind with a memory. It also provides the overview which reminds us, as Henry Steele Commager says, "that time is indeed long and our own little life fleeting; that for thousands of years each generation has thought that it was the end and the object of history; that men have known crises before and wars and turmoils and triumph and tragedy and have survived; that those issues and problems which loom so large on our horizons may not even be visible on the larger horizon of history; and that the cloud-capp'd towers, the gorgeous palaces, the solemn temples, which to us seem the very wonders of the world, may dissolve and leave not a rack behind."

Because history gives this larger perspective, it softens our prejudices and teaches us modesty and humility, patience and tolerance, and gratitude. And perhaps most of all, it reminds us by a thousand, stirring examples that it is the individual who counts, that character counts, that white men may not be complete masters of their fate, neither must they be the helpless victims of fate. At every turn of the page, it is a Gandhi or a Churchill, a Jefferson or a Lincoln, a Mohammed or a Luther who makes the difference. It is by force of individual personality rather than blind chance or iron determinism that the universe moves.

Importantly for our time, a sense of history saves us from the illusion that by the sheer exercise of intense idealism we can suddenly cure every ill of society and usher in Utopia. When the postmortem on San Francisco State's worst riots was complete, Dr. Hayakawa says he was surprised to learn that students in the field of history had not participated in the disturbances in equal proportion to students from other social science fields. "I attribute this," he explains, "to the fact that the study of history had rendered them too realistic to fall for the easy, Utopian shibboleths."

Students who examine the hard facts of history know that instant progress does not come about by mere chanting and churning. As we see the long pull--the many faiths, the cultures, the parties and philosophies--we are delivered from this illusion that we have a special corner on truth, that our lives embody the grand purpose of all history and the will of God.

The cult of contemporaneity has had an impact upon the university curriculum itself. In some places, students forego the classics for courses in ecology, philosophy for ethnic studies, and literature for a new seminar in political activism. "Forget all the traditional, theoretical stuff," goes the argument, "and teach something that's relevant and practical." As important as ecology, ethnic studies, and polit-

Part IV

ical involvement are, if we permit mere relevance to prevail in our academic planning, we will cut ourselves off from the road map which shows where we have been and how we got there and where the dead-end alleys are.

More importantly, the basic clues to today's practical problems of peace, pollution, poverty, and prejudice lie hidden in the hard lessons of the past. As Robert Maynard Hutchins recently put it: "What is relevance? The fact that something is today taught in the multiversity in an irrelevant way does not necessarily mean that it could not and ought not to be taught relevantly. Is it possible that the best practical education is the most theoretical one? Is it possible in a world which is changing every day that the object might be to find out what is not changing?"

One of the driving convictions of my life is that, in all of recorded history, the basic human predicament has not changed. And this is the primary conclusion of Will Durant's incisive book, <u>The Lessons of History</u>.

The great technological advances of our time have probably deceived us into believing that our total life situation has changed. After all, it was Henry Ford, not Eldridge Cleaver, who first made the statement, "History is more or less bunk." Ford saw himself as a man of the future, a man of automation. Because he lived at the beginning of our age of technology, we can, perhaps, excuse him for believing that the shiny new machines were to change everything.

We have now lived with technology long enough to

know that machines are causing some of our problems. We can ride around the world at 600 miles per hour in a jumbo jet, and yet we may be unsafe walking alone after dark in our own neighborhoods. We do a better job of controlling the machines than of controlling men.

It is an illusion to imagine that because we can put a man into orbit we have thereby altered his human nature. The men we have sent to the moon come back to face the ancient human problems: the need to love and be loved, the problems of avarice and selfishness, the quest for meaning in life. And they return to face the ancient specter of human death, with all that it implies.

Our chief challenge throughout the remainder of this century will not concern outer space but inner space. For this challenge, we have light from many ancient lamps to guide us. For example, Moses and Plato, Voltaire and Shakespeare, each looked deeply into the human situation and each has something to say to our world.

Recently, I visited one of the infamous Nazi extermination camps, the one in Dachau, Germany, which is now a museum. I was shaken by the ghastly artifacts of death--the pictures and documents. I would have joined those who urge us to forget the past.

Then, approaching the exit, I saw posted on the stark stone wall separating the camp from civilization a quotation from George Santayana: "Those who cannot remember the past are condemned to repeat it."

William S. Banowsky is President of Pepperdine University in Los Angeles, California.

That Attractive and Utterly Fallacious Time Machine: Futurology

Robert Nisbet

..... THE PRETENSIONS OF FUTUROLOGY..... ARE COMPOUNDED OF A CONFUSION OF prediction, AS IT IS KNOWN IN SCIENCE, AND prophesy.

I remember the way it was supposed to be: the future, that is, back in the 1930's, when a good many of us now writing were just coming of age. In no way, it seems to me, does the present -- the significant present -- bear much relation to anything we then thought of as our probable future in America. Far more important, neither does the present bear much relation to anything that can today be exhumed from the 1930's.

Recently I came across a New Republic editorial, written 40 years ago, directed against an address President Hoover had just made:

> Of particular interest was his "20-year plan" for America..... He says that in the next 20 years we shall add 20,000,000 to our population.... and improve our standard of living..
>
> It is so easy to answer Mr. Hoover on specific details that it is hardly worth doing. He is evidently ignorant of the studies made by

Reprinted with the permission of Robert Nisbet, Encounter Ltd., 1971.

population experts, which show that we are
rapidly approaching a stationary or declining
population, so that it is highly improbable
that we shall add 20,000,000 persons in the
next 20 years....

As anyone can discover quickly enough, it was
Mr. Hoover who was right: the population increased
by nearly 30,000,000 by 1951. The editors
of The New Republic fell ludicrously wide of the
mark.

Never mind, though, what editors, social scientists and statesmen were predicting back in 1931. The more important question is: Can we go back to the population and economic data of the 1930's and, working with all the techniques and instruments in our possession today, as well as with the priceless advantage of hindsight, see in those data anything that might suggest what was to be economic reality in 1951? I think not.

Nor is the matter different when we turn to other spheres, the political-ideological, for instance. Consider the near collapse in our day of the political community and the collapse of the socialist ideal among intellectuals. The Left received its coup de grace during the great Children's Crusade of the 1960's, which reduced a number of major universities to a kind of academic rubble. I do not think any of these momentous facts were either foreseen or foreseeable in the 1930's.

There are all the effluvia of affluence, as Eric Hoffer calls them: the bizarre, the decadent, the bored, the disenchanted, the mindless hedonists.

Part IV

Our most difficult problems at the present time are precisely those of affluence. These problems were unknown in the 1930's.

There is the extraordinary radicalization of the American middle class. There was not the slightest evidence in the 1930's that the time would come when to be middle class would mean being indulgent, permissive, tolerant in a wide range of political, social and moral matters to a degree that can only be called radical.

Or the astonishing recrudescence of religion, at least the trappings of religion: not in one's wildest nightmares in the 1930's could this have been expected. With this recrudescence of religion there goes what can only be called a revolt against reason. Three decades ago, or indeed a century or two ago, to be modern, to be emancipated and free meant being among the apostles of reason, science and scholarship. Today the ashes of the academic community in America contain, among other things, the ideals of science and rationality.

Let me not overlook the decline of humor in America. The editor of what was once America's most distinguished humor magazine tells us there are few willing or able to write humor. Nor are there many comedians left. The only ones who still perform bravely are Jack Benny, Bob Hope and a couple of others, all lingering products of the 1930's.

The possible listing here is nearly endless and I will stop with but one more not unimportant aspect of the present that could not possibly be derived from the 1930's: nostalgia for the 1930's. Who, in the unemployment-beset, breadlined, collapse-haunted, revolution-spectered 1930's could have possibly guessed or even dreamed that by the 1960's nostalgia for the 1930's would run rife in the land?

Let me go back for a moment to the example of President Hoover and the editors of The New Republic. It will be said that if Mr. Hoover came out more nearly right than the editors, it was luck. I will concede this. It will also be said that the editors and their social-scientist sources were operating from correct principle, that if only they had had the kinds of technology and the stores of data that can today be fed into computers, they would have come out right too.

The last won't be said by all social scientists, not even by all futurologists. What many are more likely to say is, given those correct principles of trend finding, given the stores of data and data interpretation that today's technology makes possible, they would have come out right for 1951 if certain random events such as those involved in World War II hadn't taken place and if a few maniacs like Hitler hadn't dominated the Western world from about 1935 on. But in a world in which random events are omnipresent, what does it profit us to work up constructions of the future in which these are, and have to be, ignored?

Futurology seems to me now what it appeared to be in its first efflorescent decade; an unstable combination of occasionally shrewd insights into the present, statistical extrapolation, ordinary fore-

Part IV

casting and, now and then, some worthwhile, old-fashioned prophecy, based upon the kind of fertile imagination we are likely to see at its best in first-rate science fiction.

I have all possible admiration for what technology, computer science and advanced mathematics have done for modern knowledge. But neither technology nor science as a whole will ever be able to get us any more accurately into the future than the imaginations and insights of men of common sense, of seers and forecasters and prophets and of science-fiction writers.

The reason for this is simple in statement, massive in theoretical implication. The future does not lie in the present. What is at issue here is a wide-ranging, encompassing habit of mind, one that has been deep in Western thought ever since the pre-Socratic Greeks made the momentous analogy between the biological organism and social structure, declaring that as growth is an inalienable attribute of organismic structure, so change--that is, a "natural" pattern of change needing only to be described by the sociologist as the life-cycle of growth is descried by the structure of whatever social system we may have in view. What we have all around us, as the Greeks did, is the spell of the metaphor of growth.

Closely associated is the metaphor of genealogy. Who has not been beguiled by the historian into believing that the same genetically causal relation exists from event to event, act to act and motive to motive, that so plainly exists from one generation to another?

But whereas growth and genealogy are actual enough in the world of plants and animals, a mighty act of metaphoric transference is required to give them acceptability in our theories of institutions, changes and events through time. In the biological world each is to be seen clearly and indisputably whether the canvas be small or large. In the social world, however, these two metaphors gain greatly in verisimilitude the more abstract, distant in time or vast in size the subject matter is. If the subject is civilization, or a Parsonian social system or all mankind, ideas of inexorable growth and of genealogical causality are easy enough to sustain. If the subject is the United States in the twentieth century, or the caste system in India or the Chinese family, the same ideas have a somewhat grotesque relation to subject matter.

Fundamental, it seems to me, to futurology is the attractive, but utterly fallacious, assumption that the continuity of time is matched by the continuity of change or the continuity of events. Time--at least as we record it--can easily be thought of as continuous, cumulative and directional. Seconds become minutes; minutes become hours, days, months, years. The temporal present has indeed emerged from the temporal past.

Change, however, is in no sense a necessary aspect of time. Time can coexist with absolute fixity of position or condition. When we refer to change, we are referring to a succession of differences in time in some persisting identity. The entity may be anything: a tree, language, structure of kinship or a human being. Change may be said to exist if over a period of time we can per-

Part IV

ceive differences in that persisting entity. We like to assume that these differences emerge genetically subject to uniform causation.

In the organism there is warrant for making time and change synchronous. As long as an organism is alive at all, each passing moment is simultaneous with some change, however small, that is a genetic element in the directional process we call growth. No such warrant exists, however, where the "persisting identity" is not the biological organism but the social and cultural behavior of human beings.

The essence of futurology is that the future lies in the present. Few major ideas are more obvious than this. How could the present not have lain in the past? And if this be true, how could the future not be found, if only our instruments become sharp enough, our techniques skilled enough, in our present?

It would be nice, of course, if continuity did rule in the world of change and event, if each institution or other social structure did have a pattern of change built into it. But there is not an atom of evidence to suggest that a pattern of change emerges from a social structure--that is, that change or development is an attribute of a social structure as growth is an attribute of any organism--or that any kind of cycle or trajectory for a civilization can be deduced from either intensive study of the present or as a consequent of those subjective, arbitrary and highly selective events that historians assemble in the form of narrative history.

But let us assume for a moment that there is indeed a built-in pattern of change in institutions and cultures. We would still be confronted by the all too intrusive phenomena of the historical record: random events such as wars, invasions, migrations--all catastrophes that could never be projected from analysis of structure.

Futurologists, social evolutionists and social-systems theorists say, in effect: "We are not concerned with unique or random events, with the highly individual impact of the great (or maniacal) statesman, general, prophet, inventor, creator or entrepreneur. Our concern is with those patterns of change and development that exist independently of such forces." But the kinds of change that exist independently of such forces are insignificant at best, more likely to be manifestations of simple motion, activity, flux and interaction, which are always present in social life and which are different from change.

If that is what is meant by futurology, it is bound to have a good future. All one needs is to be sufficiently general in one's "predictions," as are the practitioners of the so-called Delphi Method in the Rand Corporation, and one cannot fail to be a futurologist. The amount of certifiable change in history is extraordinarily small in comparison with the amounts of sheer persistence and inertia, which of course include much random motion that often gives the illusion of change.

Much that is often taken to be prescience or prophecy is in fact no more than distorted rendering of the observer's own present. An excellent ex-

Part IV

ample of this is the nineteenth century Frenchman the Marquis de Custine, on whose life and works George F. Kennan has just written a fascinating book.

Kennan tells us that Custine's impressions of Russia, drawn from a single visit in the summer of 1839, made the subject of a four-volume book published in 1843, "is probably in fact the best of the books about the Russia of Joseph Stalin and not a bad book about the Russia of Brezhnev and Kosygin."

> Here, as though the book had been written yesterday..... appear all the familiar features of Stalinism: the absolute power of a single man; his power over thoughts as well as actions.... the frantic fear of foreign observation; the obsession with espionage... the tendency to rewrite the past.

But, of course, the book was not about the future of Russia at all. Custine was interested in the Russia of 1839, a Russia that he detested. It was also a Russia that Custine did not report accurately.

How, we ask, did Custine, in a book that Kennan can call dreadfully and shamefully inaccurate, manage to see the Russia of 1920 to 1960 so brilliantly and prophetically? The answer is, by overlooking a great deal in the Russia of 1839 and missing completely all that was to prove crucial in Russian history from his own day to the outbreak of the Bolshevik Revolution.

Tocqueville's _Democracy in America_ is an even more imposing example of the fact that much so-called prediction turns out to be, at its best, only distorted analysis of a given present. Tocqueville did not describe the Americans of 1831-32 very accurately. He went to America to see "the image of democracy itself, with its inclinations, its character, its prejudices and its passions, in order to learn what we have to fear or to hope from its progress."

The result is one of the masterpieces of political philosophy--but not a very good book on American life in the nineteenth century. What Tocqueville so often "saw" did not really exist. What he did see were a good many attributes of "the image of democracy," and only rarely did he lapse into future tense in describing them. By the late 1950's a great many of these attributes came to seem wonderfully relevant to the America of our own day. Tocqueville is accordingly pronounced a great prophet. Actually, one could fill a small book with Tocqueville's bad prophecies and fill another one with his failures to see aspects of American culture that were vital, that were to manifest themselves for all the world to see within a decade or two.

So too, I am inclined to think, with the "predictions" by Edmund Burke of "the general earthquake in the political world" that, he tells us in his Reflections on the Revolution in France, lay ahead for Europe; by Jacob Burckhardt on the "military commandos," the "terrible simplifiers" of the future; by Max Weber on the rationalization and disenchantment of the West, or a "polar night of icy darkness and hardness," and the like. For the most part these are reflections on the society that these minds thought they could see around

Part IV

them. We tend to be indulgent to our great minds of the past, savoring their "right" prophecies, overlooking the bad ones.

Nothing in this essay should be taken to suggest that I lack confidence in the predictions of the social sciences. They have nothing to do, however, with the pretensions of futurology. These pretensions are compounded of a confusion of prediction, as it is known in science, and prophecy. Prediction in science has nothing to do with the time category of the future. When the astronomer "predicts" the eclipse, he is merely vouchsafing that part of a well-known astonomical regularity that is capable of statement in terms of a certain day, hour and even minute. The astronomer is not looking into the future of the cosmic system but only into the "future" that is contained in our conventional chronology. The astronomer's "prediction" of an eclipse is no different from "prediction" that the sun will rise at 5:29 a.m. or from the epidemiologist's "prediction" that malaria, or pellagra, will be found in a given community--the epidemiologist's "prediction" being no more than a statement of causal effect on the basis of his prior intelligence that certain conditions prevail in that community.

Can social scientists predict? We can and do. We know enough about the conditions and functional relationships of certain social phenomena to make **explanatory** propositions much like those I have borrowed from the physical sciences. To use a very important example, we have found that hardcore poverty never, by itself, leads to revolutionary behavior. We are thus in a sound position to "predict" when we come upon a new enclave of poverty that no revolutionary behavior will emerge apart from the addition of certain easily specifiable elements such as a sudden expectation-increasing rise in standard of living or the addition to the enclave of change-minded or revolutionary political intellectuals.

Futurology suggests that prediction in the social sciences, or in historiography, must take the form of preview of the future. The quest for universal generalization, for so-called unified theory, is as powerful a quest today in human thought as the quest for community is in human behavior. Genetic causality, continuity, cumulation, directionality: all of these are, it would sometimes seem, as much icons in the intellectual spheres of history and the social sciences as belonging, identity and membership are icons in other spheres of contemporary society.

Robert A. Nisbet, professor of sociology at the University of California at Riverside, is the author of Tradition and Revolt.

The Future as Myth

Daniel Roselle

"WE WERE ALL BORN IMMORTAL. WE LEARN TO DIE. WE'VE GOT TO UNLEARN THAT."

In May of 1971, the first general assembly of the World Future Society, held in Washington, D. C., drew one thousand people, instead of an anticipated five hundred. Michael Kernan reported: "They came from France, where the futurist movement started, from Israel, from Argentina, from Britain and Germany and Canada, from every corner of the United States, and their diversity, even superficially, was staggering..... The diversity ran much deeper than clothes. The futurist society, founded in Washington five years ago, has 8,000 members including social scientists, psychologists, industrialists, educators, government officials, city planners, architects, writers, physicists biologists, statisticians - and professional futurologists."

Most of these individuals do not purport to have the ability to predict the future; they are, however, deeply concerned with the necessity of speculating about possibilities and alternatives

Reprinted with the copyright permission of Social Education, Vol. 36, No. 3, March, 1972, pp. 215-16, the National Council for the Social Studies and Daniel Roselle.

for the future and planning intelligently for generations yet unborn.

In 1972, these and other individuals and groups continue to probe, and their vision of things-to-come seem miraculous. Thus, we are told that we can look forward to boats that ride a cushion of air across the Atlantic in one day, electronic highways that enable drivers to enjoy the scenery while electronic devices operate and guide their cars, bat-shaped planes that fly at three times the speed of sound, biosynthetic combinations of bacteria, algae, and turnips to meet our food needs, chemicals that freeze the minds of criminals, computers that free man for abundant leisure time, test tubes that create genetically desired species, and a full assortment of artificial organs that extend human life to a century and a half (as Arthur C. Clarke points out: "Your son may look quite young when he's 103. Human cells don't have to die, you know. We were all born immortal. We learn to die. We've got to unlearn that.").

As for the exploration of the nature of space, we are no longer stunned by Yvonne Mozee's statement: "If you took a trip around the entire run of our galaxy, averaging 99 percent of the speed of light, you would return having aged 30 years while the earth would have aged 30,000." Blaise Pascal's fear of the silent spaces between the stars now seems philosophically juvenile. It is R. Buckminster Fuller who is the man of our times, for it is he who makes clear that it is madness to think that we can still cling tenaciously to mother Earth. "When and if humanity learns how to support

Part IV

human life successfully anywhere in the universe," he writes, "the logistical economics of doing so will become so inherently efficient and satisfactory that then, and then alone, may we for the first time make all humanity a success back here aboard our space vehicle Earth."[1]

We fully support the efforts to explore the future; to break out of the stultifying environment of old patterns of thought; to experiment with the new, the untried, the unknown; to search for dynamic life styles that refuse to be bounded; to free ourselves from terrestrial inhibitions and accept the challenge of the universe.

We are concerned, however, with a peculiar side effect of our obsession with the future, an insidious infection that draws on the majuscule idea of the future and applies it illogically to the minuscule lives of individual human beings. It is what might be called the Myth of the Future, and we do not like what it is doing to people. Briefly stated, the myth is this: that the glories of the future--both immediate and long-range--provide sufficient justification for ignoring aspects of life in the present.

Here are some examples of the effects of the myth:

In nations throughout the world, people are convinced of the necessity of dying or of killing other human beings in wars on the grounds that "in the future, when your nation is safe, it will remember its debt to you and honor you for your sac- **rifices.**"

Advocates and Disclaimers of Futurology

About 60 percent of all preschool-age children in the world suffer from malnutrition today. Nevertheless, we are expected to find comfort in the promise that "projected plans for the future should enable us to reduce this percentage substantially."

One hospital bed out of four in the world is occupied by a patient disabled by polluted water. Yet we assume that something important is happening when we read in a report: "There is no reason why--using our technological knowledge-- we cannot eliminate water pollution by the year 2,000 or even earlier in the future."

In thousands of families, parents accept lives of dull, dehumanizing, and demoralizing work, sacrificing themselves "so that some day in the future our children or our children's children will have the opportunity to lead good lives."

In universities throughout the United States, graduate students spend years of their lives working on inane doctoral dissertations while their senior advisors assure them: "In the future, once you have obtained your doctoral union card, there will be more than enough time to do creative research and writing."

In social studies classes in many schools, memorization of thousands of isolated facts continues to hold top priority while parents are told "in the future, after they know the facts, the youth of our country can begin to think for themselves."

In many areas of the United States, no program of music or art is provided for elementary school

Part IV

children on the logic that "in the future, if they are interested in that sort of thing, there will be plenty of time for them to enjoy good music and art."

We seem to be suffering from a Future Syndrome in which we apply futurist thinking to presentist lives--often with disastrous results. Who was it who said: "There was jam yesterday, and there is never jam today."?

To view the situation from another angle, what has happened also is that our excitement with the world of the future--with space walks and test-tube genetics and instant communications systems--has seeped down to our lives of the present and has drained them of some of their richness and meaning. Too many of us, obsessed with the future, no longer enjoy--or even feel-- the wonder of each day, of each hour, of each minute of the present.

How many elementary teachers still enjoy leisurely sharing with a child the spontaneous intoxication that comes from his discovery of nonsensical and humorous sounds of words-- without nervously noting that they must move on at once to prepare him for a future based on words that do make sense? How many secondary schoolteachers still take pleasure in teaching daily classes without focusing on that day in the future when their doctoral degrees will bring them the respectibility of a college position? How many college professors still delight in walking up the time-worn and memory-worn staircases of an Old Main without calculating the day in the future when the new air-conditioned building will be completed? How many administrators are able to forget the future enrollment for their institution (as projected for 1980), and take the time to experience the pleasure of guiding one student lost in the corridors of the present?

What miracles we experience each day--and they have nothing to do with the future. A child's self-portrait painted in red and green and dirt; a new book that crackles crisp and clear when we turn the pages; a battered postcard from Greece with an X to mark " Me, standing in front of the Parthenon"; a telephone call, a voice, a silence at the other end; a bus trip home and a fantasy against an icy window pane; and all the tens and hundreds and thousands of delicious moments in a single day.

What are we anyway? We with our ambitions for the future, our plans for the future, our charts for the future, our statistics for the future, our lives for the future? What are we to throw away our moments in the present and prepare for our years in the future? What are we to dream new worlds and sleep away the world we live in? What are we to never realize that the touch of one dear hand--today--may be all the immortality that any of us will ever have?

Daniel Roselle is Editor of Social Education.

Notes and References

1. Quoted from Pace Magazine, Vol. V, No. 8, August 1969, p. 58

Futurism in Higher Education: Fad or Fulfillment?

John A. Creager

ALL EDUCATION CAN AND DOES HAVE A ROLE IN THE FUTURE, AND THE FUTURE HAS A ROLE IN EDUCATION.

Forty years ago, Alfred North Whitehead, in his Adventures of Ideas, expounded the role of ideas in promoting and preserving civilization. Writing on "Foresight," he remarked on the acceleration of change in the world and its implications for culture and education:

> Our sociological theories, our political philosophy, our practical maxims of business, our political economy, and our doctrines of education, are derived from an unbroken tradition of great thinkers and of practical examples. .... The whole of this tradition is warped by the vicious assumption that each generation will substantially live amid the conditions governing the lives of its fathers and will transmit those conditions to mould with equal force the lives of its children. We are living in the first period of human history for which this assumption is false.

Reprinted with the permission of the author. Change published portions of this article in its February, 1972 issue.

Advocates and Disclaimers of Futurology

The assumption had probably been false for some time before Whitehead so lectured to the Harvard Business School. After giving examples of the consequences of this false assumption for various aspects of the culture, including educational theory, he noted that mankind was trained to adapt itself to fixed conditions because the time-span of important change was considerably longer than the span of a single human life. He then drew the following contrast:

> Today this time-span is considerably shorter than that of human life, and accordingly our training must prepare individuals to face a novelty of conditions. But there can be no preparation for the unknown. It is at this point that we recur to the immediate topic, Foresight. We require such understanding of the present conditions, as may give us some grasp of the novelty which is about to produce a measurable influence on the immediate future.

With occasional exceptions, Whitehead's point seems to have been virtually ignored until Alvin Toffler elaborated the theme in Future Shock. The public, out of a combination of hope and fear, eagerly accepts anyone who offers a scapegoat for the shock of a future that is already here, or who possesses some crystal ball, whatever its clarity. Thus, Charles Reich, in The Greening of America, offers the Corporate State as one such scapegoat. According to Reich, the "system" is beginning to self-destruct, through its own internal contradictions, and the behavior of revolutionaries is a logical and consequential symptom of

Part IV

the resulting human frustration. He would "green" America by having all of us adopt a "new level of consciousness," in which each and every person would be true to the self. Wasn't that the good, but superficial, advice the senile Polonius gave Laertes? Reich would have us all sing of the free self with Walt Whitman, and behave as if we had heard the Sermon on the Mount. If Reich's sermon seems simplistic and verbose, it also contains such insights as the following comment on the "failure of education":

> We have vastly underestimated the amount of education and consciousness that is required to meet the demands and organization of technology. Most of our "education" has taught us how to <u>operate</u> the technology; how to function as a human component of an organization. What we need is education that will enable us to make use of technology, control it and give it direction, cause it to serve values which we have chosen.

As a consequence of ignoring Whitehead's point, we are currently experiencing a value crisis, marked by intensified public interest in, and fantasies about, the future. The failure of education to prepare us to cope with rapid change has led us to react violently against creativity and rational thought, as if our difficulties could be solved without them. But public awareness of such problems as overpopulation, environmental damage, the reduced viability of institutions, and social tensions has increased the anxiety underlying interest in the future at the same time that recent technological developments have intensified both hope and fear.

Advocates and Disclaimers of Futurology

For better or worse, our destiny is tied to the future we create by our present decisions. The approach of contemporary revolutionists, with their irrational rhetoric and outrageous behavior, can only lead to such chaos that humanity, further degraded, will demand some form of tyrrany. The reactionaries cannot stop the world; there is no exit, no avenue of retreat. Those who uphold the status quo, with its materialistic forms of pragmatism, have already produced a short-sighted world destructive of its own prosperity. The only alternative open to us is to improve our foresight in coordination with our human values. To do this, we must first improve the educational system. We must envisage and evaluate possible futures, giving close attention to the relations between the human values that determine the kind of future we want, those pertinent facts from which the future is to emerge, and the consequences of our current decisions.

As Whitehead notes, a neat doctrine of foresight is probably impossible. What is possible is that our special efforts to progress be coordinated by a philosophic outlook "at once general and concrete, critical and appreciative of direct intuition." Such an outlook would be "a survey of possibilities and their comparisons with actualities. In philosophy, the fact, the theory, the alternatives, and the ideal, are weighed together." But a shift in outlook is occurring, and Whitehead has stated what it implies for education and for life:

> To recreate and reenact a vision of the world, including those elements of reverence and order without which society lapses into riot,

Part IV

and penetrated through and through with unflinching rationality.

It remains for us to examine what the current shift in outlook is; how it affects, and is affected by, education (particularly higher education); and what actualities limit this risky but necessary adventure.

Human attempts to ascertain the future are at least as old as recorded history. These attempts, presumably motivated by anxiety about individual or communal destiny, have ranged from the irrational charlatanism of soothsayers, astrologers, and demagogues to highly sophisticated methods for forecasting and decision making. Historically, the rise of religious and moral values provided a normative basis for social criticism. This, in turn, led to exhortative attempts to control human affairs by reference to alternative destinies, expressed in prophetic and apocalyptic terms. The same kind of thinking may be found in some of the fantasies of modern ideologies, each with its special mix of utopian and doomsday elements. As science and technology developed, the desire to predict and control the future was, to a limited extent, fulfilled, and further fantasies about both utopia and doomsday were stimulated. Some of these fantasies were probably offered primarily as entertainment; one thinks of traditional science fiction like the novels of Jules Verne and the Buck Rogers comic strips. Other fantasies, like those of H. G. Wells, Aldous Huxley, George Orwell, and B. F. Skinner, no less entertaining, are more profoundly concerned with human values; their scenarios involve social and moral criticisms, as well as the envisagement of possible futures.

Advocates and Disclaimers of Futurology

Since World War II, the development of improved techniques for forecasting, such as trend projection, computer simulation of alternative futures, and creation of analytical models useful in dealing with multidimensional problems, has encouraged some people to believe that we can choose and control our destiny. This is a new attitude which involves a willingness to take bold implementative action rather than just to speculate and to criticize social trends. Partly as a function of their pragmatic concerns, government and industry have supported the development of techniques for anticipating and creating the future in war and peace.

The conviction that the future could be deliberately chosen and rationally controlled began to find organized expression in the sixties. The first International Future Research Conference was held in Oslo in 1967; the second in Kyoto, Japan, in 1970. The World Future Society held its first General Assembly in Washington in May 1971. The Futurist, a journal of forecasts, trends, and ideas about the future, has been published bimonthly since February, 1967, and similar periodicals have also been initiated. These research conferences, assemblies, societies, and journals are concerned with the full range of substantive, methodological, and normative issues involved in futuristics. The substantive area includes design of new aspects of the physical, biological, psychological, and social environments and relies heavily on current scientific research and technological development; artists and humanists, many of whom have some background in science, prepare scenarios of the possible futures that may result from the confluence of several trends

Part IV

and possible choices. The methodological area is concerned with developing and improving techniques for forecasting, including computer simulation of possible futures and procedures for estimating the consequences of current decision making. The normative area involves the evaluation of possible futures and judgments as to how changes in knowledge and culture may affect the quality of human life.

Warren G. Bennis has suggested that a scientific study of the future should have the following objectives: (1) survey of possible futures in terms of major alternatives, (2) ascription of the relative likelihood that a given alternative will occur by some specified date, (3) identification of preferable alternatives relative to various basic policies or values, and (4) identification of decisions subject to control, whose occurrence will have a major effect on the probability that an alternative will be realized.

It is not true that futurists have ignored values. Nevertheless, some thoughtful humanists, recognizing the hubris in the new futuristics, are asking whose goals and values will determine our choices. Peter Shrag, writing in the Saturday Review, takes the futurists to task for their elitest assumption that they know what is best for us, and believes a reaction, not solely attributable to current economic setbacks, has already set in. Clearly, the substantive and methodological aspects of futurism must be in the hands of the technically competent. In a society professing democracy, the normative aspects of the future must have a measure of public insight and support for their resolution. Neither commandments handed down ex cathedra, Talmudic legalisms designed to cover all contingencies, nor rigid hierarchies of values determining the same priorities in all situations are adequate to the task of evaluating alternate futures.

It is not wholly encouraging to note that some of the most competent and imaginative futurists share those values of the Corporate State most frequently questioned. Such persons often serve those industries sufficiently astute to employ them to consider the future in terms of those values. The evaluation of possible futures and the decision to implement one or more aspects of some scenario involve complex normative issues, in which we all have a stake, but which few persons are competent to resolve. Our novelists and dramatists often show us the human consequences of past decisions, but tell us little of how alternative values in those decisions should have been weighed and chosen. Our theologians and moralists search for new bases for normative judgments amid their dead deities and fallen idols, or try to resurrect and rejustify the old bases. What is needed is a high order of scholarly development of ethics and esthetics applicable to the complexities of modern decision making. This may require interdisciplinary terms of experienced scholars and representatives of tomorrow's leadership, a combination most likely to be found on a university campus.

The educational system, as well as government and industry, has a practical stake in the future. This interest goes well beyond projecting future enrollments or ascertaining needs and resources for

Part IV

physical plants and personnel; the concern is, as always, with student development. Today's students will be living their adult lives and working in the last quarter of this century. Consequently, in the face of rapid and worldwide change, it is the business of education to help students imagine, understand, create, and evaluate their future, so that their life styles, competencies, and values permit them to adapt to, and rationally control their worlds. The purpose of futurism in education, especially higher education, is to meet such needs.

Most futuristic activity in education occurs in well-established, accredited institutions of higher education in both their research and instructional functions. In addition, about a dozen new institutions, either still in the planning stages or just recently opened, purport to exemplify various reforms and innovative styles in education; they may, for example, incorporate futuristic content in their curricula, or they may meet the anticipated needs of their students for protection against future shock. Some institutions have been active in collecting and disseminating information on educational futuristics. For example, the Program for the Study of the Future in Education, conducted at the University of Massachusetts, published a syllabus of future studies, compiled by Billy Rojas and H. Wentworth Eldredge. The Educational Policy Research Center at Syracuse University published Michael Marien's annotated bibliography, <u>Essential Reading for the Future of Education.</u> These items, and the December 1970 issue of <u>The Futurist</u>, indicate how much is already going on across the broad spectrum of education.

Advocates and Disclaimers of Futurology

In the case of higher education, there is, of course, nothing new about universities and colleges being centers for generating and evaluating ideas about the future. The novelty lies in the deliberate and conscious effort to incorporate concern about the future into instructional programs. There are about 150 courses and seminars in futuristics offered to undergraduates in a wide variety of colleges, located in some two dozen states, with all regions in this nation represented, and in three Canadian provinces. The cliche "spreading like wildfire" seems appropriate. Moreover, a number of traditional courses explicitly incorporate futuristic ideas and methods. Although futuristics curricula per se are now rare--one institution offers an undergraduate major, another a graduate program--they may soon become more common. But, as William S. Hayes, president of Alice Lloyd College, points out:

> I think futuristics is not so much a curriculum as it is a point of view which should permeate all areas of teaching and learning, all seminars, supporting student initiatives in learning, from the point of view of its ensuring purposefulness and meaning to the topics we study so far as the future of our lives and our society are concerned.

The first course in futuristics was offered by Alvin Toffler at the New School for Social Research in 1966. Since then, courses involving futuristics have proliferated rapidly and, once initiated, have apparently suffered little or no attrition. Nearly all kinds of departments, with the exception of

Part IV

law, library science, and home economics have offered courses prior to 1971. The failure of law schools to offer such courses may be especially unfortunate in view of the high probability that rapid changes in the near future will raise serious questions for both legislation and litigation. In addition, new consumer problems arising in the future may justify some futuristics content in home economics and new knowledge and technologies may imply new dimensions for information retrieval in library science.

Prior to 1970, most course offerings were introductions to futuristics designed to expose students to the substantive, methodological, and normative issues. More recently, the trend has been to interject futuristics into specific subject-matter courses, sometimes as a technique for integrating and focusing traditional content, but more often as the major content of the course. Both traditional and innovative instructional techniques are used. Another trend is to offer interdisciplinary and problem-oriented courses and seminars which emphasize futuristics in their outlook and content.

A careful reading of course descriptions indicates that most progressive faculty members have exercised care in providing real and relevant substance and that they have sought to improve their courses when reoffered. It is, of course, more difficult to determine the existence of superficial activities, resulting either from cautious attitudes based on critical judgment or from mere dilettantism. Information so far available gives little grounds, however, for regarding the current developments as a mere fad. In such a rapidly developing situation, the attraction of dilettantes, faddists, and proprietary entrepreneurs is a strong possibility, and responsible educators must guard with vigilance against them. Such vigilance will be most useful if done in the spirit of constructive criticism.

Amitai Etzioni has raised an important question about futurism, bearing on the nature and extent to which its contents belong in the curriculum:

> I believe none of us has yet found a technique for divining the future. Reports on the year 2000 predict an environment that is too far away to allow us any real sense of the validity of these predictions. And, predictions are often made not only in an interval, which is, of course, necessary, but in such an open-ended fashion that they are not subject to testing, even at the year 2000.

Indeed, the very title of the previously cited article by Bennis, "A Funny Thing Happened on the Way fo the Future," reflects the same reservations. In answer, it is not enough to point out that most students will probably not regard the year 2000 as being that "far away." More important, futuristics is concerned with improving the validity of forecasting and with evaluating the future, as it evolves through present realities and decision making. There is, indeed, need for such improved validity and for greater precision. But, only by some sensible indulgence in futuristics will it be possible to ascertain, with time, what was and was not valid, and why. Who but the educated will be able to make this

Part IV

determination?

Already our judgment about the very near future, and its implications, is sufficiently reliable to allow us to specify some of the ways higher education can help the student develop a life style suitable to 1980, whatever the precise conditions then prevailing. For example, few can doubt that the student will need flexibility of attitudes and techniques to ward off, or cope with the future shock brought about by rapid change. He will need to know more about the sources and reliability of information than about detailed content; he will need to know more about techniques for retrieving information and synthesizing it in a problem-solving context. He will need sound critical judgment, based on semantic as well as logical insight, while retaining respect for creative ideas. He will need to become aware of the full range of individual differences, developing a working tolerance and respect for such differences as a part of his development of maximally effective inter-personal and communicative skills. Some of the current innovations and reforms in higher education appear to be useful, and instruction in futuristics may enhance the students' awareness of these needs while at the same time providing them with the cognitive and affective content to meet them. Most current visions of the future imply the broad philosophy and practice of higher education suggested by President Hayes in the comment quoted earlier.

Civilization would never have spread if adventurers had first demanded complete and accurate maps. Nevertheless, to ignore reefs and shoals is to invite shipwreck. Of course, a knowledge of fathoms is of little use if the seas are so stormy that one cannot control one's course. In that case, one lashes himself to the mast and starts praying. But where a knowledge of risks and some degree of control are possible, critical judgment is required to chart and follow the course.

Those who want to scuttle the ship forget that they can swim only so far in shark-infested waters. Frustrated by institutions and organizations that fail to function properly, disenchanted with traditional hierarchies of authority and responsibility, bored by the routine of day-to-day operations, some critics would demolish the present social structure, replacing it with a radically egalitarian, unstructured, disorganized activity of individuals, responsible--if at all--only to themselves. It may be true that "all we like sheep have gone astray" collectively; is it any better that we should do so individually?

Routine plays a useful role in individual and communal life; some kinds of institutions can accomplish what individuals need and want, but cannot achieve by themselves. There must be some lines of rational and responsive authority and responsibility, defined by some kind of social contract, whereby conflicting needs, desires, and values are resolved so that the business of life may proceed. What is needed, then, is not the total destruction of all our present institutions and ways of life, but rather a greater flexibility of approach to accomodate the full range of human differences and to allow for rapid changes in resources, risks, and attitudes. This is not to imply that we can be content with just tinkering with the

Part IV

system. We may need to find new ways of doing things in a just accomodation of humane values and realistic constraints.

The critics of our society, and those of some forms of futurism, may not always be mutineers, but they are aware of the Captain Blighs among us, who demand a much tighter ship, in which human differences and future developments would be rigidly controlled. In such a futurism, there will be no future shock because the technocrats will have programmed the computers to schedule our experiences and thereby reduce the degree and content of our awareness to that of a pecking pigeon. Nothing will be left to chance, let alone to ignorance or to possible differences of opinion. Some persons exist whose need to control, or to be controlled, determines their "utopia." As noted earlier, some sectors of the Corporate State support futurism and futurists. What will happen when specialized futurism creates scenarios and implements them with a parochial vision instead of the coordinating philosophy demanded by Whitehead forty years ago? Precisely more inhumane dysfunction.

But we cannot stay in a dead calm. Risks must be taken--but with insight and prudence. All education can and does have a role in the future, and the future has a role in education. It is at the level of higher education, with its current reforms and innovations, that informed scholarship and instruction must cope with the complex task of creating, enacting, and coordinating the future in its substantive, methodological, and normative dimensions. Half-baked ideas may need further cooking with controlled heat lest we suffer more indigestion from a future lacking genuine creativity and balanced judgment.

Futurism in higher education is a well-established fact; it is growing and is quite likely to continue to grow. Not only is it represented in a wide range of courses and seminars given in diverse and reputable institutions, but also its potential value is recognized in other ways. For example, a few colleges retain "resident futurists" on their faculties, a fact that suggests that the academic discipline of futurism or special futurism centers will emerge in a few years. Already the State University of New York has a number of futurists active in administrative as well as faculty positions. Despite the risk of attenuated quality as more persons become committed to it, futuristics in higher education is not simply a fad.

The important question is whether futurism in higher education will lead to the development of persons who can readily live with the future, who can help to shape it for human values, and who can adapt to those aspects of the future they cannot control. Will futurism in higher education render persons more capable of service, better able to shape the structure and functions of our institutions of government, industry, and the professions?

These questions cannot be answered clearly at the present time. Neither fanatical enthusiasm nor reactionary disdain is an appropriate attitude. Rather educators can assist the development of a wise and humane future in two ways. First, as

Part IV

a community of scholars, they may create and judge ideas about the future. Second, as facilitators of the learning process, they can aid their students to develop the life styles and competencies required to live in the future. There is a continuing need for the monitoring of processes and practices in higher education with evaluation of both immediate and long-range outcomes. We can ask if the development of persons exposed to futuristic content in their education differs from the development of those who have little or no such exposure. We can also evaluate the effects of such exposures on a wide range of educational objectives, both the traditional ones and those implied by the purposes of introducing futurism into higher education.

Futurism in higher education may be a fad, a useful aspect of innovation and reform, or both. It all depends on how wisely and responsibly the academic community exercises its freedom and on an informed public appreciative of the adventures of ideas.

John A. Creager is Research Associate, American Council of Education, Washington, D. C.

Trying to Know Tomorrow Today

Donald W. Robinson

.....SOME FUTURISTS ASSERT THAT IF THEY ARE TO BE SERIOUS ABOUT THEIR CONCERN FOR THE FUTURE, THEY MUST HELP CREATE IT RATHER THAN MERELY STUDY IT.

How long must we wait before free public universal education will begin at the age of two?

How soon will women fill 50% of the administrative positions in education?

When may we expect drugs to be generally available for the purpose of raising effective intelligence levels?

How many years will elapse before the four-day work week becomes universal? The 12-month school year?

How long will it be until universal worldwide literacy is achieved?

What competencies will be the most important for teachers in 1980?

What will be the most probable tax base for schools when the property tax is replaced? How soon will this take place?

Reprinted with the copyright permission of Phi Delta Kappan and the author, December, 1971.

Part IV

Some of these questions are patently speculative; others are iffy only with respect to when they will occur. The answers to all of them (and scores of similar questions) are so important to effective educational planning that it seems worth a very considerable investment of TEM's (time, energy, and money) to find the most reliable answers at the earliest possible date. Not the answer of course, but the most likely alternatives, based not on mere speculation but on precise statistical projections of carefully selected data having to do with relevant technical, psychological, demographic, sociological, and other changes recognized as imminent. The futurist moves systematically from data collecting to projection, prediction, and planning.

The obvious value of making such tentative forecasts as accurate as possible and as early as feasible has led to the mushrooming, in the past five years, of Future Planning--or, as some prefer, Futures Planning, to emphasize the importance of alternatives rather than single predictions.

Already the idea of Futures Planning has attained enough status that the president of the American Psychological Association has dared to assert in his presidential address that "all power-controlling leaders--and those who aspire to such leadership" should be required to submit to behavior modification drugs which could be perfected within a few years to control the "animalistic, barbaric, and primitive propensities in man."

If this prospect sounds a bit scary, it also underlines the need for careful, deliberate planning of the use of and control over such products as behavior modification drugs that will continue to arrive in increasing variety and potency. One of the many roles of futurism is to serve as a widespread early warning system to society, because it makes many persons aware of probable and possible futures.

When I was enrolled in a school of education, professors made a great point of explaining the changes that had taken place in the past evolution of our educational systems. "History of education" was a required course, and professors conveyed the notion that as a result of changes over the centuries, we had arrived. They seemed to say that we now had a satisfactory program of schooling, and, while there would always remain minor curriculum adjustments in order to stay abreast of technology, essentially the system had been perfected.

A little later, the dominant notion switched from stress on past changes to awareness of the need for changes in the present. The "needed now" concept took over and the history of education went into eclipse. Beginning half a dozen years ago, the "change now" emphasis swelled into a cult of innovation so popular that in some areas no superintendent could feel that he was doing his job if he was not recommending at least one innovation.

And today, while the enthusiasm for "change now" is still at its peak, the next stage in our perspectives about change has already made its appearance. It is our new concern for the future. As historicism gave way to presentism, this sense

Part IV

of immediacy is in danger of being upstaged by futurism. The World Future Society, the Institute for the Future, the International Society of Educational Planners, and other groups are recruiting members, producing books and journals, promoting conferences and projects, and otherwise doing their thing, which is perfecting techniques for predicting and planning the future.

The Institute for the Future cooperates in publishing the quarterly Futures ($22.50 per year, $7.50 per copy, printed in England), of whose 2,000 subscribers 27% are American and 27% British, with the remaining 46% divided among 42 other countries. Futures' concern is with "the development and application of forecasting techniques or to subjects appropriate to long-term policy making."

The Institute for the Future, head-quartered in Middletown, Connecticut, and Futures recently published Educational Planning in Perspective, edited by Thomas Green of the Educational Policy Research Center at Syracuse. (IPC Science and Technology Press, Ltd., 300 East 42nd St., New York, N.Y. 10019. $5.)

The World Future Society (1629 K Street, Washington, D.C. 20006) claims 6,000 members in 50 countries and publishes the Futurist (bi-monthly, $7.50 per year).

As early as July, 1970, at least 90 institutions of higher learning were offering futurism or forecasting courses -- most of them in sociology, economics, or business administration, but a few in education.

At least one sociologist who has surveyed the futures scene suggests that "explicitly in most courses, implicitly in others, the instructors were out to 'improve' the world in a planful way." This can be as scary as the mind-altering drugs. Some of the instructors, according to the same sociologist, are "young radical social scientists..... out to 'bust' the status quo."

Only an affluent society could afford to produce a science of futurism which its own adherents admit is not always considered a serious intellectual activity, since it deals with possible alternative futures or "futuribles" rather than with directly verifiable data.

Already some futurists are realizing that the mere perfection of statistical techniques for predictive purposes is slight contribution to a world so sorely in need of direction. Its effect might in fact be a contribution to despair by suggesting that the future simply happens, and the best we can do is try to foresee it. To escape this brand of fatalism, some futurists, assert that if they are to be serious about their concern for the future, they must help to create it rather than merely study it. In pursuance of this notion, much serious social planning is under way, with many model "future" cities on the drawing boards, including Arcosanti, New Mexico; Synanon City, California and Auroville, India.

Having no crystal ball, no great talent for statistics, and no close friends among this new breed

Part IV

of forecasters, this commentator is loath to predict their destiny. However, it seems safe, at least for the short-range future, to predict a prosperous future for futurism.

Donald W. Robinson is Director of Special Publications, Phi Delta Kappan, Bloomington, Indiana. This article appeared in a regular Kappan column he writes, "Scraps From A Teacher's Notebook."

INDEX

Academic reform, 84-89
Administration (also see
 administrators and
 governance)

  attendance unit, 23-24
  organization, 98-102
  programs, 102-04
  reshaping the role of

    central staff, 17-19
    principal, 14-17
    specialists, 9-14
    superintendent, 20-23

  supplies committee, 50-51

Administrators

  leadership, 42-43, 51-53,
  253-54, 256-59
  principals, 14-17, 45-54
    professional prep-
    aration, 53-54
    staff relations, 9-14,
    17-19, 46-50
  superintendents, 20-23

Alberta Academy, 150-65

  learning strategies,
  159-62
  organization, 162-65

Arbolino, Jack, 102
Ashby, Sir Eric, 84, 132-33
Aspirations of humans, 174-75
Astin, Alexander, 89

Bacon, Sir Francis, 135
Bellamy, Edward, 133-34, 145
Ben-David, Joseph, 84
Bennis, Warren G., 300
Biofeedback training, 198-99
Bowles, Frank, 90
Brown, George, 159
Business in education, 192-94, 232

Capitol and the Campus: State Responsibility for Postsecondary Education, The, 90, 94-95
Carnegie Commission, 71, 78-97, 223
Certificate of Opportunity, 196
Chance to learn: An Action Agenda for Equal Opportunity in Higher Education, A, 80-81
Cheit, Earl, 93
Choice of Futures, A, 150-65
Cities of Education, 140-41
CLEP, 101-03
Costs of higher education, 73-74
Counselors, 189, 198
Credentialing, 111 183-84, 188, 228

Cult of contemporaneity, 268, 273
Curriculum, 12, 61-62, 237-43, 273-74

  futuristics, 303-05, 309-10
  higher education, 120-21, 163-65, 184, 189, 193, 303, 309-10
  programs, 102-04
  work experience, 224-25

DeCosta, Frank, 90
Dennis, Lawrence, E., 100
De Tocqueville, Alexis, 125, 284-85

Drucker, Peter, 268
Dunham, Alden, 85

Early school years, 250
Enrollments, 72-73, 89-90, 93-94
ESP, 199
Etzioni, Amitai, 305

Facilities, 38-40, 261-64
Financing education

  general, 223, 254-55
  medical, 83
  problems, 31-32, 73-74

From Isolation to Mainstream: Problems of the Colleges Founded for Negroes, 91
Fuller, Buckminister, 57-64
Futuristics, 303-05, 309-10

Galbraith, John Kenneth, 130
Goals, 104-05
Goodman, Paul, 136-37, 142, 144
Governance, 34-36, 87-89, 113-14, 117-20, 122-25, 127, 186-88, 202-05
Graubard, Stephen R., 140

Hall, G. Stanley, 40
Heist, Paul, 129
Higher education

costs, 73-74
curriculum, 83-84, 120-21, 163-65, 184, 189, 193, 303, 309-10
depression in, 93-94
growth and development, 89-90
non traditional, 100, 103, 105, 144-46, 229
utopias, 133-36

Higher Education and the Nation's Health: Policies for Medical and Dental Education, 83-84
Hoffer, Eric, 277
Hoover, Herbert, 276-77, 279

Hopkins, John, 142
Hutchins, Robert M.,
  42, 137, 139, 144,
  146-47, 204, 274
Huxley, Aldous, 25,
  145, 298

Illich, Ivan, 159
Institutional redesign-
  ing, 175-79

Kant, Immanuel, 135, 147
Katz, Joseph, 129

Keniston, Kenneth, 129
Kennan, George, 284
Kerr, Clark, 233

Ladd, Dwight, 85
Leadership, 42-43,
  51-53, 253-54, 256-59
Learning

  capacity, 60-61
  extended, 33-34, 91-93,
    97-110, 224-26, 228-29
  strategies, 159-62, 193,
    250

Lee, Calvin, 89
Less Time, More Options:
  Education Beyond the High
  School, 81-82, 86-87
Librarians, 217-18
Libraries, 218-20, 227
Lieberman, Bernhardt, 102
Lippman, Walter, 140-41

Mann, Horace, 27
McLuhan, Marshall, 218
Meyerson, Martin, 70
Mood, Alexander M.,
  100-01

Negro colleges, 90-91

New Students and New
  Places: Policies for the
  Future Growth and
  Development of American
  Higher Education, 89-90
Non traditional education,
  33-34, 91-93, 97-110,
  224-26, 228-29

Open university (open
  ended, college without
  walls, etc), 33-34, 100,
  103, 105, 144-46, 229
Orwell, George, 25, 27, 298

Principals, 14-17, 45-54
Professional preparation,
  53-54

Quality and Equality:New
  Levels of Federal
  Responsibility, 78-80
Questions for the 1970's,
  108-11

Reich, Charles A., 268,
  295-96
Riesman, David, 76

Shrag, Peter, 300
Skinner, B. F., 139, 143,
  298

Specialization, 58-60
Staff relations, 9-14,
  17-19, 46-50
Stoddard, Alexander, 4
Students

  attitudes, 74-77, 115-17,
  123-24
  black, 116-17
  development, 23, 89-90
  learning, 60-61, 82-84

Superintendent of schools,
  20-23

Taylor, Harold, 129

Teachers

  attitudes, 74-77, 122-23, 127, 182-83
  reshaping the role of, 4-9, 136-37, 259-61
  teaching, 188, 189
  training, 23, 53-54, 198

Teaching, 159-62, 188-89, 193, 250
Technology, 5-98, 112-13, 163-65, 192-93, 197, 202, 233-34, 246-48, 274-75, 280
Toffler, Alvin, 268, 295, 303
Trained manpower, 82-84
Tyler, Ralph, 34, 43

Urbanization, 121-22

Utopia

  confusion, 146-48
  higher education, 133-36
  significance, 141-44

Valley, John, 102
Values, 206-07
Veblen, Thorsten, 135, 146
Verne, Jules, 298
Vouchers, 188

Wells, H. G., 25, 298
Whitehead, Alfred North, 294-98
Work experience, 224-25
Wycoff, Deborah, 102